GLOBAL STOCK EXCHANGES: STABILITY, INTERRELATIONSHIPS, AND ROLES

GLOBAL STOCK EXCHANGES: STABILITY, INTERRELATIONSHIPS, AND ROLES

PAOLO B. CASSEDES
EDITOR

Nova Science Publishers, Inc.
New York

For permission to use material from this book please contact us:
Telephone 631-231-7269; Fax 631-231-8175
Web Site: http://www.novapublishers.com

Library of Congress Cataloging-in-Publication Data

Global stock exchanges : stability, interrelationships, and roles / [edited by] Paolo B. Cassedes.
p. cm.
Includes index.
ISBN 978-1-60692-184-5 (hardcover)
1. Stock exchanges. I. Cassedes, Paolo B.
HG4551.G636 2009
332.64'2--dc22

2009010125

Published by Nova Science Publishers, Inc. ✢ New York

CONTENTS

PREFACE

This book explores the ways in which global stock exchanges work. A stock exchange or share market is a corporation or mutual organization which provides "trading" facilities for stock brokers and traders to trade stocks and other securities. Stock exchanges also provide facilities for the issue and redemption of securities as well as other financial instruments and capital events including the payment of income and dividends. The initial offering of stocks and bonds to investors is by definition done in the primary market and subsequent trading is done in the secondary market. This new book is dedicated to understanding the stability, interrelations and roles of these global stock markets. The various factors which drive the supply and demand in stock markets, and subsequently affect the price of stocks, is examined as well.

Chapter 1 - The authors conducted a time-series and cross-sectional examination of institutional ownership in a panel of 171 publicly traded financial firms obtained from the *S&P500*, *MidCap400* and *SmallCap600* indices from 1997 to 2002. The authors found that institutional ownership of financial firms has steadily increased over time, and yearly changes in institutional ownership have shown a negatively skewed distribution across different types of S&P indices and financial corporations. The authors found significant evidence that institutional ownership is higher in financial firms with better firm performance, higher capital asset ratios (lower leverage), larger firm size, higher stock return variance, lower market to book ratio, and in financial firms that do not pay dividends. Further evidence shows that the determinants of institutional holdings vary across financial and non-financial firms, bull and bear markets, different S&P indices, and different types of financial corporations.

Chapter 2 - The authors analyzed the presence of rational bubbles in Istanbul Stock Exchange (ISE) between 1998-2006 period by implementing linear and nonlinear unit root tests to 7 different indices. The first analysis is based on implementing augmented Dickey-Fuller unit root and KPSS stationary tests to the price-dividend ratios of the indices. The results are in favor of the presence of rational bubbles in the indices. The authors implemented a further test which enables time-varying discount rates. Generally the results of the loglinear model also support the previous results. The potential weaknesses of linear test methods as well as the advantages of nonlinear models motivated to use the bilinear test method. The evidence from the nonlinear test is in favor of the existence of rational bubbles in all indices in the sample period of 2nd March 1998–29th December 2006. But the results of the sub periods are contradictory for some indices. In the first and second sub periods the authors cannot accept unit root bilinearity for ISE National-Services index. The results also reject the significance of the bilinear term for ISE National-Industrials and ISE Investment Trusts indices in the second sub period. As a result, the authors can conclude that as a general structure, the rational bubbles present in ISE.

Chapter 3 - The conduct of policy under floating exchange rates is becoming an increasingly important concern for developing countries. The challenge facing the central banks is to contain the volatility of the exchange rate while achieving low inflation and stimulating output growth. As a complement, the governments must implement sound policies to bring the fiscal and legal environments close to those of the advanced economies so as to enhance long-term economic growth. One recent example of an emerging economy that confronts this challenge is Turkey with a history of high inflation and a collapse of a fixed exchange rate based stabilization program that resulted in a market-forced devaluation. After a review of the literature, this chapter analyzes the developments in the foreign exchange market in Turkey in light of the Central Bank's policies during the floating exchange rate system between February 2001 and November 2003. The results indicate that the Central Bank had been successful in containing volatility and reducing the average inflation rate. However, the accumulated risks in the economy, such as the extreme appreciation of the currency and high real interest rates make the system vulnerable to adverse shocks.

Chapter 4 - The globalization of the world stock markets is the one of the new significant development occurred during the last decade. Various factors contributed to the globalization of financial organizations including: First, advancement of technology and remote access which have been utilized in the stock trading. Second: Emerging of international financial institutions, which offer financial services regardless of the geographical and jurisdictions boarders. Third: Introducing new trends of liberalization and removing restrictions on foreign ownership, trading and cross border transactions. Fourth: the movement occurred in the world stock markets towards regional integration of stock exchanges, clearing and settlements organizations, and other financial institutions.

Accordingly, the world stock markets are moving so rapidly towards globalization. The concept of globalization simply means the free movement of goods, technology, labor and capital flow. Our main concern is related to the globalization of capital flow through the world stock trading. The globalization of financial sector means the integration of the local financial system to international financial systems and institutions through cross borders financial transactions, products, and instruments. The globalization phenomenon may be a blessing which is embraced by the majority of economic experts due to the expected benefits of such economic opening. Many experts believe that globalization may bring market to more efficiency, lowering its risk due to the possibility of diversifications, more convenience, and using arbitrage in a relevant way. On the other side, many believe that globalization may harm the interests of some groups of society, such as farmers, labors, and small-scale industries.

Chapter 5 - This paper investigates the relative performance of local, foreign, and expatriate financial analysts on Latin American emerging markets. The authors measure analysts' relative performance with three dimensions: (1) forecast timeliness, (2) forecast accuracy and (3) impact of forecast revisions on security prices. Our main findings can be summarized as follows. First, there is strong evidence that foreign analysts supply timelier forecasts than their peers. Secondly, analysts working for foreign brokerage houses (i.e., expatriate and foreign ones) produce less biased forecasts than local analysts. Finally, after controlling for analysts' timeliness, the authors find that foreign financial analysts' upward revisions have a greater impact on stock returns than both followers and local lead analysts forecast revisions. Overall, our results suggest that investors should better rely on the research produced by analysts working for foreign brokerage houses when they invest in Latin American emerging markets.

Chapter 6 - Congress passed the Sarbanes-Oxley Act of 2002 (P.L. 107-204) to remedy weaknesses in accounting and corporate governance exposed by massive fraud at Enron Corp. and other firms. Criticism of the law, which has been fairly widespread among business groups, academics, and accountants, focuses on the costs of compliance, which are said to outweigh the benefits. Several studies and comments have argued that the rising cost of regulation has created incentives for firms to list their shares on foreign markets or to withdraw from the public markets altogether, weakening the international competitive position of U.S. stock exchanges.

Specific evidence cited includes the fact that 24 of the largest 25 initial public stock offerings (IPOs) in 2005 took place on foreign exchanges, and that there has been a boom in the private equity market, where U.S. securities regulation is minimal. This article attempts to put instances like these in context by presenting comparative data on the world's major stock markets over the past decade.

In terms of the number of corporations listing their shares, several foreign markets have shown faster growth than the major U.S. exchanges (the New York Stock Exchange (NYSE) and Nasdaq). However, these increases appear to be fueled primarily by growth in the number of domestic firms listing on their own national markets. While major foreign markets have seen significant declines in foreign listings as a percentage of all listings, U.S. exchanges have not been abandoned by foreign companies in significant numbers.

Perhaps the most common reason for firms to delist, or leave a stock exchange, is a merger with another firm. Lower costs of regulation may be a side benefit of many mergers, but trends in interest rates and stock prices appear to be the primary determinants of merger activity. A rising number of corporate acquisitions result in the acquired firms "going private" — becoming exempt from most regulation — but this trend is also largely driven by economic conditions. Private equity investment has boomed since 2000 because debt financing has been abundant and relatively cheap, and because institutional investors have sought higher yields than what the stock and bond markets have provided.

Figures on new issues of stock (including IPOs) are volatile, and annual data may be skewed by a few large deals. Certain foreign exchanges have recovered more quickly from the 2000-2002 bear market, but, on the whole, there is little evidence that the U.S. stock market is becoming less attractive to companies seeking to raise capital. When the bond markets are included, the role of the U.S. securities industry in capital formation appears to be as strong as ever.

The data surveyed here suggest that rising regulatory costs have not precipitated any crisis in U.S. markets, and that the outcome of global competition among stock exchanges depends more on fundamental market conditions than on differentials in regulatory costs.

Chapter 7 – The authors propose a two-stage approach for estimating Value-at-Risk (VaR) that can simultaneously reflect two stylized facts displayed by most asset return series: volatility clustering and the heavy-tailedness of conditional return distributions over short horizons. The proposed method combines the bias-corrected exponentially weighted moving average (EWMA) model for estimating the conditional volatility and the extreme value theory

(EVT) for estimating the tail of the innovation distribution. In particular, for minimizing bias in the estimation procedure, the proposed method makes minimal assumptions about the underlying innovation distribution and concentrates on modeling its tail using the non-parametric Hill estimator and uses the moment-ratio Hill estimator for the shape parameter of the extreme value distribution. To validate the model, the authors conducted an empirical investigation on the daily stock market returns of eight emerging Asian markets: China, India, Indonesia, Malaysia, Philippines, South Korea, Taiwan, and Thailand. In addition, the proposed method was compared with J.P. Morgan's RiskMetrics approach. The empirical results show that the proposed method provides a more accurate forecast of VaR for lower probabilities of VaR violation from 0.1% to 1%. Furthermore, the authors demonstrate that applying the Hill estimator to estimate the tail of the innovation distribution can better capture additional downside risk faced during times of greater fluctuation than the second-order moment-ratio Hill estimator.

Chapter 8 - Our panel data analysis (1988-2002) of a sample of 31 less developed countries shows that the stock market capitalization as a percentage of GDP- an important indicator of stock market development- has no relationship with the growth rates of gross fixed capital formation. Our time series analysis (1976-2005) of 15 countries shows that in at least 10 cases the authors observe no positive long-run relationship between the stock market turnover ratio and the growth of capital accumulation. Interestingly the countries experiencing the developmental function of stock market are by and large civil law origin countries with alleged poor shareholder protection.

Chapter 9 - This paper empirically analyzes the relationship between international stock prices and international business cycles, specifically focusing on the number of cointegration vectors of each variable. The empirical data were taken from statistics on Germany, Japan, the UK, and the USA tabulated from January 1980 to May 2001. No cointegrating vectors were identified in indices of international stock prices, whereas several were identified in indices of international industrial production. These empirical results suggest that international stock prices do not necessarily reflect international business cycles.

In: Global Stock Exchanges: Stability, Interrelationships… ISBN: 978-60692-184-5
Editor: Paolo B. Cassedes

Chapter 1

INSTITUTIONAL OWNERSHIP IN S&P INDEX FINANCIAL CORPORATIONS*

***Wallace N. Davidson III*[1], *Yixi Ning*[2†] *and Sameh Sakr*[3]**
[1]Southern Illinois University, Carbondale, IL, USA
[2]University of Houston-Victoria, TX, USA
[3]Sultan Qaboos University, Oman

Abstract

We conducted a time-series and cross-sectional examination of institutional ownership in a panel of 171 publicly traded financial firms obtained from the *S&P500*, *MidCap400* and *SmallCap600* indices from 1997 to 2002. We found that institutional ownership of financial firms has steadily increased over time, and yearly changes in institutional ownership have shown a negatively skewed distribution across different types of S&P indices and financial corporations. We found significant evidence that institutional ownership is higher in financial firms with better firm performance, higher capital asset ratios (lower leverage), larger firm size, higher stock return variance, lower market to book ratio, and in financial firms that do not pay dividends. Further evidence shows that the determinants of institutional holdings vary across financial and non-financial firms, bull and bear markets, different S&P indices, and different types of financial corporations.

JEL Classifications: G21, G22, G23, G32

Key Words: Financial Institutions Security Ownership S&P Indices

---

* A version of this chapter was also published in *New Developments in Banking and Finance,* edited by Linda M. Cornwall published by Nova Science Publishers, Inc. It was submitted for appropriate modifications in an effort to encourage wider dissemination of research.

† Correspondence author.

1. Introduction

Corporate control mechanisms consist of both internal and external monitoring factors (Jensen, 1993). External factors include capital markets, product and factor markets, and the legal/regulatory environment. Control factors for financial institutions are different from their non-regulated counterparts. Unlike non-financial corporations, financial institutions are subject to regulations and regulatory monitoring and supervision at both the state and national levels. This regulatory control has a mixed effect on the external and internal corporate control mechanisms. On the one hand, the control exercised by regulatory monitoring and supervision may reduce control required from other sources. On the other hand, regulatory restrictions reduce the ability of the capital markets to control corporations by decreasing the ability of bidders to engage in hostile-disciplinary takeovers because acquisitions of financial institutions require time-consuming regulatory approval. In addition, regulatory restriction in the product market may allow inefficient financial institutions to survive, a privilege that is denied to unregulated corporations.

Institutional ownership is only one among several mechanisms in both the internal and external markets for corporate control. The interaction of various mechanisms in the corporate control market is documented in the literature under the substitute hypothesis and the substitute monitoring hypothesis (e.g. Brickly & James, 1987; Mishra & Nielsen, 2000). Impediments to the corporate control market leave ownership by institutions and other blockholders as the primary capital market monitors for financial institutions. Institutions have become the majority stakeholders of most large publicly-traded firms in recent years and given their important role as monitors, it is important to examine the extent and possible determinants of institutional holdings in financial institutions.

We examine the recent trends and determinants of institutional ownership of financial institutions in this paper. Relatively few papers have examined institutional ownership in the financial firms. Roth and Saporoschenko (2001), with a sample of 65 large publicly traded banks in 1993, has found that bank size, capital adequacy, stock return variance, and CEO pay-performance sensitivity have significant effects on the proportion of a bank's shares held by institutional investors. We build on their research in several ways. Besides examining determinants of ownership in commercial banks, we examine institutional shareholdings of other types of financial institutions such as investment banks and insurance companies. Second, we consider additional factors such as firm performance and dividend yield as explanations of institutional ownership. Third, we examine how the determinants of institutional holdings vary in bull and bear markets and across different S&P indices. Fourth, our sample of 171 listed financial firms from the *S&P500*, *Midcap400* and *SmallCap600* indices from 1997 to 2002 allows us to conduct both a time-series and cross-sectional examination of institutional ownership.

We find that institutional ownership of financial firms steadily increased from 1997 to 2002. Institutional ownership is significantly higher in *S&P500* firms and in insurance and real estate companies than in other financial firms. The distribution of yearly changes in institutional ownership shows a negative skewness instead of a normal distribution. This distribution pattern indicates that the proportion of medium/large increases in institutional ownership is much larger than that of medium/large decreases.

We also find evidence that institutional holdings are significantly higher in financial firms with better firm performance, higher capital asset ratios (lower leverage), larger firm size, and higher risk (measured by the annualized value of stock return variance). However, the determinants of institutional ownership change across bull and bear markets, different S&P indices, and different types of financial corporations. We also find that improvement in firm performance, increases in firm size, and decreases in the stock return variance in the prior year will lead to an increase in institutional holdings in the following year.

Comparing our findings with Grinstein and Michaely's (2005) sample of non-financial firms, we find that institutional investors prefer some different firm-specific characteristics when choosing financial versus industrial stocks. Institutional ownership is higher in financial corporations with lower market to book ratios and in firms that do not pay dividends, which is different from their ownership of non-financial firm stock. We present further evidence that the differences between financial and non-financial firms are influenced by stock market trend, different S&P indices, and different types of financial corporations.

Additionally, we find evidence that a greater number of institutional investors are attracted to financial firms when it is relatively large, has a better capital ratio, a higher dividend yield, and a more volatile stock price. We find, however, a negative relation between financial firm size and the average size of investment made by each institutional investor. When a financial firm has a better performance, a higher capital asset ratio, and a greater CEO pay-performance sensitivity, the average shares held by each individual institutional investor tend to be larger.

We have organized the remainder of the paper as follows. In section 2, we review previous literature and develop related hypotheses. Data selection and methodologies are presented in Section 3. Section 4 presents the empirical analysis. A conclusion is drawn in Section 5.

2. Literature Review and Hypothesis Development

Regulatory control, especially in deposit institutions, may both exacerbate and mitigate agency problems in financial institutions. Prowse (1997) noted that regulators' least cost resolution objective differs from shareholder wealth maximization. Since mergers are subject to regulatory control and delay, market control through takeovers is reduced. In addition, financial firms had a lower concentration of ownership than non-financial corporations and, as result, less discipline imposed by institutional investors (Demsetz & Lehn, 1985). On the other hand, financial institutions are subject to regulatory monitoring and supervision thereby decreasing the necessary control required from other internal and external corporate control mechanisms.

There has been considerable research concerning institutional ownership in non-financial firms. Previous studies have documented that institutional ownership in non-financial firms is greater in high-quality firms (Del Guercio, 1996; McConnell & Servaes, 1990) and greater in low-dividend firms (Cready, 1994; Dahlquist & Robertsson, 2001; Grinstein & Michaely, 2005). Relatively few papers have examined institutional holding in financial firms, and some studies, such as Grinstein and Michaely (2005), excluded financial firms from their final sample. Utilizing the findings from these studies on non-financial firms, we expect institutional ownership in financial firms will be related to firm performance, capital ratio (leverage), and dividend yield.

Unlike individual investors, institutional investors invest on behalf of others and are constrained by regulations aimed at preventing them from speculating with others' money. Directed by "prudent-man" rules, they generally have invested a large proportion of their holdings in high-quality stocks (Del Guercio, 1996) such as firms with high Tobin's Q ratios (McConnell & Servaes, 1990) and firms with positive abnormal earnings forecasts (Brous & Kini, 1994). Based on these findings, we expect good performance to attract institutional investors in financial firms.

The role of capital for commercial banks, savings institutions, and credit institutions is critical. A lack of sufficient capital can lead to financial distress and would be associated with tangible and intangible costs for a firm. The Federal Deposit Insurance Corporation Improvement Act (FDICIA) of 1991 mandates a minimum capital ratio (8%) for U.S. commercial banks and threatens prompt corrective action (PCA) of undercapitalized banks and early closure of financially troubled banks. Berger (1995) has found earnings to be positively related to capital ratios in a sample of U.S. banks in the 1980s. Given institutional investors' desire for quality investments, deposit institutions with adequate capital may be more likely to attract institutional investors than those with capital adequacy issues.

However, if the risk reduction inherent in large capital ratios reduced expected return, large capital ratios could potentially reduce institutional ownership in financial firms. Several studies have shown banks with low capital ratios can overcome outside discipline better than other banks (e.g., Hovakimian & Kane, 2000; Roth & Saporoschenko, 2001). These results from prior studies suggest that the relation between institutional ownership and capital ratios may be more complex than expected by a linear model. We expect, therefore, that the relation may be nonlinear.

For investment banks, insurance companies, and real estate companies, the capital asset ratio is not as critical as that for deposit institutions since they are not subject to the same regulatory controls. Non-deposit financial firms may be more like their corporate counterparts in this regard. Prior studies have documented the relation between ownership and leverage. Friend and Lang (1988) found that managerial shareholdings are negatively related to debt ratio. Several studies (e.g., Shyam-Sunder & Myers, 1999; Fama & French, 2002) provided evidence to support pecking order theory, in which more profitable firms use less financial leverage. We, therefore, expect more profitable firms to attract more institutional shareholdings and institutional ownership to be higher in non-deposit financial firms with higher capital ratios (less leverage).

Dividend yield has been widely documented to be an important factor influencing professional investor decisions. Empirical results regarding this issue are mixed as well. Dividend changes usually lead analysts to change their earnings forecasts, which in turn affect institutional holdings (Denis, Denis, & Sarin, 1994; Caroll, 1995). Allen, Bernardo, and Welch (2000) found that institutional investors are more likely to invest in dividend-paying stocks due to their relative tax advantage treatment over individual investors. Grinstein and Michaely (2005) also found that institutional holdings are higher in dividend-paying firms than in non-dividend-paying firms, but dividend yield has a negative association with institutional ownership. Cready (1994) also provided evidence that institutional investors prefer low-dividend-yield firms. Dahlquist and Robertsson (2001) documented that foreign investors, most of which are institutional investors, prefer Swedish firms that pay relatively low dividends. Based on these findings for non-financial firms, we expect a negative relation between institutional ownership and dividend yield, but a positive association with the presence of dividend payments.

During the sample period of this study (1997 to 2002), the Glass-Steagall Act of 1933 that was aimed at separating investment and commercial banking activities, was repealed in the late 1999. The reduction in regulation from the repeal of this act may have increased the need for outside monitoring. Institutional ownership in financial firms may increase to fill this void.

3. Data, Methodology and Variable Definitions

3.1. Sample Selection

We obtain our sample using all financial firms from the *S&P500*, *MidCap400* and *SmallCap600* indices in 1997. There are a total of 179 financial firms (SIC codes from 6021 to 6799) in the three S&P indices. These firms are publicly traded commercial banks, savings institutions, credit institutions, investment banks, security brokers, dealers, insurance, and real estate companies. There are 73 firms from *S&P500*, 43 firms from *S&P MidCap400*, and 63 firms from *S&P SmallCaP600*. When a firm is de-listed from one of the indices after 1997, we keep it in the sample. We obtain data about the number of institutional investors, total institutional shares, total shares outstanding, index categories for these firms from *S&P Security Owner's Stock Guide* during a six-year period from 1997-2002. We delete 8 firms which had no available institutional ownership data in the *Stock Guide*. The final sample of this study consists of 171 publicly traded financial firms, which consists of 86 deposit institutions, 17 investment banks, 62 insurance companies, and 6 real estate companies. We obtain financial data for these firms from the *COMPUSTAT* database and CEO compensation data from the *EXECUCOMP* database.

3.2. Empirical Methodology

To examine institutional ownership in publicly traded financial firms, we use both time-series and cross-sectional tests. We analyze the average institutional ownership over time from 1997 to 2002 and use a frequency distribution analysis to examine yearly changes. We measure the relation of firm characteristics to institutional holdings with several tests. First, we employ univariate comparisons to determine whether firm characteristics affect institutional holdings. Second, we use year-by-year OLS regressions[1] for each year from 1997 to 2002 (shown in Appendix Table 3). Third, we use a fixed-effects model to examine the full sample of pooled time-series/cross-sectional data. The fixed-effects model is appropriate for our panel data because we may miss some potential determinants (i.e., macroeconomic factors) of institutional ownership (Hausman & Taylor, 1981). We only consider the company-specific determining variables in this study.

[1] Since the dependent variable is the percentage of institutional ownership and it is a two-sided Tobit variable, so we also conduct Tobit regressions for robustness check and get similar results as OLS.

Then we follow the approach in Grinstein and Michaely (2005), and construct a lagged-variables model with one-year lagged explanatory variables. Grinstein and Michaely (2005) argued that a static relation between institutional ownership at time t and firm characteristics at time t is not appropriate because institutional investors cannot change their holdings dramatically just after the changes of firm characteristics. Finally, we examine changes in firm characteristics on changes in institutional holdings.

3.3. Variable Definitions

The dependent variable in our paper is *the percent of institutional ownership,* which is equal to total shares owned by institutions divided by total shares outstanding. Independent variables consist of firm performance, capital asset ratio (leverage), dividend yield, and other control variables. We use the book-value *return on assets* to measure firm performance and expect it to have a positive association with institutional ownership. To measure the impact of capital (leverage) on institutional ownership, we use the *capital asset ratio,* which is the book value of equity divided by total assets. We expect a positive relation between capital asset ratios and institutional ownership. To measure the effect of undercapitalization status on institutional ownership in deposit institutions, we also employ a dummy variable, *undercapitalization dummy*, which equals to 1 when the capital asset ratio is less than 8% and 0 otherwise. We use two variables to proxy for a firm's dividend payout policy: *dividend yield*, and *dividend-payment dummy*, which equals to 1 when a firm pays cash dividends, or 0 when it does not. We expect a negative relation between institutional ownership and dividend yield, but a positive relation with the dividend-payment dummy variable.

3.4. Other Control Variables

Since institutional investors have often tilted their portfolios towards large firms (Falkenstein, 1996; George, 1996; Dahlquist & Robertsson, 2001; Cready, 1994; Roth & Saporoschenko, 200; Grinstein & Michaely, 2005), we use the *log of market capitalization,* which equals to the number of shares outstanding times the year-end stock price of the firm, to measure the size of the firm and expect it to have a positive relation with institutional ownership.

The market-to-book ratio and Tobin's Q are often used to measure a firm's growth potential (Lakonishok, Shleifer, & Vishny, 1994). Institutional investors seem to prefer firms with low market-to-book ratios (Gompers & Metrick, 2001; Grinstein & Michaely, 2005). We use the *market-to-book ratio*, measured as the market value of a firm's equity divided by book-value of equity, to capture value/growth characteristics of these traded financial firms. We expect institutional investors to prefer financial firms with low market to book ratios.

Equity holdings of professional money managers may be related to momentum trading strategies. For example, Grinblatt, Titman, & Wermers (1995) found that about 77% of the mutual funds were "momentum investors", and these funds are found to perform better than other funds in the intermediate term. Jegadeesh and Titman (1993, 2001) documented that stocks performing well in the past 3 to 12 months generate significant positive abnormal returns and stocks performing poorly generate significantly negative abnormal returns. Similar results also appear in Davidson and Dutia (1989) who documented stocks performing well (poorly) in one calendar year continue to perform well (poorly) in the next year. We, therefore, expect that the institutional investors will buy into past winners and sell out past losers to realize abnormal returns in the intermediate horizon. We use a *1-year abnormal stock return* of a financial firm to capture the intermediate-horizon momentum characteristic and expect it to have a positive relation with institutional ownership.

On the other hand, contrarian trading strategies seem to work well in the long run. Many studies has found that long-term past losers outperform past-winners over the subsequent three to five years (DeBondt & Thaler, 1985, 1987; Jegadeesh & Titman, 2001). So we argue that institutional investors should have lower holdings of such stocks that have higher abnormal return in the past three to five years. We use a *3-year abnormal stock return* of a financial firm to capture the characteristics of a contrarian trading strategy, and expect the variable to have a negative relation with institutional ownership. We calculate 1-year (3-year) stock abnormal return by using 1-year (3-year) total stock return minus NYSE/AMEX/NASDAQ value-weighted benchmark return from CRSP database.

Firm risk may affect institutional holdings, although the results of past research are equivocal and have found a positive relation between risk and institutional holdings (Grinstein & Michaely, 2005) and a negative relation (Roth & Saporoschenko, 2001). We employ annualized value of *stock return variance* to measure stock risk, and expect professional money managers to buy stocks of financial firms with low risk. We expect this relation because money managers are guided by "prudent-man" rules. We use twelve months' stock closing prices to calculate the annualized stock return variance.

Roth and Saporoschenko (2001) found that CEO pay-performance sensitivity has a significant impact on institutional investors' choice. A compensation package with high pay-performance sensitivity may signal the high quality of bank assets, and/or CEO's commitment to maximizing shareholder wealth. They did not find a relation between institutional ownership and affiliated block ownership, proportion of outside directors, outside director share ownership, board size, and CEO duality. We, therefore, include only *CEO pay-performance sensitivity* as a control variable to account for the internal governance structure. Following Jensen and Murphy (1990), we define CEO pay-performance sensitivity as the annual dollar change of CEO wealth relative to each $1000 change in the shareholder wealth.

Because our sample consists of the publicly traded financial firms from *S&P500*, *S&P MidCap400*, and *S&P SmallCap600*, the type of indices on which a financial firm is listed may affect institutional holdings, especially for the portfolios of index funds. Listing on the *S&P500* index increases trading volume (Shleifer, 1986; Harris & Gurel, 1986) and increases institutional ownership (Pruitt & Wei, 1989). Cready (1994) and Del Guercio (1996) found that institutional investors, guided by the "prudent-man" rules prefer *S&P500* listed firms. In this paper, a categorical variable, *index type*, is used to measure the effects of S&P indices on the ownership when we conduct some additional regressions. In addition, different types of financial firms may attract different levels of institutional holdings. We use another categorical variable, *FI type*, to control the type of financial corporations, such as deposit institutions, investment banks, insurance companies, and real estate firms.

4. Empirical Analysis

4.1. Summary Statistics

The summary statistics of institutional ownership in financial firms appears in the Table 1. Panel A shows institutional ownership across our sample period, 1997-2002. The mean number of institutional investors in financial firms more than doubled from 361 to 905 during this 6-year period. The mean (median) values of the percent of institutional ownership steadily increase from 53.42% (53.03%) in 1997 to 64.89% (65.90%) in 2002. The average number of shares held by each institutional investor increased each year from 1997 to 2000 but began to decrease in 2002 perhaps due to the onset of a bear market. The percent of average institutional holdings has a decreasing monotonic trend from 1997 to 2002 as can be seen from the last two rows of panel A. In 1997, the average institutional shareholder held about 0.23% of a financial firm's total outstanding shares, but this number decreased to only 0.12% in 2002. The increasing number of institutional investors and the decrease in average shareholdings could cause an increasing in free-riding problem among institutional investors and could demonstrate their desire to exploit the benefits of diversification.

Table 1. Summary statistics of institutional ownership

Panel A: Institutional ownership across years from 1997-2002

		1997	1998	1999	2000	2001	2002
# of institutional shareholders	Mean	361	443	540	524	650	905
	median	254	338	384	374	460	716
Shares of institutional ownership (million shares)	Mean	67.48	99.45	155.51	191.77	241.04	269.23
	median	34.20	48.30	58.08	72.21	85.44	104.18
Total shares outstanding (million shares)	Mean	122.19	176.01	267.67	325.91	392.04	423.69
	median	71.28	99.38	110.27	127.54	137.32	152.45
Percent of institutional ownership (%)	Mean	53.42	56.06	56.38	55.81	61.44	64.89
	median	53.03	55.08	56.15	57.73	62.51	65.90
Average shares by each institutional shareholder (000)	Mean	149.57	173.88	198.12	245.24	250.17	206.29
	median	120.97	146.01	147.19	172.02	173.94	146.80
Percent of average institutional shares (%)	Mean	0.23	0.20	0.17	0.17	0.15	0.12
	median	0.18	0.16	0.14	0.14	0.12	0.09

Panel B: Institutional ownership across different S&P indices

		Full Sample	S&P500	S&P MidCap	S&P SmallCap	Non-S&P firm-years
# of institutional shareholders	Mean	549	868	303	170	120
	median	402	731	271	160	125
Shares of institutional ownership (million shares)	Mean	160.92	292.34	46.38	16.04	23.56
	median	63.60	144.73	40.15	14.15	18.13
Total shares outstanding (million shares)	Mean	269.76	484.12	86.62	31.19	40.74
	median	107.54	242.76	79.09	28.15	34.68
Percent of institutional ownership (%)	Mean	57.53	61.64	53.98	53.11	51.61
	median	59.18	61.89	49.46	51.37	41.47
Average shares by each institutional shareholder (000)	Mean	199.83	276.05	152.77	93.40	165.60
	median	149.24	213.57	133.05	88.77	138.46
Percent of average institutional shares (%)	Mean	0.18	0.09	0.19	0.34	0.41
	median	0.14	0.08	0.17	0.30	0.36

Panel C: Institutional ownership across different types of financial firms

		Deposit institutions	Investment banks	Insurance companies	Real estate & others
# of institutional shareholders	Mean	623	486	476	369
	median	425	368	401	142
Shares of institutional ownership (million shares)	Mean	212.00	124.55	99.56	174.96
	median	68.22	41.06	63.30	15.15
Total shares outstanding (million shares)	Mean	363.87	235.95	152.00	242.26
	median	145.72	81.09	88.33	28.52
Percent of institutional ownership (%)	Mean	51.33	51.74	67.31	60.81
	median	52.23	49.32	68.85	71.77
Average shares by each institutional shareholder (000)	Mean	224.81	174.43	168.50	254.62
	median	167.84	118.83	147.35	113.55
Percent of average institutional shares (%)	Mean	0.13	0.18	0.23	0.35
	median	0.11	0.14	0.17	0.33

This sample of financial firms is obtained from *S&P500, S&P MidCap400, and S&P SmallCap600* . We obtain the institutional ownership data from the *S&P Security Owner's Stock Guide*. The final sample consists of 171 financial firms from 1997 to 2002. *# of institutional shareholders* is the total number of institutional investors in a financial firm. *Shares of institutional ownership* are total number of shares held by all institutional investors. *Total shares outstanding* are total number of outstanding shares by a financial firm. *Percent of institutional ownership (%)* is total shares held by all institutions over total shares outstanding. *Average shares by each institutional shareholder* are defined as total shares held by all institutions divided by total number of institutional investors. *Percent of average institutional shares (%)* is proportion of average shares held by each institutional investor over total shares outstanding by a financial firm.

Panel B displays institutional ownership data across different S&P indices. *S&P500* financial firms have the highest institutional ownership at 61.64%, while that for *S&P MidCap* firms is 53.98%, for *S&P SmallCap* firms is 53.11%, and for non-S&P firms, which are financial firms de-listed from one of the indices during the sample period, is only 51.61%. This finding is consistent with Cready (1994), who has documented institutional investors' preference for *S&P500* firms. The mean (median) institutional ownership for all S&P financial firms during a 6-year period is 57.53% (59.18%), suggesting that institutions held more than half of the total financial firms' equity in the U.S. On average, *S&P500* firms have the largest number of institutional investors (868) when compared to those in the other indices. However, they have the lowest percent of average shares held by each institutional shareholder, which is only 0.09% of total shares and far less than the 0.18% for the full sample and 0.34% for *S&P SmallCap* firms. Institutional investors' smaller ownership in S&P 500 as compared to other indices could perhaps be attributed to the variations in the size of companies comprising each index.

Panel C reports ownership structure across different types of financial firms. The average institutional ownership for insurance companies is 67.31%. For deposit institutions and investment banks, the average institutional holdings are 51.33% and 51.74%. We also find that average institutional shareholder holds a lower proportion of total shares for deposit institutions (0.13%) and investment banks (0.18%), as compared to insurance companies (0.23%) and real estate firms (0.35%).

4.2. Time-Series Analysis of Changes in Institutional Ownership

Following Denis and Sarin (1999), we examine average changes in institutional ownership between 1997 and 2002. Then we conduct a frequency distribution analysis of yearly changes in ownership and explore whether stock market trend affects the pattern of yearly changes.

4.2.1. Average Changes in Institutional Ownership over Time

We plot median levels of institutional ownership for the first year, 1997, and the last year, 2002, based on different ownership levels, types of S&P indices, and financial firms and show them in Figure 1.

Panel A of Figure 1 shows that institutional ownership increased from 1997 to 2002 across all ownership levels. While low ownership firms (under 20% in 1997) increased substantially, high ownership firms (above 80% in 1997) also increased slightly. We do not observe a mean reversion trend here. Institutional ownership in financial firms from each S&P index (Panel B) increases over these years. *S&P500* firms have the highest ownership in 1997 and still increase slightly in 2002. *S&P MidCap* firms have the lowest ownership in 1997 but have a greater increase in 2002. This pattern of increasing ownership across the years could perhaps be explained by financial institutions' attempt to fill the gap left behind after the increased deregulation and the decrease in monitoring that accompanied deregulation of the financial institutions sector. For example, the repeal of Glass-Steagall Act in late 1999 eliminated the legal framework for the separation of commercial banking and investment banking business. Panel C shows that, of the various types of financial firms, insurance and real estate firms have the greatest proportion of institutional ownership in both 1997 and 2002.

Panel A: Median percentage institutional ownership across different ownership levels

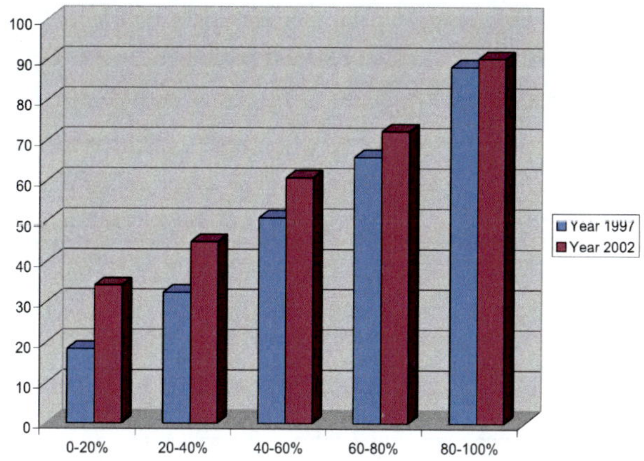

Panel B: Median percentage institutional ownership across different S&P indices

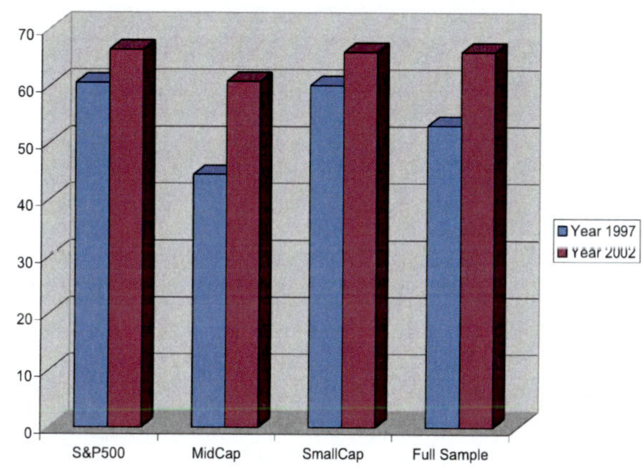

Panel C: Median percentage institutional ownership across different FI types

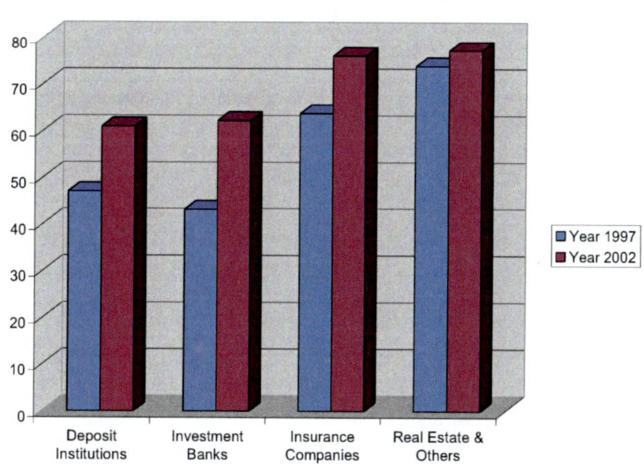

Figure 1. Changes in institutional ownership between 1997 and 2002.

4.2.2. Frequency Distribution Analysis of Yearly Changes in Institutional Ownership

Table 2 presents a frequency distribution analysis of yearly changes in institutional ownership from 1997 to 2002. To describe patterns of yearly changes, we define a large change of institutional ownership as either an increase of 10%, or a decrease of 10% relative to previous year[2]. A medium change is from -10 to -2% or 2 to 10%, and a small change is from −2% to 2%.

Table 2. Frequency distribution analysis of annual changes in institutional ownership

Panel A: Percentage of institutional ownership across different ownership levels

Changes in ownership	Previous institutional ownership			
	Full sample	0-30%	30-70%	>70%
Less than -10%	5.0	2.1	2.7	12.5
-10% to -2%	13.4	8.3	12.3	18.4
-2% to 2%	33.6	33.3	32.5	36.8
2% to 10%	40.2	48.0	42.5	30.9
Greater than 10%	7.8	8.3	10.0	1.4

Panel B: Percentage of institutional ownership across different S&P indices

Changes in ownership	S&P Index Type		
	S&P 500	S&P MidCap	S&P SmallCap
Less than -10%	3.1	4.3	10.3
-10% to -2%	13.4	13.7	13.5
-2% to 2%	39.3	36.0	19.4
2% to 10%	40.2	36.0	43.9
Greater than 10%	4.0	10.0	12.9

Panel C: Percentage of institutional ownership across different FI types

Changes in ownership	FI Type			
	Deposit Institutions	Investment Banks	Insurance Companies	Real Estate Companies
Less than -10%	4.9	1.6	6.4	6.7
-10% to -2%	12.2	7.9	15.7	26.7
-2% to 2%	37.3	33.3	29.2	20.0
2% to 10%	39.4	47.6	39.4	33.3
Greater than 10%	6.2	9.5	9.3	13.3

[2] We also conduct frequency distribution analysis using other definitions of large increases/decreases (i.e., 8%, 12%) in institutional ownership and obtain the similar distribution pattern as that in Table 2.

Table 2. Continued

Panel D: Percentage of institutional ownership from 1997 to1999 (Bull market)

Changes in ownership	Previous institutional ownership			
	Full sample	0-30%	30-70%	>70%
Less than -10%	5.6	0.0	2.4	20.0
-10% to -2%	16.7	4.3	18.2	16.4
-2% to 2%	35.9	30.4	35.4	40.0
2% to 10%	33.1	52.2	34.0	21.8
Greater than 10%	8.7	13.1	10.0	1.8

Panel E: Percentage of institutional ownership from 2000 to2002 (Bear market)

Changes in ownership	Previous institutional ownership			
	Full sample	0-30%	30-70%	>70%
Less than -10%	4.0	4.0	3.0	7.3
-10% to -2%	8.6	12.0	6.9	13.2
-2% to 2%	32.7	36.0	22.9	41.2
2% to 10%	46.9	44.0	51.1	36.8
Greater than 10%	7.8	4.0	9.1	1.5

This sample of financial firms is obtained from *S&P500, S&P Midcap400, and S&P SmallCap600* indices. We obtain the institutional ownership data from the *S&P Security Owner's Stock Guide*. The final sample consists of 171 financial firms from 1997 to 2002. We classify the years from 1997 to 1999 as the bull market period and the years from 2000 to 2002 as the bear market period. The annual return of CRSP NYSE/AMEX/NASDAQ value-weighted market index was 30.3%, 22.3%, and 25.4% from 1997 to 1999, then decreased to -11.1%, -11.3%, and -21.0% from 2000 to 2002.

Panel A of Table 2 displays the frequency distribution results of yearly changes in institutional ownership across different previous ownership levels. First, we find an asymmetric distribution of yearly changes. For the full sample of firm-years, 7.8% of firm-years display large annual increases (above 10% growth) and 40.2% show medium increases (2 to 10%), while only 5.0% of total firm-years display large decreases (less than 10%) and 13.4% show medium decrease (−10 to −2%). The yearly changes in institutional ownership show a negatively skewed distribution. This asymmetric distribution pattern exists across various ownership levels (Panel A), S&P indices (Panel B), and types of financial firms (Panel C). Since the ownership increased gradually over the sample period from 1997 to 2002, the distribution of annual changes has a positive mean (1.75%). The largest proportion of changes (40.2%) occurs in the category with annual increases of 2% to 10%. However, large annual increases in institutional ownership are not uncommon for U.S. financial corporations (7.8%). These results suggest that portfolio managers continue to buy into financial stocks in the sample period from 1997 to 2002.

Panel B and C report frequency distribution results across different S&P indices and types of financial firms respectively. Ownership in *S&P500* financial firms appears more stable over time than for firms in other *S&P indices*. As Panel B shows, 39.3% of these *S&P500* firms have ownership changes of −2% to 2%, which is greater than that of other categories. As shown in Panel C, deposit institutions and investment banks seem to be less likely to have large changes in institutional ownership than other types of financial corporations.

4.2.3. Yearly Changes in Institutional Ownership across Bull and Bear Markets

The U.S. had a strong "bull" market in the 1990s, followed by a "bear" market that started in 2000. This market trend can be identified in our sample period based on the annual return of CRSP NYSE/AMEX/NASDAQ value-weighted market index, which was 30.3%, 22.3%, and 25.4% from 1997 to 1999, then decreased to −11.1%, −11.3%, and −21.0% from 2000 to 2002. Our sample period is from 1997 to 2002, so one concern is that the U.S. stock market trend may affect the distribution pattern of yearly changes in institutional ownership. We expect that institutional investors will buy more in the bull market and sell more shares in the bear market. So we divide the full sample of firm-years into two subsamples, bull-market subsample from 1997 to 1999, and the bear-market subsample from 2000 to 2002. We, then, perform a frequency distribution analysis of the two subsamples (Table 2). We indeed find evidence that the yearly changes in institutional ownership differ between bull-market and bear-market subsamples, but the evidence is different from our original expectation.

The results in Panel D and Panel E (Table 2) shows that, from 1997 to 1999, the proportion of large decreases (less than −10%) and medium decreases (−10 to −2%) in institutional ownership is as high as 22.3%, while that in bear market is only 12.6%. On the other hand, the percent of large increases (larger than 10%) and medium increases (2 to10%) in the bull market is smaller than that in bear markets (41.8% vs. 54.7%). The seemingly inconsistent findings may suggest institutional investors are more likely to buy into financial stocks even in a "bear" market because these stocks may be considered safe havens and less risky than other stocks, such as those in high-tech firms. In addition, the Federal Reserve Bank reduced interest rates numerous times between 2000 and 2003. Low interest rates generally benefit financial corporations, perhaps making them more attractive to institutional investors. Finally, the Glass-Steagall Act separating investment and commercial banking activities was repealed in the late 1999, just before the start of bear market in 2000. Deregulation in financial sector may have made investments in financial corporations attractive even in the "bear" market.

4.3. Univariate Analysis

To examine whether firm characteristics affect institutional ownership in financial corporations, we divide the full sample of firm-years into two subsamples based on median values of the firm variables, and then use t tests to compare institutional ownership between the above-median and below-median groups.

The results in Table 3 suggest that the level of institutional ownership is affected by many market and firm characteristics. The t-statistics are highly significant (at 0.01 levels) for return on assets, capital asset ratio, firm size, and dividend yield, which are consistent with our hypotheses. We find, however, that institutional ownership is significantly higher in financial firms with lower market to book ratio (t=-2.65, significant at 0.01 level) and non-dividend-paying firms (t=−4.95, 0.001 level). This finding is inconsistent with Grinstein and Michaely (2005), who document that institutional holdings are higher in industrial firms with

Table 3. Univariate comparison of a firm's characteristics on the institutional ownership

	Mean of Institutional ownership (%)	Mean difference (%)	t statistic
High return on assets firms	60.93	6.32	4.80***
Low return on assets firms	54.61		
Adequately-capitalized firms	58.98	3.69	2.61**
Undercapitalized firms	55.29		
High capital ratio firms	63.46	11.11	8.73***
Low capital ratio firms	52.35		
Dividend-paying firms	56.57	−11.13	−5.26***
Non-dividend paying firms	67.70		
High dividend yield firms	52.70	−10.32	−8.14***
Low dividend yield firms	63.02		
Large market capitalization firms	59.79	4.20	3.18**
Small market capitalization firms	55.59		
High market-to-book firms	55.93	−3.51	−2.65**
Low market-to-book firms	59.44		
High 1-year abnormal return firms	57.31	−0.99	−0.75
Low 1-year abnormal return firms	58.30		
High 3-year abnormal return firms	58.32	1.21	0.92
Low 3-year abnormal return firms	57.10		
High risk firms	59.87	4.63	3.59***
Low risk firms	55.24		
High CEO pay-performance firms	58.26	0.24	0.18
Low CEO pay-performance firms	58.02		
1997-1999	55.20	−5.30	−4.15***
2000-2002	60.50		

***, **, *, and † denote significance at the 0.001, 0.01, 0.05, and 0.10 levels, respectively.

This sample of financial firms from *S&P500, S&P Midcap400, and S&P SmallCap600* indices consists of 171 financial firms from 1997 to 2002. The institutional ownership data are obtained from the *S&P Security Owner's Stock Guide*, and firm characteristics data are drawn from *COMPUSTAT, CRSP,* and *EXECUCOMP* database. We divide the full sample of firm-years into two subsamples based on median values of those firm variables respectively, and then use t tests to compare institutional ownership in high-median subsample and low-median subsample.

a higher growth opportunity and paying dividends. This inconsistent finding could be explained by the difference between regulated and non-regulated firms. Corporations' dividend payout may be designed to accommodate the preferences of some large institutional shareholders (e.g., pension funds, university endowment funds) with tax advantage versus those shareholders whose dividends are taxed as regular income. There is evidence that the non-dividend paying firms are typically smaller in firm size, and own a smaller number of institutional shareholders than the dividend paying firms[3].

The t-test results also strongly suggest that institutional ownership is higher in high-risk financial firms measured by the variance of the stock price. The finding supports that of Grinstein and Michaely (2005) yet contradict those of Roth and Saporoschenko (2001) who argue that a risk-averse institutional investor is more likely to be attracted by bank stocks with low volatility. We do not find evidence to support the finding by Roth and Saporoschenko (2001) that institutional ownership is higher in firms with higher CEO pay-performance sensitivity. However, this result is consistent with Booth, Cornett, and Tehranian (2001). They indicate that higher CEO pay performance sensitivity in financial institutions may not entice institutional investors to hold more of financial institutions' stock because the presence of regulatory surveillance undermines the importance of internal control mechanisms. We also find that institutional ownership is significantly higher in the "bear" market (60.50%) from 2000 to 2002 as compared to the "bull" market (55.20%) from 1997 to 1999. The difference is strongly significant at 0.001 level (t=−4.15), indicating money managers' escape to relatively safe investment havens. We further conduct t tests of institutional ownership across different S&P indices and different FI types and find some different results[4].

As we discussed in the literature review, the effects of a firm's capital status on institutional ownership is different between deposit institutions and non-deposit financial firms. The role of capital for commercial banks, savings institutions, and credit unions is more important than for other financial firms. The undercapitalization variable (which equals to 1 if a firm's capitalization is less than 8%) is statistically significant only for deposit firms (t=−2.14, 0.05 level), but not for other non-deposit financial firms. The undercapitalized deposit institutions have a higher institutional ownership than the adequately capitalized firms (53.19% vs. 49.48%). We also find that the average institutional ownership is significantly (t =−2.21, 0.05 level) higher in the below-median capital ratio deposit firms than that in the above-median capital ratios deposit firms (53.23% vs. 49.42%). These findings are consistent with several previous studies which employed commercial banks as their research samples (i.e., Hovakimian & Kane, 2000; Roth & Saporoschenko, 2001). But for non-deposit firms, such as insurance companies, institutional ownership is significantly higher (t = 4.84, 0.001 level) if they have a higher capital asset ratio (72.24% vs. 63.27%), supporting a negative relation between institutional ownership and leverage.

---

[3] We find that the non-dividend-paying firms are typically smaller than the dividend-paying firms (the mean difference of market value o f equity is −$10.44 billion, t = −5.31, significant at 0.001 level), therefore it has a smaller number of institutional owners (the mean difference of the number of institutional investors is 184.80 thousands, t = −5.50, significant at 0.001 level).

[4] We further conduct t tests of institutional ownership across different S&P indices (Appendix Table 1) and different FI types (Appendix Table 2), and find some different results. When we control for S&P index types, the significant effects of firm size on the institutional ownership disappear. The positive relation between institutional ownership and stock risk is only significant (t = 3.20, significant at 0.001 level) for *S&P500* firms, but not for *S&P Midcap* and *SmallCap* firms (t = 0.25 and 0.13 respectively). The t test results across different types of financial firms are obviously different from those of total sample of firms. For example, institutional shareholdings is significantly higher in insurance companies with a better firm performance (t = 3.31, significant at 0.001 level) and in investment banks with a lower dividend yield (t=−8.13, significant at 0.001 level), but not in other types of financial firms.

4.4. Multiple Regression Results Across Bull and Bear Markets

To further document the effects of firm factors on the institutional ownership in the listed financial firms, we employ a multivariate model to explore the issue. We use *the percent of institutional ownership to total shares outstanding* as the dependent variable. Our independent variables are the return on assets, dividend yield, capital asset ratio (leverage) while controlling for firm size, market-to-book, stock return, risk, and CEO pay-performance sensitivity.

Table 4. Fixed-effects Regression Results across Bull and Bear Markets

	Full sample		Bull-market		Bear-market	
	Model 1	*Model 2*	*Model 3*	*Model 4*	*Model 5*	*Model 6*
Return on assets	0.002 (1.71)†	0.003 (2.18)*	-0.005 (-1.66)†	-0.005 (-1.78)†	0.003 (2.18)*	0.004 (2.75)**
Capital asset ratio	0.381 (7.96)***	0.357 (6.79)***	0.387 (4.81)***	0.415 (4.93)***	0.333 (5.24)***	0.279 (4.09)***
Undercapitalization dummy	-- --	0.017 (1.15)	-- --	0.015 (0.79)	-- --	0.025 (1.25)
Dividend yield	-0.007 (-2.45)*	−0.004 (−1.28)	-0.043 (-5.41)***	-0.049 (-5.45)***	-0.001 (-0.23)	0.003 (1.12)
Dividend-paying dummy	-- --	−0.102 (−4.14)***	-- --	0.056 (1.46)	-- --	-0.185 (-5.82)***
Log of market capitalization	0.029 (6.05)***	0.032 (6.67)***	0.035 (5.40)***	0.033 (5.12)***	0.018 (2.68)**	0.027 (4.17)***
Market-to-book	-0.003 (-1.76)†	−0.004 (−1.97)†	0.001 (0.56)	0.001 (0.67)	-0.015 (-4.06)***	-0.018 (-5.11)***
1-year abnormal return	-2.2E-4 (-1.00)	−3.1E−4 (−1.44)	-2.5E-4 (-0.68)	-1.6E-4 (-0.42)	-4.9E-5 (-0.19)	-1.4E-4 (-0.57)
3-year abnormal return	-4.1E-4 (-0.91)	5.0E−5 (0.11)	-0.002 (-2.99)**	-0.002 (-3.38)***	0.002 (2.64)**	0.002 (3.88)***
Stock return variance	1.27E-4 (3.22)***	1.1E−4 (2.71)**	4.43E-5 (1.17)	5.5E-5 (1.37)	0.001 (5.38)***	0.001 (5.80)***
CEO pay-performance	-5.4E-6 (-0.07)	−9.3E−6 (−0.12)	3.80E-4 (2.26)*	3.9E-4 (2.31)*	-5.6E-5 (-0.65)	-8.0E-5 (-0.98)
Adjusted R^2	18.7%	20.5%	23.7%	23.8%	25.5%	32.7%
F	12.89***	12.71***	12.33***	10.65***	11.01***	13.02***

***, **, *, and † denote significance at the 0.001, 0.01, 0.05, and 0.10 levels, respectively.

This sample of financial firms from *S&P500, S&P Midcap400, and S&P SmallCap600* indices consists of 171 financial firms from 1997 to 2002. The dependent variable is *the percent of institutional holdings to total shares outstanding*. We divide the full sample of firm-years into two subsamples: the bull-market sample from 1997 to 1999 and the bear-market sample from 2000 to 2002.The *capital asset ratio* is the book value of equity to total assets. The *undercapitalization dummy* is equal to 1 when the capital asset ratio is less than 8% and 0 otherwise. The *dividend-payment dummy* is equal to 1 when a firm pays dividend, or 0 otherwise. We calculate *1-year* and *3-year stock abnormal return* relative to CRSP NYSE/AMEX/NASDAQ value-weighted benchmark. The *stock return variance* is defined as the annualized value of monthly stock return variance. The *CEO pay-performance sensitivity* is defined as the dollar change of CEO wealth relative to each $1000 change in the shareholder value. t values are reported in parenthesis. Variance Inflation Factors (VIF) indicates multicollinearity is not a problem.

To examine whether regression results differ over time, we first run OLS regression year by year from 1997 to 2002 (Shown in Appendix Table 3). The year-by-year OLS results provide evidence supporting that institutional ownership is higher in financial firms with lower dividend yields, greater capital asset ratio, larger market capitalization, smaller market to book ratio, and higher risk. The estimated coefficients for these variables are significant in some of the six years, and the significance levels change in different years, indicating the existence of yearly effects. We, therefore, use a fixed-effects model to regress the pooled data. A fixed-effects model is appropriate because we may miss some potential determinants of institutional ownership (i.e., macroeconomic factors). Hausman and Taylor (1981) argued that the fixed-effects framework represents a common, unbiased method of controlling for omitted variables in a panel data set. The fixed-effects regression results are in Table 4.

The fixed-effects regression results from the full sample of pooled data in Model 1 continue to support most findings that were obtained from the t tests and year-by-year OLS regressions. The estimated coefficients for the return on assets (t=1.71, significant at 0.10 level), capital asset ratio (t=7.96, 0.001 level), log of market capitalization (t=6.05, 0.001level), and stock return variance (t=3.22, 0.01 level) are positive, and the estimated coefficients for dividend yield (t=-2.45, 0.05 level) and market-to-book ratio (t=−1.76, 0.10 level) are negative.

We then add an undercapitalization dummy (equals to 1 when the capital asset ratio is less than 8% and 0 otherwise), and a dividend-payment dummy (equals to 1 when a firm pay dividend and 0 otherwise) as explanatory variables in Model 2. We use the undercapitalization dummy to test the expected nonlinear relation between capital asset ratio and institutional holdings in financial corporations. However, we do not find a significant coefficient for the dummy variable for the full sample of all types of financial institutions. The nonlinear relation may exist only in deposit institutions, and we address this in the next section. The estimated coefficient for dividend-payment dummy is negative and strongly significant (t=−4.14, significant at 0.001 level), suggesting that professional money managers prefer financial firms without dividend payments, which is contrary to the results from non-financial firms found in Grinstein and Michaely (2005).

As we previously documented, our sample spans both the "bull" market and "bear" market in the U.S., and the frequency distribution pattern of annual changes in institutional holdings varies across the bull and bear markets. At the same time, the Glass-Steagall Act (GSA) was repealed in the late 1999 and the increasing deregulation in financial sector is also expected to influence professional money mangers. So we divide the full sample of firm-years into two subsamples: the bull-market sample from 1997 to 1999 (pre-GSA) and the bear-market sample from 2000 to 2002 (post-GSA).

The fixed-effects regression results for the bull and bear samples have some differences. First, institutional investors are more likely to invest in quality financial stocks with larger return on assets (t=2.75, significant at 0.01 level) and lower market to book ratios (t= -5.11, 0.001 level) in the bear market than in the bull market. Second, institutional holdings are higher in financial firms with a lower dividend yield (t=-5.41, 0.001 level), and a greater CEO pay-performance sensitivity (t=2.31, 0.05 level) in the bull market. But in the bear market, institutional ownership is higher in financial institutions with higher stock return variance (t=5.80, 0.001 level), and in firms that do not pay dividends (t=-5.82, 0.001 level). Third, institutional investors are more likely to be "momentum investors" in a bull market than in a bear market. The estimated coefficient for 3-year abnormal return is negative (t=-3.38, 0.001

level) in the bull market, but the sign changes to positive (t=3.88, 0.001 level) in the bear market.

On the other hand, some variables have been found to be highly consistent across both the bull and bear markets. The estimated coefficients for the capital asset ratios (t=4.93 for the bull-market sample and t=4.09 for the bear-market sample) and firm size (t=5.12 for the bull-market sample and t=4.17 for the bear-market sample) are both positive and highly significant.

4.5. Multiple Regression Results Across Different S&P Indices and Financial Firm Types

As we previously discussed, the S&P index types (Cready, 1994; Del Guercio, 1996) and different types of financial firms have attracted different levels of institutional holdings. We utilize the fixed-effects model across different types of indices and financial firms. Table 5 contains the results.

The fixed-effects regression results across different S&P indices (Table 5) provide evidence that the association between institutional ownership and firm variables varies slightly across different index types. For *S&P500* firms, the most significant factors are dividend yield (t=−6.33, significant at 0.001 level), market-to-book ratio (t=−4.48, 0.001 level), and stock return variance (t=2.71, 0.01 level). But for *S&P MidCap* and *SmallCap* firms, the positive effects of capital asset ratio are highly significant at 0.001 levels (t = 4.96). The difference may suggest that institutional investors do not care as much about the capital status of large *S&P500* financial firms because these firms generally have strong capital financing abilities, or perhaps rely on government's implicit or explicit "too big to fail" guarantees. An interesting finding is that the log of market capitalization has a significant (t =−2.46, 0.05 level) negative relation for *S&P MidCap* firms. It seems that institutional investors prefer small-size financial firms listed on *S&P MidCap400* index. The positive association between institutional ownership and CEO pay performance sensitivity documented by Roth and Saporoschenko (2001) is only supported when using the *S&P MidCap* financial firms (t = 2.35, 0.05 level). Recall that the return on assets and the log of market capitalization had positive and strongly significant estimated coefficients for the full sample of firms, but the significance of these explanatory variables for three subgroups of *S&P500, MidCap,* and *SmallCap* firms disappears.

The fixed-effects regression results across different type of financial firms (Table 5) show that, for deposit institutions, the significant factors are undercapitalization dummy (t=2.72, significant at 0.01 level), firm size (t=6.11, 0.001 level) and stock return variance (t=2.51, 0.05 level). For investment banks, most of the independent variables are insignificant, but the market to book ratio (t=−1.72, 0.10 level) and dividend-payment dummy (t=−7.40, 0.001 level) have a negative association with institutional ownership. These results suggest that professional managers prefer investment bank stocks with low market to book ratio and that do not pay dividend. For insurance companies, the capital asset ratio (t=5.66, s 0.001 level), undercapitalization dummy (t=3.71, 0.001 level), firm size (t=2.54, 0.05 level) and stock return variance (t=3.36, 0.001 level) have significant estimated coefficients. Institutional ownership has a positive relation with log of market capitalization and capital asset ratio, suggesting professional money managers favor large insurance companies with higher equity ratio. This finding is similar that in other types of financial firms.

Table 5. Fixed-effects Regression Results across Different S&P Indices and Different Types of Financial Institutions

Independent Variables	S&P index type			Financial firms type		
	S&P500	MidCap	SmallCap	Deposit institutions	Investment banks	Insurance companies
Return on assets	−0.003	−0.006	−0.007	0.004	2.8E−4	−0.002
	(-0.47)	(-1.27)	(-1.61)	(0.94)	(0.09)	(-0.63)
Capital asset ratio	0.243	0.678	0.505	0.620	−0.108	0.476
	(1.97)†	(4.96)***	(4.04)***	(1.95)†	(−1.07)	(5.66)***
Undercapitalization dummy	0.007	0.079	−0.010	0.053	0.059	0.117
	(0.40)	(2.65)**	(-0.010)	(2.72)**	(1.29)	(3.71)***
Dividend yield	−0.044	−0.004	0.001	3.4E−4	−0.023	−0.009
	(−6.33)***	(−0.97)	(0.11)	(0.11)	(−0.76)	(−1.15)
Dividend-payment dummy	−0.027	−0.163	−0.093	−0.068	−0.392	−0.010
	(−0.58)	(3.97)***	(-1.81)†	(−0.63)	(−7.40)***	(−0.31)
Log of market capitalization	0.007	−0.068	0.007	0.039	−0.009	0.019
	(0.83)	(−2.09)*	(0.23)	(6.11)***	(−0.63)	(2.54)*
Market-to-book	−0.023	−0.013	0.003	0.003	−0.005	0.007
	(−4.48)***	(−2.46)*	(1.26)	(0.11)	(−1.72)*	(1.30)
1-year abnormal return	−6.8E−6	3.6E−4	−5.2E−4	−1.7E−4	−4.7E−5	−1.7E−4
	(−0.02)	(0.86)	(−1.27)	(−0.52)	(−0.12)	(−0.55)
3-year abnormal return	0.001	0.003	−2.3E−4	9.3E−4	5.9E−4	−2.1E−4
	(1.52)	(2.41)*	(−0.22)	(1.10)	(0.66)	(−0.32)
Stock return variance	4.0E−4	4.4E−4	2.4E−5	1.2E−4	2.9E−4	4.5E−4
	(4.44)***	(1.12)	(0.49)	(2.51)*	(0.75)	(3.36)***
CEO pay-performance	−1.4E−4	6.4E−4	8.6E−5	−1.2E−4	1.3E−4	3.0E−4
	(−1.57)	(2.35)*	(0.62)	(−1.41)	(0.80)	(1.60)
Adjusted R^2	25.8%	38.4%	22.1%	21.4%	65.1%	24.9%
F	8.88***	8.31***	3.89***	7.10***	9.64***	6.78***

***, **, *, and † denote significance at the 0.001, 0.01, 0.05, and 0.10 levels, respectively.

This sample of financial firms from *S&P500, S&P Midcap400, and S&P SmallCap600* indices consists of 171 financial firms from 1997 to 2002. The dependent variable is the percent of institutional holdings to total shares outstanding. The *capital asset ratio* is book value of equity to total assets. The *undercapitalization dummy* is equal to 1 when the capital asset ratio is less than 8% and 0 otherwise. The *dividend-payment dummy* is equal to 1 when a firm pays dividend, or 0 otherwise. We calculate *1-year* and *3-year stock abnormal return* relative to CRSP NYSE/AMEX/NASDAQ value-weighted benchmark. The *stock return variance* is defined as the annualized value of monthly stock return variance. The *CEO pay-performance sensitivity* is defined as the dollar change of CEO wealth relative to each $1000 change in the shareholder value. t values are reported in parenthesis. Variance Inflation Factors (VIF) indicates multicollinearity is not a problem.

4.6. Endogenous Model with Lagged Variables

Grinstein and Michaely (2005) argued that a static relation between institutional ownership at time t and firm characteristics at time t is not appropriate because institutional investors cannot change their holdings dramatically immediately after changes in firm characteristics. So we examine determinants of institutional ownership by using institutional ownership variable at year t+1and explanatory variables at year t. The lagged-variables model is:

$$\text{Institutional ownership}_{i,t+1} = f\,(\text{explanatory variable}_{i,t}).$$

We use ordinary least square to estimate these models (Greene, 2000). The regression results appear in Table 6.We find that the estimated coefficients for one-year lagged capital asset ratio (t=6.79, significant at 0.001 level), dividend-payment dummy (t=−3.59, 0.001 level), log of market capitalization (t = 8.68, 0.001 level), and market-to-book ratio (t=−2.10, 0.05 level) all are significant. These results are consistent with the fixed-effects model in Table 5 which utilized contemporaneous values for the independent variables.

Some differences between the two models are that the estimated coefficients for dividend yield become significant at 0.001 levels (t=−3.24) only in the lagged-variables model, suggesting that professional managers changes their holdings in financial firms based on previous year's dividend yield data. On the other hand, the estimated coefficients for return on assets and stock return variance and, whose estimated coefficients are significant in the fixed-effects model, become insignificant in the lagged-variables model, indicating that contemporary firm performance and stock return volatility tend to be more important factors affecting portfolio managers' investment decision. The fixed-effects regression results across different S&P indices and different type of financial firms are also shown in Table 5 and some different findings between the fixed-effects model and lagged-variables model have been observed.

4.7. Effects of Changes in Firm Characteristics on Institutional Ownership

In this section, we examine changes in institutional ownership on changes in firm variables. We argue that changes in ownership may not occur with changes in firm variables simultaneously, so we follow Grinstein and Michaely (2005) and estimate a model with changes in institutional ownership from year t to year t+1 on changes in firm characteristics from year t−1 to year t. The regression results are reported in Table 7.

The regression results from the full sample of firms in Table 7 show that some firm variable changes in the prior year have significant effects on the changes in institutional ownership in the following year. The increase in the institutional ownership is associated with an improvement in a financial firm's firm performance (t = 2.74, significant at 0.01 confidence level), increase in firm size (t=2.70, 0.01 level), and decrease in dividend yield (t = −1.69, 0.10 level) and stock return variance (t = -1.93, 0.10 level).

As before, we then split the full sample of firm-years into two subsamples: the bull-market sample from 1997 to 1999 and the bear-market sample from 2000 to 2002 and re-estimate the model. We find slightly different results across bull and bear markets.

Table 6. Lagged-Variables Models with One-year Lagged Right-side Variables

Independent Variables	Full Sample	S&P index type			Financial firms type		
		S&P500	MidCap	SmallCap	Deposit institutions	Investment banks	Insurance companies
Constant	-0.285 (-2.71)**	0.490 (2.46)*	1.940 (3.08)**	0.129 (0.25)	-0.556 (-3.48)***	0.399 (1.30)	0.224 (1.26)
Return on assets(t)	0.001 (0.61)	-0.004 (-0.74)	0.007 (1.22)	-0.005 (-1.82) †	0.021 (2.20)*	0.002 (0.62)	0.003 (1.36)
Capital asset ratio(t)	0.364 (6.79)***	0.309 (2.61)**	0.421 (2.85)**	0.396 (3.95)***	0.581 (1.66) †	-0.168 (-1.42)	0.268 (3.58)***
Undercapitalization dummy(t)	0.010 (0.69)	0.018 (1.11)	0.087 (2.97)**	-0.290 (-0.78)	0.063 (3.31)***	-0.025 (-0.53)	0.097 (3.01)**
Dividend yield(t)	-0.010 (-3.24)***	-0.044 (-5.99)***	-0.010 (-2.74)**	-0.018 (-1.35)	-0.003 (-0.92)	0.016 (0.44)	-0.035 (-3.58)***
Dividend-paying dummy(t)	-0.088 (-3.59)***	-0.015 (-0.33)	-0.163 (-3.54)***	-0.061 (-1.25)	-0.141 (-1.73) †	-0.443 (-7.08)***	0.018 (0.52)
Log of market capitalization(t)	0.041 (8.68)***	0.009 (1.09)	-0.060 (-2.08)*	0.020 (0.78)	0.049 (7.84)***	0.025 (1.76) †	0.018 (2.26)*
Market-to-book(t)	-0.004 (-2.10)*	-0.015 (-0.33)	-0.014 (-2.52)*	0.001 (0.43)	2.0E-4 (0.03)	-0.006 (-1.74) †	1.4E-4 (0.03)

Table 6. Continued

Independent Variables	Full Sample	S&P index type			Financial firms type		
		S&P500	MidCap	SmallCap	Deposit institutions	Investment banks	Insurance companies
1-year abnormal return(t)	2.4E-4 (1.45)	3.1E-4 (1.39)	5.6E-4 (1.77)†	1.6E-4 (0.54)	2.9E-4 (1.29)	-8.0E-5 (-0.22)	2.6E-4 (1.16)
3-year abnormal return(t)	-4.3E-4 (-1.07)	-3.2E-4 (-0.54)	3.2E-4 (0.35)	3.4E-4 (0.41)	-2.6E-4 (-0.41)	0.001 (1.13)	-4.0E-4 (-0.64)
Stock return variance(t)	-2.4E-5 (-0.60)	2.4E-4 (2.26)*	-5.1E-5 (-0.13)	-6.4E-5 (-1.33)	-1.2E-5 (-0.27)	1.1E-4 (0.30)	2.0E-4 (1.19)
CEO Pay performance	-9.6E-5 (-1.27)	-1.7E-4 (-1.86)†	6.1E-6 (0.02)	-5.9E-5 (-0.46)	-2.1E-4 (-2.59)**	1.4E-4 (0.78)	-6.5E-5 (-0.40)
Adjusted R^2	20.0%	22.8%	32.7%	19.0%	22.7%	49.6%	20.2%
F	18.20***	10.49***	9.25***	5.23***	11.05***	7.99***	7.57***

***, **, *, and † denote significance at the 0.001, 0.01, 0.05, and 0.10 levels, respectively.

This sample of financial firms from *S&P500, S&P Midcap400, and S&P SmallCap600* indices consists of 171 financial firms from 1997 to 2002. We use one–year lagged values of variables at year t on the right side of equations. The dependent variable is the percentage of institutional ownership at Year t+1. The OLS technique is employed to estimate the models. The *undercapitalization dummy* is equal to 1 when the capital asset ratio is less than 8% and 0 otherwise. The *dividend-payment dummy* is equal to 1 when a firm pays dividend, or 0 otherwise. We calculate *1-year* and *3-year stock abnormal return* relative to CRSP NYSE/AMEX/NASDAQ value-weighted benchmark. The *stock return variance* is defined as the annualized value of monthly stock return variance. The *CEO pay-performance sensitivity* (PPS) is defined as the dollar change of CEO wealth relative to each $1000 change in the shareholder value. t values are reported in parenthesis. Variance Inflation Factors (VIF) indicates multicollinearity is not a problem.

The significant levels for some explanatory variables are different. For example, the significance levels for the improvement in return on assets and increase in firm size disappear in the bear market, but the signs for the estimated coefficients remain the same.

4.8. Additional Analysis

We further perform the analysis of additional institutional ownership variables, something that relatively very few studies have done. The number of institutional investors and average shares held by each institutional shareholder may also contain information about ownership characteristics. We examine this issue and use the log of the number of institutional investors, and the percent of average shares as dependent variables. We define the percent of average shares as PAIS= IS / (AIS × TS). In the equation, IS is the shares held by all institutional

Table 7. The effects of changes in explanatory variables on institutional ownership

Independent Variables	Full Sample	Bull-Market	Bear-Market
Constant	0.013	-0.005	0.030
	(2.77)**	(-0.69)	(3.63)***
Return on assets(t) - Return on assets(t-1)	0.004	0.005	0.004
	(2.74)**	(2.74)**	(1.48)
Capital asset ratio(t) - Capital asset ratio(t-1)	-0.151	-0.157	-0.374
	(-1.46)	(-1.26)	(-1.93) †
Dividend yield(t)- Dividend yield(t-1)	-0.004	-0.006	-0.005
	(-1.69) †	(-0.56)	(-2.17) †
Log of market capitalization MV(t) – log of MV(t-1)	0.040	0.072	0.029
	(2.70)**	(3.23)***	(1.18)
Market-to-book(t) – market-to-book(t-1)	-0.002	-0.002	-0.002
	(-1.61)	(-1.11)	(-0.63)
1-year abnormal return(t) – 1-year abnormal return(t-1)	-3.96E-5	-3.45E-4	1.10E-4
	(-0.52)	(-2.21)*	(1.04)
3-year abnormal return(t) - 3-year abnormal return(t-1)	3.82E-4	8.54E-5	-1.10E-4
	(1.23)	(0.16)	(-0.19)
Stock return variance(t) – Stock return variance(t-1)	-4.17E-5	-4.67E-5	-1.67E-4
	(-1.93) †	(-2.04)*	(-1.71) †
CEO pay-performance (t) – CEP pay-performance(t-1)	-6.69E-5	-1.58E-4	-2.14E-5
	(-1.43)	(-1.86) †	(-0.39)
Adjusted R^2	7.4%	7.4%	9.9%
F	6.19***	4.32***	3.55***

***, **, *, and † denote significance at the 0.001, 0.01, 0.05, and 0.10 levels, respectively.

This sample of financial firms from *S&P500, S&P Midcap400, and S&P SmallCap600* consists of 171 financial firms from 1997 to 2002. We divide the full sample of firm-years into two subsamples: the bull-market sample from 1997 to 1999 and the bear-market sample from 2000 to 2002. The dependent variable is changes of percent of institutional ownership from year t to year t+1 in model 2. We calculate *1-year* and *3-year stock abnormal return* relative to CRSP NYSE/AMEX/NASDAQ value-weighted benchmark. The *stock return variance* is defined as the annualized value of monthly stock return variance. The *CEO pay-performance sensitivity* is defined as the dollar change of CEO wealth relative to each $1000 change in the shareholder value.

investors, AIS is the number of institutional investors, and TS is total shares outstanding. We estimate models with these dependent variables and firm-specific variables using both a fixed-effects model and a lagged-variables model. We present all the regressions results in Table 8.

Table 8. Multiple regression of the number of institutional investors and average institutional holdings

Independent Variables	Log of number of institutional investors at		Percent of average shares by each institutional investor at	
	Year t	*Year t+1*	*Year t*	*Year t+1*
Return on assets(t)	-0.002	0.003	1.47E-5	-1.27E-5
	(-1.34)	(0.97)	(2.36)*	(-1.47)
Capital asset ratio(t)	0.419	0.397	0.001	0.001
	(5.31)***	(4.24)***	(2.70)**	(3.76)***
Undercapitalization dummy(t)	0.075	0.043	-1.08E-5	1.29E-5
	(3.33)***	(1.70)†	(-0.14)	(0.17)
Dividend yield(t)	0.012	0.012	-1.10E-5	-3.97E-5
	(2.70)**	(2.30)*	(-0.74)	(-2.62)**
Dividend-payment dummy(t)	-0.109	-0.084	-3.84E-4	-3.49E-4
	(-2.96)**	(-1.97)*	(-3.03)**	(-2.76)**
Log of market capitalization(t)	0.503	0.541	-0.001	-0.001
	(70.66)***	(66.88)***	(-26.68)***	(-29.38)***
Market-to-book(t)	-0.001	-0.004	3.16E-6	-1.75E-6
	(-0.36)	(-1.09)	(0.33)	(-0.18)
1-year abnormal return(t)	-0.002	4.70E-4	3.50E-6	-6.75E-7
	(-7.49)***	(1.64)	(3.16)**	(-0.79)
3-year abnormal return(t)	-0.003	-0.002	-7.74E-7	9.04E-7
	(-4.08)***	(-2.46)*	(-0.32)	(0.43)
Stock return variance(t)	2.23E-4	7.59E-5	-1.20E-7	-4.40E-7
	(3.81)***	(1.10)	(-0.59)	(-2.16)*
CEO pay-performance(t)	-1.71E-4	-4.24E-4	8.07E-7	9.24E-7
	(-1.48)	(-3.23)***	(2.03)*	(2.37)*
Adjusted R^2	90.5%	87.4%	62.6%	63.1%
F	430.38***	477.36***	76.80***	118.66***

***, **, *, and † denote significance at the 0.001, 0.01, 0.05, and 0.10 levels, respectively.

This sample of financial firms from *S&P500*, *S&P Midcap400*, and *S&P SmallCap600* indices consists of 171 financial firms from 1997 to 2002. The dependent variable is the log of number of institutional investors and the percent of average shares held by each institutional investor to total shares outstanding at year t or t+1. The capital asset ratio is book value of equity to total assets. The undercapitalization dummy is equal to 1 when the capital asset ratio is less than 8% and 0 otherwise. The dividend-payment dummy is equal to 1 when a firm pays dividend, or 0 otherwise. We calculate 1-year and 3-year stock abnormal return relative to CRSP NYSE/AMEX/NASDAQ value-weighted benchmark. The stock return variance is defined as the annualized value of monthly stock return variance. The CEO pay-performance sensitivity is defined as the dollar change of CEO wealth relative to each $1000 change in the shareholder value.

When the log value of number of institutional investors is used as the dependent variable for the fixed-effects model, we find significant estimated coefficients at 0.01 levels or better for firm size (t=70.66, significant at 0.001 level) and capital asset ratio (t=5.31, 0.001 level), suggesting that more institutional investors tend to invest in financial firms with a larger market capitalization and a better capital status. These results continue hold in the lagged-variables model (t=66.88 and 4.24 respectively). The stock return variance is found to have a strongly significant (t=3.81, 0.001 level) and positive estimated coefficients in the fixed-effects model, but not in the lagged-variables model, indicating that the volatility of stock price and the number of institutional investors may have simultaneous relation. There is some evidence that a financial firm without dividend-payments (t=-2.96, 0.01 level) tend to attract more institutional shareholders. But if a firm does pay dividends, a higher dividend yield (t=2.70, 0.01 level) is preferred by more institutional investors.

When the percent of average shares is used as the dependent variable, the regression results show a different picture. First, we find strong evidence (t= -26.68, significant at 0.001 levels) that the larger the firm size, the lower the proportion of shares held by each institutional shareholder. This is somewhat consistent with Faccio and Lasfer (2000), who suggest that UK pension funds only hold large stakes mainly in small companies. Second, the percent of average shares in a financial firm is higher if the company has better firm performance, either measured by accounting-based return on assets (t=2.70, 0.05 level), or measured by market-based 1-year abnormal return (t=3.16, 0.10 level). This is consistent with our expectations. Third, if a financial corporation has a better capital status (t=2.70, 0.001 level), and more effective corporate governance characterized by a greater CEO pay-performance sensitivity (t=2.03, 0.05 level), it tends to have a larger average shares held by each institutional investor. These results are mostly consistent in both the fixed-effects model and the lagged-variables model.

5. Conclusions

Using a panel of 171 listed financial corporations from the *S&P500*, *MidCap400* and *SmallCap600* indices from 1997 to 2002, we conduct a time-series and cross-sectional examination of institutional ownership in *S&P* index financial corporations. Since many similar studies excluded financial firms (Grinstein & Michaely, 2005), we attempt to fill this gap in the literature. First, we perform time-series analysis of institutional ownership over time. We find that institutional ownership in financial firms steadily increase over time, even in the obvious “bear” stock market from 2000 to 2002. This trend occurs across different ownership levels, different types of *S&P* indices, and different types of financial firms, and it seems to be different from results for industrial firms reported elsewhere. Institutional ownership was higher in *S&P500* firms than that in either *S&P MidCap* or *S&P SmallCap* firms (Pruitt & Wei, 1989). We also find that institutional ownership is higher in insurance and real estate companies relative to deposit institutions and investment banks. The frequency distribution analysis of yearly changes in ownership shows a negatively skewed pattern. The largest proportion of yearly changes is an increase of 2 to 10% (40.2%). Large annual changes (over 10% and less than −10%) in ownership are not uncommon (12.8%) for U.S. financial firms.

Second, we perform univariate comparisons, year-by-year OLS, and fixed-effects models to examine the relation between institutional ownership and a broad range of firm-specific variables. We find strong evidence that institutional ownership is higher in financial firms with better firm performance, better capital status (lower leverage), lower dividend yield, larger market capitalization, and higher stock return variance. Some of these findings are consistent with Grinstein and Michaely (2005), who used a large sample of non-financial firms. However, we find that institutional holdings of financial firms are higher when there is a lower market to book ratio, and for non-dividend-paying firms. These results are not the same as those found for non-financial firms (Grinstein & Michaely, 2005).

We do not confirm the findings of Roth and Saporoschenko (2001) that institutional holdings were higher in firms with lower capital ratio, and lower stock return variance, but confirm their positive association between institutional ownership and CEO pay-performance sensitivity.

We further provide evidence to support the notion that institutional investors use different investment strategies in the bull and bear markets. They are more likely to invest in quality financial stocks with larger return on assets and lower market to book ratios, and they prefer financial firms with a lower dividend yield and a greater CEO pay-performance sensitivity in the bear market than in the bull market. In the bear market, however, institutional ownership is higher in financial institutions with higher stock return variance and in firms that do not pay dividends. Furthermore, institutional investors are more likely to use technical (contrarian) trading strategies in the bull market than in the bear market. The estimated coefficient for 3-year abnormal return is negative in the bull market but finally changes to a positive sign in the bear market.

We expand our study in institutional ownership by examining the lagged variables issues as well as the changes in ownership. We find somewhat similar results from the lagged-variables model as those from the fixed effects model, but the significant and positive associations between firm performance, stock return variable, and institutional ownership in the fixed effects models disappear when we use the lagged variable model with one-year lagged explanatory variables. Second, by regressing changes in institutional ownership on changes in firm characteristics with a lagged-variables model, we find that improvement in firm performance, increase in firm size, and decrease in the stock return variance in the previous year lead to an increase in the institutional ownership during the following year. Additionally, we examine determinants of two additional institutional variables, the number of institutional investors and the average shares held by each institutional shareholder. We find evidence that these institutional variables contain additional information about ownership characteristics which was not found when we examine the percent of institutional holdings to total shares outstanding.

Additionally, to delve into our study regarding characteristics of institutional ownership, we examine the number of institutional investors and the average shares held by each institutional shareholder. Relatively very few papers have documented this issue before. We find evidences that a greater number of institutional investors are attracted to stock in financial firms that are large and have high capital ratios and dividend yield. For the percent of average shares by each institutional shareholder, we find that the larger the firm size, the lower the proportion of shares held by each institutional shareholder. The proportion of average shares is higher when a firm has better firm performance, higher capital asset ratio, and more effective corporate governance characterized by CEO pay-performance sensitivity.

In summary, this study is among relatively few empirical studies to examine institutional holdings in financial corporations. However, limitations still exist in this study and deserve further research. First, since the Glass-Steagall Act was repealed in the late 1999, which is just before the start of the bear market in 2000, we cannot distinguish the effects of stock market situations and increasing deregulations in financial sector. Second, due to the limited information in our database, we cannot examine the institutional clientele effects in the sample of financial corporations.

Appendix Tables

These appendix tables are not a formal part of the paper, but they will be made available to readers upon request. We included these tables with the formal paper for the benefit of the referees.

Table 1. T test of firm characteristics on the institutional ownership across S&P Indices

	S&P500		S&P MidCap		S&P SmallCap	
	Owner-ship (%)	Mean dif. (t value)	Owner-ship (%)	Mean dif. (t value)	Owner-ship (%)	Mean dif. (t value)
High ROA firms	63.27	2.70	62.17	14.94	58.01	10.36
Low ROA firms	60.57	(1.79)†	47.23	(5.50)***	47.65	(3.60)***
Adequately-capitalized firms	63.20	3.21	55.75	4.34	54.94	8.01
Undercapitalized firms	59.99	(2.08)*	51.41	(1.29)	46.93	(2.39)*
High capital ratio firms	65.57	7.32	63.45	17.48	59.12	12.46
Low capital ratio firms	58.25	(4.98)***	45.96	(6.65)***	46.66	(4.39)***
Dividend-paying firms	61.38	-12.35	51.04	-24.94	50.52	-14.02
Non-dividend paying firms	73.73	(-3.20)***	75.98	(-6.63)***	64.54	(-3.85)***
High dividend yield firms	56.90	-9.92	44.85	-19.52	49.13	-7.89
Low dividend yield firms	66.82	(-6.96)***	64.37	(-7.74)***	57.02	(-2.76)**
Large market equity firms	61.35	-0.89	56.20	3.38	51.95	-2.63
Small market equity firms	62.24	(-0.58)	52.82	(1.17)	54.58	(-0.89)
High market-to-book firms	59.73	-3.80	52.70	-3.65	51.67	-3.32
Low market-to-book firms	63.53	(-2.51)*	56.35	(-1.27)	54.99	(-1.12)
High 1-year return firms	60.79	-2.06	54.51	0.00	50.85	-4.91
Low 1-year return firms	62.85	(-1.36)	54.51	(-0.00)	55.76	(-1.69)†
High 3-year return firms	62.41	1.20	57.07	5.17	52.03	-2.19

	S&P500		S&P MidCap		S&P SmallCap	
	Owner-ship (%)	Mean dif. (t value)	Owner-ship (%)	Mean dif. (t value)	Owner-ship (%)	Mean dif. (t value)
Low 3-year return firms	61.21	(0.79)	51.90	(1.81)†	54.22	(-0.75)
High risk firms	64.19	4.70	54.48	0.71	53.29	0.37
Low risk firms	59.49	(3.20)***	53.77	(0.25)	52.92	(0.13)
High CEO PPS firms	62.28	1.00	54.35	-0.75	56.71	5.52
Low CEO PPS firms	61.28	(0.65)	55.10	(-0.25)	51.19	(1.77)†
1997-1999	60.18	-2.98	49.23	-10.16	52.27	-2.72
2000-2002	63.15	(-2.06)*	59.39	(-3.71)***	54.99	(-0.88)

***, **, *, and † denote significance at the 0.001, 0.01, 0.05, and 0.10 levels, respectively.

This sample of financial firms from *S&P500, S&P Midcap400, and S&P SmallCap600* indices consists of 171 financial firms from 1997 to 2002. The institutional ownership data are obtained from the *S&P Security Owner's Stock Guide*, and firm characteristics data are drawn from *COMPUSTAT, CRSP*, and *EXECUCOMP* database. We divide the full sample of firm-years into two subsamples based on median values of those firm variables respectively, and then use t tests to compare institutional ownership in high-median subsample and low-median subsample across different types of S&P indices.

Table 2. T test of firm characteristics on the institutional ownership across different FI types

	Deposit Institutions		Investment banks		Insurance companies	
	Owner-ship (%)	Mean dif. (t value)	Owner-ship (%)	Mean dif. (t value)	Owner -ship (%)	Mean dif. (t value)
High ROA firms	52.30	1.99	51.60	-0.59	70.84	6.27
Low ROA firms	50.31	(1.14)	52.18	(-0.17)	64.57	(3.31)***
Adequately-capitalized firms	49.48	-3.71	50.67	-3.88	67.54	-0.96
Undercapitalized firms	53.19	(-2.14)*	54.55	(-1.03)	68.50	(-0.33)
High capital ratio firms	49.42	-3.81	52.55	1.25	72.24	8.97
Low capital ratio firms	53.23	(-2.21)*	51.30	(0.35)	63.27	(4.84)***
Dividend-paying firms	51.25	2.75	48.45	-36.04	66.98	-4.15
Non-dividend paying firms	48.50	(0.43)	84.49	(-8.13)***	71.13	(-1.61)
High dividend yield firms	47.24	-7.96	50.96	-1.34	64.36	-6.67
Low dividend yield firms	55.20	(-4.77)***	52.30	(-0.38)	71.03	(-3.59)***
Large market equity firms	56.94	11.54	51.38	-0.58	69.98	4.92
Small market equity firms	45.40	(7.14)***	51.96	(-0.17)	65.06	(2.58)**
High market-to-book firms	51.87	1.72	53.82	3.84	67.55	-0.07

Table 2. (Continued)

	Deposit Institutions		Investment banks		Insurance companies	
	Ownership (%)	Mean dif. (t value)	Ownership (%)	Mean dif. (t value)	Ownership (%)	Mean dif. (t value)
Low market-to-book firms	50.15	(1.01)	49.98	(1.11)	67.62	(-0.04)
High 1-year return firms	50.44	-1.49	52.42	0.28	68.07	0.87
Low 1-year return firms	51.93	(-0.87)	52.14	(0.08)	67.20	(0.46)
High 3-year return firms	52.83	3.50	51.69	-1.23	69.01	2.92
Low 3-year return firms	49.33	(2.04)*	52.92	(-0.36)	66.09	(1.54)
High risk firms	53.14	3.92	50.33	-2.96	70.87	6.96
Low risk firms	49.22	(2.34)*	53.29	(-0.88)	63.91	(3.76)***
High CEO PPS firms	51.02	-1.15	54.15	4.51	67.82	0.11
Low CEO PPS firms	52.17	(-0.66)	49.64	(1.28)	67.71	(0.06)
1997-1999	48.85	-5.65	47.52	-9.37	65.54	-4.06
2000-2002	54.50	(-3.47)***	56.89	(-2.90)**	69.60	(-2.14)*

***, **, *, and † denote significance at the 0.001, 0.01, 0.05, and 0.10 levels, respectively.

This sample of financial firms from *S&P500, S&P Midcap400, and S&P SmallCap600* consists of 171 financial firms from 1997 to 2002. The institutional ownership data are obtained from the *S&P Security Owner's Stock Guide*, and firm characteristics data are drawn from *COMPUSTAT, CRSP,* and *EXECUCOMP* database. We divide the full sample of firm-years into two subsamples based on median values of those firm variables respectively, and then use t tests to compare institutional ownership in high-median subsample and low-median subsample across different types financial institutions.

Table 3. Year-by-year ordinary least square regression results

	1997	1998	1999	2000	2001	2002
Constant	−0.078	−0.109	−0.238	−0.002	0.107	0.338
	(-0.29)	(-0.05)	(-0.80)	(−0.01)	(0.46)	(1.33)
Return on assets	−0.005	0.001	−0.003	0.004	0.004	−0.014
	(−1.05)	(0.15)	(−0.53)	(1.07)	(2.63)**	(−1.66)
Capital asset ratio	0.395	0.271	0.323	0.052	0.209	0.665
	(2.70)**	(1.59)	(1.89)†	(0.34)	(1.88)†	(3.50)***
Undercapitalization dummy	0.018	0.040	0.008	0.100	−0.012	0.070
	(0.53)	(1.24)	(0.21)	(0.27)	(−0.36)	(1.95)†
Dividend yield	−0.060	−0.061	−0.050	0.006	−0.057	−0.003
	(-2.93)**	(-3.84)***	(-3.53)***	(1.76)	(-4.18)***	(-0.31)
Dividend-payment dummy	0.106	0.072	0.092	−0.260	−0.102	−0.152
	(1.48)	(1.06)	(1.28)	(−4.31)***	(−1.90)†	(−2.74)**
Log of market capitalization	0.027	0.027	0.034	0.035	0.032	0.014
	(2.25)*	(2.56)*	(2.69)**	(2.80)**	(3.09)**	(1.31)
Market-to-book	−0.001	−0.009	0.002	−0.014	−0.035	−0.002
	(−0.31)	(−1.61)	(0.26)	(−2.80)**	(−5.09)***	(−0.10)
1-year abnormal return	−0.002	0.002	0.001	0.004	−0.0002	−0.001
	(−2.93)**	(2.69)**	(0.89)	(1.07)	(−0.54)	(−1.83)†

	1997	1998	1999	2000	2001	2002
3-year abnormal return	0.0001 (0.09)	−0.005 (−3.82)***	−0.004 (−2.58)*	0.002 (1.47)	0.003 (2.60)*	0.002 (2.05)*
Stock return variance	5.17E−5 (0.44)	5.19E−5 (1.23)	−2.1E−4 (-0.50)	6.8E−4 2.36*	8.90E−4 (3.21)**	4.6E−4 (2.18)*
CEO pay-performance	0.0004 (0.64)	0.007 (2.02)*	−5.8E−5 (−0.21)	2.8E−4 (0.44)	−4.7E−5 (−0.61)	−1.2E−4 (−0.12)
Adjusted R^2	27.1%	29.8%	18.3%	30.0%	47.5%	28.1%
F	5.84***	6.18***	3.51***	5.28***	9.72***	4.71***

***, **, *, and † denote significance at the 0.001, 0.01, 0.05, and 0.10 levels, respectively.

This sample of financial firms from *S&P500, S&P Midcap400, and S&P SmallCap600* indices consists of 171 financial firms from 1997 to 2002. We employ OLS to estimate yearly regression from 1997-2002. The dependent variable is the percent of institutional holdings to total shares outstanding. The independent variables are shown in the following table. The *capital asset ratio* is book value of equity to total assets. The *undercapitalization dummy* is equal to 1 when the capital asset ratio is less than 8% and 0 otherwise. The *dividend-payment dummy* is equal to 1 when a firm pays dividend, or 0 otherwise. We calculate *1-year* and *3-year stock abnormal return* relative to CRSP NYSE/AMEX/NASDAQ value-weighted benchmark. The *stock return variance* is defined as the annualized value of monthly stock return variance. The *CEO pay-performance sensitivity* is defined as the dollar change of CEO wealth relative to each $1000 change in the shareholder value. T values are reported in parenthesis. Variance Inflation Factors (VIF) indicates multicollinearity is not a problem.

References

Allen, F., Bernardo, A., & Welch, I. (2000). A Theory of Dividends Based on Tax Clienteles. *Journal of Finance* 55, 2499-2536.

Berger, A. (1995). The Relationship between Capital and Earnings in Banking. *Journal of Money, Credit, and Banking* 27(2), 432-456.

Booth, J., Cornett, M., & Tehranian, H. (2002). Board of Directors, Ownership, and Regulation. *Journal of Banking and Finance* 26, 1973-1996.

Brickly, J., & James C. (1987). The Takeover Market, Corporate Board Composition, and Ownership Structure: the Case of Banking. *Journal of Law and Economics* 30, 161-180.

Brous, P., & Kini O. (1994). The Valuation Effects of Equity Issues and the Level of Institutional Ownership: Evidence from Analysts' Earnings Forecasts, *Financial Management*, Spring 1994, 33-46.

Caroll, T. (1995). The Information Content of Quarterly Dividend Changes: Professional Adaptation. *Journal of Accounting, Auditing and Finance* 10, 293-319.

Cready, W. (1994). Determinants of Relative Investor Demand for Common Stocks. *Journal of Accounting, Auditing and Finance* 10, 487-507.

Dahlquist M., & Robertsson, G. (2001). Direct Foreign Ownership, Institutional Investors, and Firm Characteristics. *Journal of Financial Economics* 59, 413-440.

Davidson III, W., & Dutia, D. (1989). A Note on the Behavior of Security Returns: a Test of Stock Market Overreaction and Efficiency. *Journal of Financial Research* 12, 245-252.

DeBondt, W., & Thaler R. (1985). Does the Stock Market Overreact? *Journal of Finance* 40, 793-805.

DeBondt, W., & Thaler, R. (1987). Further Evidence on Investor Overreaction and Stock Market Seasonality. *Journal of Finance* 42, 557-581.

Del Guercio, D. (1996). The Distorting Effect of the Prudent-Man Laws on Institutional Equity Investments. *Journal of Financial Economics* 40, 31-62.

Demsetz, H., & Lehn, K. (1985). The Structure of Corporate Ownership: Causes and Consequences. *Journal of Political Economy* 93, 1155-1177.

Denis, D., Denis, D., & Sarin, A. (1994). The Information Content of Dividend Changes: Cash Flow, Signaling, Overinvestment, and Dividend Clienteles. *Journal of Financial and Quantitative Analysis* 29, 567-587.

Denis, D., & Sarin, A. (1999). Ownership and Board Structure in Publicly Traded Corporations. *Journal of Financial Economics* 52, 817-223.

Faccio, Mara, and Ameziane Lasfer. (2000). Do Occupational Pension Funds Monitor Companies in Which They Hold Large Stake? *Journal of Corporate Finance* 6, 71-110.

Falkenstein, E. (1996). Preferences for Stock Characteristics as Revealed by Mutual Fund Portfolio Holdings. *Journal of Finance* 51, 111-135.

Fama, E., & French, K. (2002). Testing Trade-off and Pecking Order Predictions about Dividends and Debt. *Review of Financial Studies* 15, 1-33.

Friedman, B. (1996). Economic Implications of Changing Share Ownerships. *Journal of Portfolio Management* 23(3), 59-70.

Friend, I., & Lang, L. (1988). An Empirical Test of the Impact of Managerial Self-Interest on Corporate Capital Structure. *Journal of Finance* 43, 271-281

George, R. (1996). Selecting Small-Cap Stocks. *Journal of Investing* 5(2), 79-86

Gompers, P., & Metrick, A. (2001). Institutional Investors and Equity Prices. *The Quarterly Journal of Economics* 116, 229-259

Greene, W. (2002). *Econometric Analysis*, New York: Prentice-Hall.

Grinblatt, M., Titman, S., & Werners, R. (1995). Momentum Investment Strategies, Portfolio Performance, and Herding: a Study of Mutual Fund Behavior. *American Economic Review* 85, 1088-1105.

Grinstein, Y., & Michaely, R. (2005). Institutional Holdings and Payout Policy. *Journal of Finance* 65 (3), 1389-1426.

Harris, L. & Gurel, E. (1986). Price and Volume Effects Associated with Changes in *S&P500*: New Evidence from the Existence of Price Pressures. *Journal of Finance* 41, 815-829.

Hausman, J., & Taylor, W. (1981). Panel Data and Unobservable Individual Effects. *Econometrica* 49, 1377-1398.

Hovakimian, A., & Kane, E. (2000). Effectiveness of Capital Regulation at U.S. Commercial Banks from1985 to 1994. *Journal of Finance* 55, 451-468.

Jegadeesh, N., & Titman, S. (1993). Returns to Buying Winners and Selling Losers: Implications for Stock Market Efficiency. *Journal of Finance* 48, 65-91.

Jegadeesh, N., & Titman, S. (2001). Profitability of Momentum Strategies: an Evaluation of Alternative Explanations. *Journal of Finance* 56, 699-720.

Jensen, M., & Murphy, K. (1990). Performance Pay and Top Management Incentives. *Journal of Political Economy* 98, 225-264.

Jensen, M. (1993). Presidential Address: the Modern Industrial Revolution, Exit, and the Failure Internal Control System. *Journal of Finance* 48, 831-880.

Lakonishok, J., Shleifer A., & Vishny, R. (1994). Contrarian Investment, Extrapolation, and Risk. *Journal of Finance* 49, 1541-1578.

McConnell, J., & Servaes, H. (1990). Equity Ownership and Corporate Value. *Journal of Financial Economics* 27, 595-612.

Mishra, C., & Nielsen, J. (2000). Board Independence and Compensation Policies in Large Bank Holding Companies. *Financial Management,* Autumn 2000, 51-70.

Parrino, R., Sias, R., & Starks, L. (2003). Voting with their Feet: Institutional Ownership Changes around Forced CEO Turnover. *Journal of Financial Economics* 68, 3-46.

Pruitt, S., & Wei, J. (1989). Institutional Ownership and Changes in the *S&P500. Journal of Finance* 44, 509-514.

Roth, G., & Saporoschenko, A. (2001). Institutional Ownership of Bank Shares. *Financial Analyst Journal,* July/August 2001, 27-36.

Shleifer, A. (1986). Do Demand Curves for Stock Slope Down? *Journal of Finance* 41, 579-590.

Shyam-Sunder, L., & Myers, S. (1999). Testing Static Tradeoff Against Pecking Order Models of Capital Structure. *Journal of Financial Economics* 51, 219-224.

In: Global Stock Exchanges: Stability, Interrelationships... ISBN: 978-60692-184-5
Editor: Paolo B. Cassedes

Chapter 2

RATIONAL BUBBLES IN ISTANBUL STOCK EXCHANGE: LINEAR AND NONLINEAR UNIT ROOT TESTS[*†]

Erdinç Altay
Istanbul University, Faculty of Economics,
Department of Business Administration, Turkey

Abstract

We analyzed the presence of rational bubbles in Istanbul Stock Exchange (ISE) between 1998-2006 period by implementing linear and nonlinear unit root tests to 7 different indices. The first analysis is based on implementing augmented Dickey-Fuller unit root and KPSS stationary tests to the price-dividend ratios of the indices. The results are in favor of the presence of rational bubbles in the indices. We implemented a further test which enables time-varying discount rates. Generally the results of the loglinear model also support the previous results. The potential weaknesses of linear test methods as well as the advantages of nonlinear models motivated to use the bilinear test method. The evidence from the nonlinear test is in favor of the existence of rational bubbles in all indices in the sample period of 2nd March 1998–29th December 2006. But the results of the sub periods are contradictory for some indices. In the first and second sub periods we cannot accept unit root bilinearity for ISE National-Services index. The results also reject the significance of the bilinear term for ISE National-Industrials and ISE Investment Trusts indices in the second subperiod. As a result, we can conclude that as a general structure, the rational bubbles present in ISE.

[*] A version of this chapter was also published in *Economics of Emerging Markets,* edited by Lado Beridze published by Nova Science Publishers, Inc. It was submitted for appropriate modifications in an effort to encourage wider dissemination of research.

[†] The present work was supported by the Research Fund of Istanbul University: Project No:581/14082006.

1. Introduction

The stock market efficiency and the rational behavior of investors are two of the most important hypotheses in explaining investor behavior and stock price formation in the finance literature. The efficient markets hypothesis depends on the immediate flow of the news to the market participants and instantaneous reflection of all relevant information to the stock prices. Such an efficient market environment with rationally behaving market participants result in ensuring the market prices of stocks equal to their fundamental values. However, since 1980's there is a continuous academic interest on a phenomenon which is called as the stock price bubble: deviation of the market prices from the fundamentals.

The models developed in the neoclassical finance framework ensure the absence of stock price bubbles by the assumption of transversality condition in infinite horizon models and backwards induction argument in finite horizon models. According to the theory, all market participants need not to be rational in order to keep the market prices equal to fundamentals. Any deviation, because of the irrational behavior of noise traders can be offset in a short time by the arbitrage procedure which will be started by the sufficient number of rational market participants. Although the market efficiency and the rational behavior hypotheses prevent the presence of the bubbles in the theory, empirical analysis of capital markets and the evidence of various market anomalies show that the strong form of efficient market hypothesis does not always hold. On the other hand, recent studies of behavioral finance present serious evidence of irrational or boundedly rational behavior, which causes significant effects on the stock pricing process. A brief glance to the history of capital markets also provides interesting examples of sharp increases without market justification, which are followed by abrupt market collapses. Among the others, some of the classical examples of bubbles can be given as Tulip mania of the 1630's, South Sea bubble of 1710-1720, Mississippi bubble of 1718-1720 and the internet bubble of 1992-2000. Such sharp increases in the market prices unrelated with the fundamentals are followed by market crashes causing deep problems in the economy.

Properly functioning capital markets have critical roles not only for financial sector but also for the overall economy. Taipalus (2006) states four different channels of how stock prices affect whole economy. These are the effects of stock markets on investments, firms' balance-sheets, household wealth and household liquidity. The close relationship between stock prices and overall economy shows the importance of correct formation of the market prices and hence the potential problems that may occur because of a bubble process. This relation between the overall economy and the capital markets are especially important for emerging markets with their instable and vulnerable economic structures. In order to understand why bubbles occur in capital markets it may be a good starting point to analyze previous bubbles' driving forces. Taipalus (2006) stated detailed information about these driving forces under five titles: 1) breaks or major changes in the regulatory environment, 2) growth prospects within a sector or a country, 3) policy changes concerning taxation, monetary operations, financial liberalization etc, 4) market infrastructure, and 5) overtrading as a result of speculation for profit.

The above stated first three issues generally create optimistic effects on traders and push stock prices upward. But on the other hand they are hard to be correctly evaluated and reflected to the stock prices by the supply and demand process of the market. The difficulty in correctly evaluating the changes in the regulatory environment, growth prospects and policy changes can result in the overreaction of traders and stimulates a bubble process in the market. Abreu and Brunnermeier (2003) also define one of the driving forces of bubbles as the structural change which causes productivity increase and give the examples of the railway, electricity, internet and telecommunication booms. Over-optimistic traders' lack of understanding the fact that the implementation of structural changes and thus the returns of productivity increase may take a long time and may be on the benefit of only a small number of firms, incorrectly increase the stock prices over their fundamental values.

While the stock price bubble is generally defined as the deviation of market prices from the fundamentals, the question arises from how one can estimate the fundamental value. If the model which is used for the estimation of the fundamental value omits some of the revelant variables, it becomes impossible to argue whether the difference between the observed market price and the estimated fundamental price is because of the bubble or the omited variables (Dezhbakhsh and Demirguc-Kunt, 1990). Related with the specification problem in detecting the bubbles, Siegel (2003) make an operational definition of the bubble. This definition is based on the explanation of Rosser (2000): the fundamental value is the long run equilibrium price level. To which extend the expected cash flows and discount factor are correctly estimated and the length of the estimation period has a critical importance. According to the operational definition of Siegel (2003), the estimation period for expected return is the duration of the stock and in order to decide on the existence of the bubble, the realized rate of return of the stock should be two standard deviations greater than its expected return.

In this research we investigated the existence of the rational bubbles in Istanbul Stock Exchange (ISE) by implementing linear and bilinear unit root test procedures to ISE National-All, ISE National-100, ISE National-30, ISE National-Industrials, ISE National-Services, ISE National-Financials and ISE Investment Trusts indices data. The results are consistent with the existence of rational bubbles in ISE. The chapter is organized as follows. The following section briefly defines the types of the stock price bubbles. The third section presents the present value model and rational bubbles. In section four, various empirical tests of rational bubbles are explained. The fifth section presents the linear and bilinear unit root test methodologies that are implemented in order to test existence of the rational bubbles in ISE. The section six summarizes the empirical findings. The last section contains the conclusion.

2. Types of Stock Price Bubbles

Boucher (2003) defines three types of bubbles according to the behavior of traders and informational efficiency. These are 1) non rational bubbles, 2) rational bubbles and 3) inefficiencies due to imperfect and heterogeneous information.

2.1. Non Rational Bubbles

The non rational bubbles occur in the markets that are not fully rational so their existence can be attributed to the presence of the irrational traders. The possible reasons of non rational bubbles can be explained in the framework of two different models: the two-traders model and the investor psychology.

2.1.1. Two-traders Model

According to the two-traders model (see Shleifer and Summers, 1990; De Long et al., 1990a; De Long et al., 1990b and De Long et al., 1991) there are two different types of traders in the market: the rational investors and the irrational noise traders. The rational investors base their trading decisions on the economic fundamentals and their motivation is to earn profit by detecting the stocks which are incorrectly priced relative to their risk levels. On the other hand, the noise traders have systematically wrong evaluations about the stock prices and base their trading decisions on the erroneous beliefs and signals which donot carry revelant information. According to the model, such a violation of the homogeneous agents assumption may cause deviation of market prices from fundamentals and the stock price bubbles arise from the interaction of these two kinds of traders.

The presence of noise traders in the maket increases the risk of stocks by their systematic biases in pricing the stocks and cause bubbles. On the other hand, if the rational arbitragers' investment horizons are infinite, they invest according to their expectations about future dividends. But if their investment horizons are not infinite and noise traders exist in the market then the rational traders also trade irrationally. Because when a non-rational bubble occurs because of the presence of the irrational trading of noise traders, as a first reaction rational arbitragers start an arbitrage process in order to profit from the misevaluation of the stocks by the noise traders. But a shorter investment horizon of rational arbitragers protects the adjustment of the over priced stocks to their fundamental level because when the investment horizon of the noise traders is longer they persist in the market and able keep the stock prices over their fundamental levels even for a longer period then the arbitragers liquidate their positions. As a result, arbitrage position becomes far away from a profitable strategy. Under these conditions, spotting market trends and benefiting from the increasing market by trying to liquidate the investments before the bubble bursts, that is trading like a noise trader becomes the real "rational" strategy for the rational investors and feeds the irrational bubble.

2.1.2. Investor Psychology

Another source of non rational bubbles is related with investor psychology and behavior. Overconfidence, incorrect weighting of information, entrapment, overreaction and herding behaviour are some of the phenomena that are related with investor psychology which may start a bubble processes.

The overconfidence is the self-deception of investors that they make the right decision among the other. The overconfidence leads the investors to over assess their information, under estimate their risks and exaggerate their ability to control the happenings. Once an overconfident irrational investor enters into the market, he thinks that his decision of investment is right, his investment is profitable and less risky. This kind of a market wide speculation which is based on overconfident behavior of investors can result in stimulating a non rational bubble.

The incorrect weighting of information can be described as the bias in estimating the probability distribution of information. The irrational investors often overweight some rarely probable happenings and underweight highly probable ones leading to the bias in expectations. If incorrect weighting of information is common in the market, this can cause a deviation of market prices from their fundamental values. This kind of a psychologic bias in the market may increase the overpriced stock's demand by creating the expectation of a further increase in its market price and may result in a non rational bubble.

The entrapment is also another kind of psychological bias which is based on the past mistakes of irrational investors. These past mistakes may affect the future decisions although they are irrelevant information. A decrease in the price of the stock of the irrational trader may result in a further demand of that stock in order to decrease the average cost of the investment, ignoring its risk and expected return.

Investor reactions to information may be different from what is stated by the efficient market hypothesis. According to the efficient market hypothesis, rational investors correctly assess the full information set and reflect it to the market prices. On the other hand, empirical findings of De Bondt and Thaler (1985) support the evidence that the investors violate bayesian rationality, overreact to the unexpected news and overweight the last information.

Another psychological phenomenon is herding. Brunnermeier (2001) describes the herding as the behaviour of people blindly following the decisions of others. The herding behavior, combined with the other psychological biases may drive market prices above their fundamental values and cause non rational stock price bubbles.

2.2. Rational Bubbles

Bubbles do not arise only because of market biases and non rational behavior of market participants. A kind of stock price bubble, rational bubble, may be consistent with the rational behavior of the investors when they expect capital gains from stock trading. Even if all the investors are rational, the presence of finite investment horizon, non limited number of investors and/or non limited number of stocks may start a rational bubble process. Rational bubbles occur if the investors are willing to pay for the stock higher than its fundamental value with the expectation of selling it at an even higher price to another investor.

If the investors are rational and have infinite investment horizons, they buy the stocks and hold them for an infinite period. One result of such a situation is the no trade structure of the market. In this case all stocks will be priced at the present value of their infinite number of future dividends and nobody would pay higher than the fundamental values of these stocks. As a result, there would be no bubble in the stock prices. Tirole (1982) shows the nonexistence of bubbles under the condition of the presence of finite number of infinite lived rational investors in a general equilibrium framework. While the arbitragers play the role of precluding the bubbles in the economy of finite number of investors with infinite investment horizons, higher interest rates than the growth rate of the economy also avoids the existence of the bubbles in an overlapping-generations economy with infinite number of investors that have finite investment horizons (Tirole, 1985). But if the number of investors increase and their investment horizons are not infinite, rational bubbles may arise.

If the investors are rational, they increase in number and their invesment horizons are finite, the only way of buying a stock for the new investors becomes to offer a price which is higher than its fundamental value. Because the previous owner of the stock would not sell it lower than its fundamental price and prefer holding it until the end of investment horizon. Thus trading in the market may result in a rational bubble. In this case the important point for an investor becomes whether the price of the stock at the end of the investment horizon will be above than its cost or not, rather than whether the market price is deviated from fundamental value or not. If the investor expects to sell his/her stocks higher than their costs, which are higher than the fundamental value, rational bubbles may continue to exist in the market. This is a kind of self-fulfilling expectations about future increases in market prices. Under these conditions, the rational strategy for an investor becomes to hold the stocks as long as the prices increase and sell them just before the bubble bursts. The motivation of such an investor is the anticipation that the stock can be resold at a higher price to another investor who has the same anticipation. This is called as the "greater fool theory". Brooks and Katsaris (2003) define this as the inclusion of the expectation of stock's future price into the information set of investors. The expectation of the stock's future price becomes a more important factor on its supply and demand than the comparison of its market price with the fundamental value.

According to Koustas and Serletis (2005), the rational bubbles may be initially started by exogenous shocks or rumors and continued by self-fulfilling expectations of market participants. Such a bubble structure arising from the investor expectations about the possibility of reselling the stocks which are bought higher than their fundamental values must continuously expand in order to survive. Because the expectation is based on reselling the stocks at a higher price to some other investors who also expect to sell them even at a higher price in the future.

Diba and Grossman (1988b) points out two problems about this kind of continuously diverging rational bubbles: 1) a negative bubble cannot exist, and 2) it can never disappear and reappear. But previous observations of stock markets show that bubbles are followed by crashes and new bubbles may start and burst. These critisms, cause generation of new models of rational bubbles which are consistent with the reality of their periodically diminishing charateristics. Two of these rational bubble versions are the intrinsic bubbles[1] and the periodically collapsing bubbles.[2] (Boucher, 2003: 2)

2.3. Inefficiencies due to Imperfect and Heterogeneous Information

The third group of the explanation of stock price bubbles can be considered in the class of inefficiencies due to imperfect and heterogeneous information. According to this explanation, the main reason of the bubbles is the informational asymmetricies among market participants.

3. Present Value Model and Rational Bubbles

While one of the basic questions about bubbles is why market prices deviate from fundamentals, the other question is how can the fundamental value correctly calculated in order to understand whether there is a deviation or not. The finance theory explains this problem by the present value model of Lucas (1978).

---

[1] See Froot and Obsfeld (1991), and Ikeda and Shibata (1992).

[2] See Evans (1991), and van Norden and Schaller (1993).

According to the present value model, the fundamental value of a stock for a rational investor is the present value of all its cash flows, namely the dividends and future market price:[3]

$$P_t^* = E_t\left[\sum_{i=1}^{k} \beta^i D_{t+i}\right] + E_t\left[\beta^k P_{t+k}\right] \tag{1}$$

where P_t^* is the fundamental value of the stock at time t, P_{t+k} is the market price of the stock at time $t+k$, D_{t+i} is dividend of the stock paid between time t and time $t+i$, β^i coefficient is the discount factor and $E[\cdot]$ is the expectation operator conditional to the information available at time t.

In order to have a unique solution from the equation (1), expected present value of the price has to converge to zero while it is going to infinity. This is called as the transversality condition and it can be expressed as follows:

$$Lim_{k\to\infty} E_t\left[\beta^k P_{t+k}\right] = 0 \tag{2}$$

Another condition for calculating the fundamental value is the requirement of a lower growth rate of prices and dividends than the discount rate. Otherwise the stock price goes to infinity in the case of infinite investment horizon. When the transversality condition holds and the discount rate is sufficiently low (lower than the dividend growth rate), the fundamental value which has a unique solution can be written as follows:

$$P_t^* = \sum_{i=1}^{\infty} \beta^i E_t\left[D_{t+i}\right] \tag{3}$$

If the transversality condition does not hold, we get infinite number of solutions of the equation (1) which lead to the differences between market prices and the fundamental value. The difference or the stock price bubble can be shown as follows:

$$P_t = P_t^* + B_t \tag{4}$$

where, B_t is the bubble at time t. This kind of a formulation shows two components of asset prices. The first compenent is the fundamental value and the second component is the bubble term. The bubble process satisfies the following equation:

$$B_t = \beta^i E_t\left[B_{t+i}\right] \tag{5}$$

[3] We utilized heavily from Campbell, Lo and MacKinlay (1997), Koustas and Serletis (2005), and Cajueiro and Tabak (2005) for explaining the present value model and the rational bubble model.

The above stated bubble process is called as the rational bubble, because it is only one solution of the present value model which is compatible with the rational behavior among the other possible solutions. Thus the presence of rational bubbles is not contradictory to the rational expectations model. (Lardic and Priso, 2004: 560) In other words, the reason of the presence of the bubble term in the model is the expectation of its presence in the next period. Such an expectation of a difference between the fundamental value and the market price of the stock in the future motivates the rational investor to continue to demand the stock at a higher price then its fundamental value. This behavior contains the aim of profiting by reselling the stock even at a higher price to another one so it can be described as a rational behavior.

4. Empirical Tests of Rational Bubbles

The tests of Shiller (1981), Blanchard and Watson (1982), and West (1987) provide some of the first bubble tests which investigate the consistency between dividends and market prices. There is still a growing number of research to detect rational bubbles in the finance literature. Brooks and Katsaris (2003) categorize the bubble tests into three groups: 1) bubble premium tests, 2) excess volatility tests, and 3) stationary (unit root) and cointegration tests.

4.1. Bubble Premium Tests

Hardouvelis (1988), and Rappoport and White (1993) implemented bubble premium tests in their research. According to this test methodology, the bubble premium is defined as the excess return above the fundamental return which is demanded by the investors in the presence of a bubble. In this definition, fundamental return can be explained by the sum of three components: risk free rate, risk premium which is related with the undertaking of a risky investment and a random disturbance. The method depends on the calculation of the difference between the excess returns of bubble period and no bubble period and detecting the bubble premium. However there are two critical problems in the implementation of such a methodology. First, how can one be sure that the period which is assumed as bubble free is really a bubble free period? Second, in the prediction of excess returns, the slope coefficients are assumed to be equal in order to subtract the excess returns of bubble and bubble free periods but this assumption may also not be true. (Brooks and Katsaris, 2003: 327)

4.2. Excess Volatility Tests

Another method of testing the rational bubbles depends on the comparison between the volatilities of fundamental value and market price of the stocks. The research of Flood and Garber (1980), Shiller (1981), LeRoy and Porter (1981), Hart and Kreps (1986), Kleidon (1986), West (1987), and Dezhbakhsh and Demirguc-Kunt (1990) are the examples of excess volatility or variance bounds tests. According to this methodology, a higher market price volatility relative the volatility of fundamental value is accepted as indicative of stock price bubbles.

Excess volatility test is previously developed by Shiller (1981) and Grossman and Shiller (1981) in order to critize the present value model. Following the initial results that present the evidence of violation of the present value model, Tirole (1985) and Blanchard and Watson (1982) presented another perspective to the model. This perspective depends on the idea of the higher variance of the asset prices may be due to the existence bubbles. According to the excess volatility tests, the asset price under the no bubble condition can be shown as the present value model as follows (Gurkaynak, 2005):

$$P_t = \sum_{i=1}^{\infty} \beta^i E_t \left(D_{t+i} \right) \tag{6}$$

On the other hand the ex-post rational price is the present value of actual dividends:

$$P_t^* = \sum_{i=1}^{\infty} \beta^i D_{t+i} \tag{7}$$

The difference between actual and expected dividends, forecast error (ε) is zero mean and unforecastable:

$$P_t^* = \sum_{i=1}^{\infty} \beta^i \left[E_t \left(D_{t+i} \right) + \varepsilon_i \right] \tag{8}$$

$$P_t^* = P_t + \sum_{i=1}^{\infty} \beta^i \varepsilon_{t+i} \tag{9}$$

The variance of the ex-post rational price can be written as:

$$\sigma\left(P_t^*\right) = \sigma\left(P_t\right) + \varphi\sigma\left(\varepsilon_t\right) \tag{10}$$

thus; $\sigma\left(P_t^*\right) \geq \sigma\left(P_t\right)$ (11)

where, $\sigma\left(P_t^*\right)$ is the variance of the ex-post rational price, $\sigma\left(P_t\right)$ is the variance of the market price and $\sigma\left(\varepsilon_t\right)$ is the variance of the difference between actual and expected dividends. Such a framework presents an upper bound for the volatility of asset prices: variance of ex-post rational prices should be equal or greater than the variance of the observed market prices.

However one of the basic problems in such a variance bound test methodology is the sensitivity of the test results to the assumptions in the estimation of the dividends for calculating the fundamental value. Inappropriate assumptions may seriously decrease the dependability of the test results and conclusions about the presence of the bubbles. For example if the dividends are generated from a non-stationary process and if the discount rate which is used in the construction of the fundamental price is assumed to be unrealistically constant, the test results can lead to the wrong conclusions. Unless the assumptions and information set used in the modelling of the fundamental value cover the real information set of the investors, it would be very hard to talk about the robustness of the test methodology. Another critique about the volatility test is the possibility of a bubble effect in the proxy of the fundamental value because the cut off prices are used as the proxy of the present value of future dividends. The critique of Kleidon (1986) is also another important point to consider. Kleidon points out the possibility of the irrationality of the investors and the misspecification of the model used in the construction of the fundamental value as the reasons of excess volatility. (Brooks and Katsaris, 2003: 328-330)

4.3. Unit Root and Cointegration Tests

Among the others, Campbell and Shiller (1987, 1988), Diba and Grossman (1988a), Froot and Obstfeld (1991), Craine (1993), Timmermann (1995), Horvath and Watson (1995), Lamont (1998), Bohl (2003), and Cunado, Gil-Alana and Gracia (2005) implemented unit root and cointegration tests in order to investigate the rational bubbles in stock markets. In this test methodology, the non stationarity in the logarithm of the dividend price ratio time series is consistent with the presence of rational bubbles. Because Diba and Grossman (1988a) show that if the stock prices are exclusively depend on future dividends, if there is no rational bubble in the stock market and if the dividend time series is stationary in the mean, then the price series should also be stationary.

In the literature, another kind of rational bubble test is the cointegration test between dividend and market price data. A cointegration between dividend and market price implies that fundamental value and market price cannot drift apart indefinitely. A nonstationary deviation between these two time series indicates nonexistence of a long-run equilibrium condition in the market which is an evidence of the presence of rational bubbles. (Koustas and Serletis, 2005: 2524)

If the fundamental value is equal to the market price, then market price and dividend series are cointegrated. This means, although the market price and dividend time series are nonstationary, their linear combination should be stationary. In order to test the existence of the bubbles, unit root tests are implemented to the price and dividend time series. Non rejection of unit root hypothesis for both series is followed by a cointegrating regression between these two series for implementing another unit root test on the residual process. The presence of a unit root in the residual process is considered as the evidence of no cointegration relation between market prices and dividends which results to the conclusion that there is a rational bubble in the stock prices. (Boucher, 2003: 5-6)

Campbell and Shiller (1987) also implement such a cointegration test to the annual data of Standard and Poor's 500 Index. The test period is 1871-1986 and the results are in favor of the presence of rational bubbles but they find that the results are sensitive to the discount factor which is used in the present value model. On the other hand, Froot and Obsfeld (1991) also implement a unit root test procedure to the price-dividend ratio of Standard and Poor's index and find the evidence of the existence of rational bubbles due to the lack of cointegration relationship between these two variables.

However Diba (1990) and Evans (1991) think that in finite samples, the nonstationarity can be masked and cointegration tests cannot detect all kinds of bubbles. The exclusion of significant variables in the fundamental value model may also result in wrong conclusions. Another pitfall of such a linear stationarity procedure is that it is only capable of detecting the bubble in the expanding phase. However periodically collapsing bubbles have both expanding and collapsing phases. Therefore the bubble structure becomes hard to be detected by a linear unit root procedure.

The test procedures like unit root and cointegration are inadequate especially in detecting the periodically collapsing bubbles and may result in incorrect conclusions. This is also true for not only periodically collapsing bubbles but also for the non-negative rational bubbles and intrinsic bubbles, which contain linear fundamental value and nonlinear bubble terms. Another weakness of these linear stationarity test procedures is their assumption of a linear discount rate in the fundamental value modeling. In his research in Japan Stock Market, Fukuta (2002) points out this problem. He argues that the discount factor which is employed in determining the present value of future dividends should not be constant but rather it should be a stochastic process, so a time-varying cointegration vector should be employed in the model. Boucher (2003) also employs time-varying risk premium in rational bubble tests. Referring to the no necessary reason of assuming the economic systems as linear as well as the nonlinear dependencies of financial time series, Chang et al. (2005) implemented a nonparametric cointegration test to Taiwan Stock Market data and rejected the presence of rational bubbles.

In order to overcome the above stated problems of linear unit root and cointegration tests, various nonlinear test procedures are started to be employed. Among the others, Bohl (2003) employed MTAR (Momentum Threshold Autoregressive) model for testing the periodically collapsing bubbles and Charemza, Lifshits and Makarova (2005) employed bilinear stochastic unit root procedure for testing the rational bubbles.

Peel and Davidson (1998) state that bilinear unit root test has advantages in capturing the sudden and unexpected changes in the time series relative to the TAR (Threshold Autoregressive) models such as SETAR (Self-Exciting Threshold Autoregressive) and MTAR models. Thus in this research, we also employed a bilinear unit root test in investigating the rational bubble in Istanbul Stock Exchange.

5. Testing Rational Bubbles in Istanbul Stock Exchange

In order to test the presence of rational bubbles in ISE, we implemented linear and nonlinear unit root test methodologies to daily and monthly data of 7 indices of ISE in March 1998- December 2006 period.

5.1. Linear Unit Root Test Methodology

Linear unit root test methodology is based on the stationarity of the price-dividend ratio. If the discount factor and the dividend growth rate are stationary, than the price-dividend ratio is also stationary under no rational bubble conditions. The equations through (12) to (16) show the derivation of price-dividend ratio (Lardic and Priso, 2004: 564-565):

$$P_t^* = \sum_{i=1}^{\infty} \beta^i E_t\left[D_{t+i}\right] \tag{12}$$

$$P_t = P_t^* + B_t \tag{13}$$

$$B_t = \beta^i E_t\left[B_{t+i}\right] \tag{14}$$

$$\frac{P_t}{D_t} = E_t\left(\sum_{i=1}^{\infty} \beta^i \frac{D_{t+i}}{D_{t+i-1}}\right) + E_t\left(\beta^i \frac{B_{t+i}}{D_{t+i-1}}\right) \tag{15}$$

$$\frac{P_t^*}{D_t} = \left(\sum_{i=1}^{\infty} \beta^i \frac{D_{t+i}}{D_{t+i-1}}\right) + \left(\beta^i \frac{B_{t+i}}{D_{t+i-1}}\right) + \varepsilon_t \tag{16}$$

where, ε_t is the error term. Lardic and Priso (2004) indicate two basic advantages of this famework. The first advantage is the inclusion of the error term in the model. The error term in the equation (16) enables to compansate the specification errors by including the forgotten or the excluded but significant variables in the pricing model. The second advantage of the model is stated as the importance in the implementation of the unit root tests to the left hand side of the model (P_t / D_t). This is indeed an important advantage because the right hand side of the model is closely related with the specification of the utility function of the representative agent and testing the left hand side of the model may cause specification problems.

The implementation of unit root tests like augmented Dickey-Fuller or KPSS tests on the above price-dividend ratio provide evidence about the existence or nonexistence of rational bubbles in the stock markets. The null hypothesis of augmented Dickey-Fuller test is the price-dividend ratio time series is unit root, thus the rejection of the null hypothesis is indicative of the non existence of stock price bubbles. On the other hand, the null hypothesis of KPSS test is the stationary price-dividend ratio time series, therefore the rejection of null hypothesis is a sign of the presence of stock price bubbles.

One pitfall of the linear unit root test arises from the assumption of constant discount rate which is contradictory to the reality. Campbell and Shiller (1988) implement a methodology in order to allow for the time-varying discount factor in the model. The methodology is based on the following loglinear approximation:[4]

$$r_{t+1} \approx k + \rho p_{t+1} + (1-\rho) d_{t+1} - p_t \tag{17}$$

[4] We utilized from Taipalus (2006; 39-40) for the loglinear model.

where, r_{t+1} is the first logarithmic difference of market price at time $t+1$, p_{t+1} is the market price at time $t+1$, d_{t+1} is the dividend at time $t+1$, $k \equiv -\log(\rho)-(1-\rho)\log\left[\frac{1}{\rho-1}\right]$ and $\rho \equiv \frac{1}{\left[1+\exp(d-p)\right]}$. Imposing no rational bubble to equation (17) yields to the following equation:

$$p_t = \frac{k}{1-\rho} + \sum_{i=0}^{\infty} \rho^i \left[(1-\rho) d_{t+1+i} - r_{t+1+i}\right] \tag{18}$$

Taking the expectations of the equation (18), we obtain the following equation which is the dynamic generalization of the Gordon model:

$$p_t = \frac{k}{1-\rho} + E_t\left[\sum_{i=0}^{\infty} \rho^i \left[(1-\rho) d_{t+1+i} - r_{t+1+i}\right]\right] \tag{19}$$

We can derive the logarithmic dividend price ratio from the equation (19) as follows:

$$d_t - p_t = -\frac{k}{1-\rho} + E_t\left[\sum_{i=0}^{\infty} \rho^i \left[-\Delta d_{t+1+i} + r_{t+1+i}\right]\right] \tag{20}$$

where, Δ is the first difference. Craine (1993) states that if Δd_t and r_t are stationary processes and the no rational bubble condition holds, then the logarithmic dividend price ratio $(d_t - p_t)$ should also be stationary. Thus the rational bubble test has a two stage process. At the first stage the stationary of Δd_t and r_t are tested, then in the second stage, the stationary of logarithmic dividend price ratio $(d_t - p_t)$ is tested. If the Δd_t and r_t are stationary and $(d_t - p_t)$ is unit root, then this is consistent with the presence of the rational bubbles in the market. (Taipalus, 2006: 40)

5.2. Bilinear Unit Root Test Methodology

Recent developments in the bubble test methodology document that linear unit root test procedures may fail to conclude about the existence of the rational bubbles especially which are collapsing periodically. The problems due to the linear test procedures lead to the utilization of nonlinear models in order to get stronger evidence.

According to the model of Diba and Grossman (1988a), the object of the household is to maximize the utility of the comsumpion over an infinite horizon (Cajueiro and Tabak, 2005: 4-5):

$$C_t = P_t\left(S_{t+1} - S_t\right) \leq Y_t + D_t S_t \tag{21}$$

where, C_t is the consumption at time t, P_t is the market price of the stock at time t, S_t is the amount of the stock bought at time t, Y_t is the periodic income, and D_t is the dividend at time t. The object of the individuals is to choose the amount of stocks $\left(S_t\right)$ that maximizes their utility. If we assume that the statistical distribution of stock prices and consumption are independend, we get the following equilibrium:

$$P_t U'\left(C_t\right) = \beta E_t\left[\left(P_{t+1} + D_{t+1}\right)\right] E_t\left[U'\left(C_{t+1}\right)\right] \tag{22}$$

If we use dividend adjusted stock prices, the equation (22) can be rewritten as follows:

$$P_t U'\left(C_t\right) = \beta E_t\left[P_{t+1}\right] E_t\left[U'\left(C_{t+1}\right)\right] \tag{23}$$

The ratio of the discounted marginal utility of the future consumption and the marginal utility of current consumption is the preference of the investor between current consumption and expected future consumption. Diba and Grossman (1988a) and Charemza, Lifshits and Makarova (2005) define this ratio as a random variable that is affected by the mistakes in stock pricing which are made in the previous periods. This ratio can be shown as follows:

$$\frac{\beta E_t\left[U'\left(C_{t+1}\right)\right]}{U'\left(C_t\right)} = 1 + \psi\left(P_t - E_{t-1}\left[P_t\right]\right) \tag{24}$$

where, ψ is the adjustment coefficient and indicates to which extend investors are affected by their previous pricing mistakes. Charemza, Lifshits and Makarova (2005) show that the following bilinear unit root test procedure can be utilized in order to test whether the adjustment coefficient is statistically equal to zero:

$$p_t = \left(a + b\varepsilon_{t-1}\right)p_{t-1} + \varepsilon_t \tag{25}$$

where, p_t is the logarithm of the price of the stock at time t, a is the constant and b is the adjustment factor.

Considering the well known problem of unit root in financial time series, when a is assumed as equal to 1, the equation (25) can be rewritten as follows in order to test the significance of b (Charemza, Lifshits and Makarova, 2005: 63-93):

$$\Delta p_t = b p_{t-1} \Delta p_{t-1} + \varepsilon_t \tag{26}$$

where, Δ is the first difference, p_t is the logarithmic stock prices and Δp_{t-1} is the return of the stock. The test statistic which is utilized in order to test the significance of the adjustment coefficient (b) can be shown as follows:

$$t_{\hat{b}} = \frac{\sum_{t=2}^{T} p_{t-1}\Delta p_{t-1}\Delta p_t}{\hat{\sigma}_e \sqrt{\sum_{t=2}^{T} p_{t-1}^2 \Delta p_{t-1}^2}} \tag{27}$$

In this research we employ the two stage test procedure of bilinear unit root test of Charemza, Lifshits and Makarova (2005) in order to investigate the rational bubble in Istanbul Stock Exchange. In the first stage augmented Dickey-Fuller and KPSS (Kwiatkowski, Philips, Schmidt, and Shin) tests are implemented. The condition for passing through the second stage is rejection of the stationarity hypothesis. In the second stage, the model in equation (26) is utilized for testing a statistically significant and positive b coefficient. A positive and statistically significant adjustment coefficient is accepted as an evidence of nonlinear property of the unit root.

6. Empirical Findings

6.1. Empirical Findings of Linear Unit Root Model

In this part of the research, we analyzed the presence of rational bubbles in ISE by employing the linear unit root test procedures to the data of ISE National-All, ISE National-100, ISE National-30 and 4 different sector indices. The daily data of indices cover the period between 1st March 1998-29th December 2006. The data are provided by the Istanbul Stock Exchange. The codes and the names of the indices are presented in Table 1.

Classical examples of rational bubble tests implement linear unit root test procedures as it is mentioned above. Thus we also utilized linear unit root tests to the price-dividend ratio in order to implement the classical bubble tests to the indices of ISE as initial analyses.

Following the methodology of Taipalus (2006), the price-dividend ratio is derived from the daily total return index and price index series. According to the methodology, return of the index is the sum of dividend return and capital gains return:

$$\frac{TRI_t}{TRI_{t-1}} = \frac{D_t}{P_{t-1}} + \frac{P_t}{P_{t-1}} \tag{28}$$

where, TRI_t is the value of total return index at time t, D_t is the dividend at time t and P_t is the value of price index at time t. Thus the daily dividend (D_t) can be approximately derived from the following equation:

$$D_t = P_{t-1} \cdot \left[\frac{TRI_t}{TRI_{t-1}} - \frac{P_t}{P_{t-1}} \right] \tag{29}$$

Considering the fact that in ISE dividends are not paid evenly in whole year and usually accrue over a one-year period, the monthly dividends can be derived by the sum of rolling previous 364 days dividends for the end of each month.[5] Similarly the dividend yield (DY_t) can also be calculated as the sum of rolling previous 364 days dividends and dividing by end of the month value of the price index as follows:

$$DY_t = \frac{\sum_{t}^{t-364} D_t}{P_t} \tag{30}$$

Table 1. List of Indices

Code	Index
N-All	ISE NATIONAL - ALL SHARES
N-100	ISE NATIONAL - 100
N-30	ISE NATIONAL - 30
N-Ind	ISE NATIONAL - INDUSTRIALS
N-Serv	ISE NATIONAL - SERVICES
N-Fin	ISE NATIONAL - FINANCIALS
InvTrst	ISE INVESTMENT TRUSTS

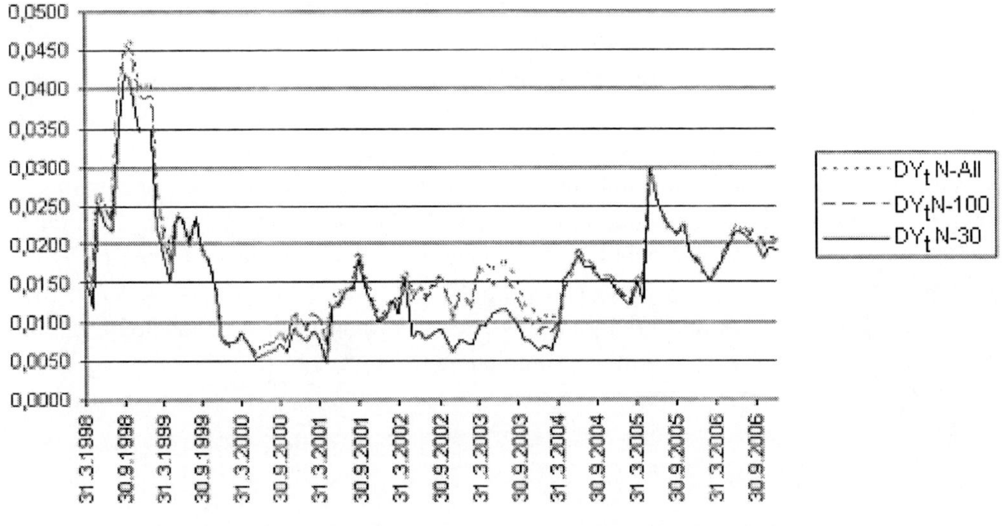

Figure 1. Dividend Yields of N-All, N-100 and N-30 Indices (March 1998–December 2006).

[5] See Taipalus (2006) for the same monthly dividend time series generating method for the Finnish stock market.

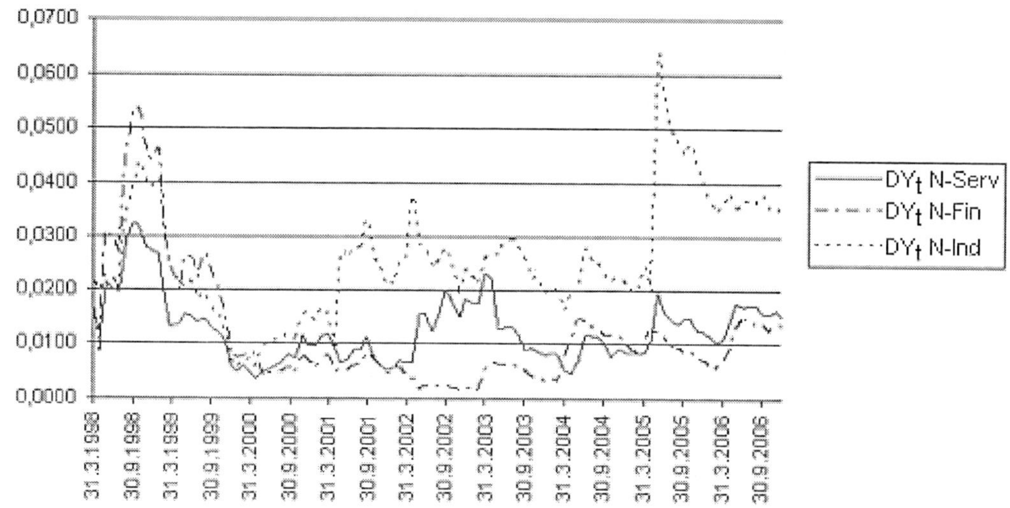

Figure 2. Dividend Yields of N-Serv, N-Fin and N-Ind Indices (March 1998–December 2006).

The dividend yields of the indices between March 1998 – December 2006 are shown in Figure 1, Figure 2 and Figure 3.

We also produced the monthly data of P_t and D_t from the daily data of total return and price indices. Although the total sample period of monthly data is decided between March 1998-December 2006, we considered the possible effects of two economic crises on the Turkish economy for our analysis. These crises are experienced in November 2000 and February 2001. Considering the sensitivity of unit root tests to the structural breaks, we divided the total sample period into two subperiods: March 1998-October 2000 and March 2001-December 2006. Summary statistics of monthly price indices, dividends and price-dividend ratios are presented in Table 2.

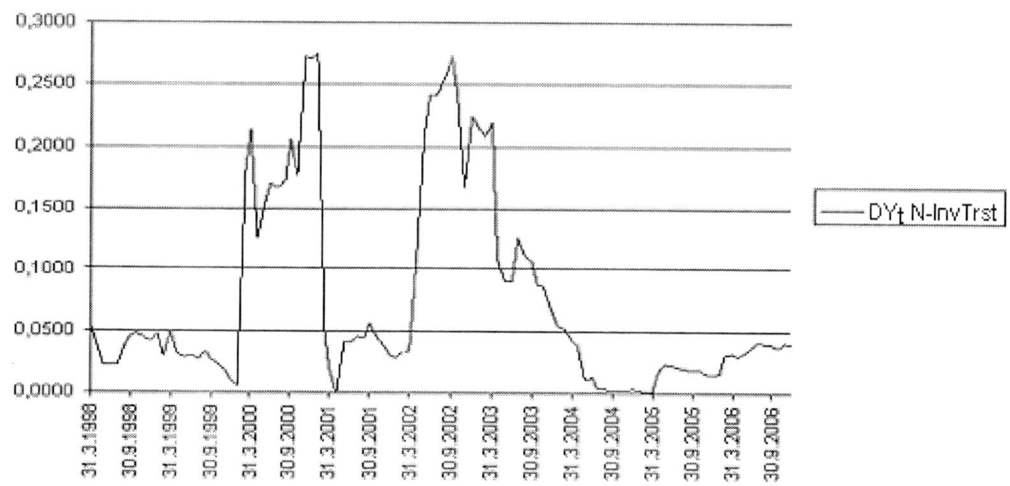

Figure 3. Dividend Yield of InvTrst Index (March 1998 – December 2006).

When we look at the summary statistics presented in Table 2, it is seen that the variables are not normally distributed in the full sample period of March 1998 – December 2006, and the second subperiod of March 2001-December 2006. However this is not the same for the first subperiod.

Referring to the equation (16), we implemented augmented Dickey-Fuller unit root tests and KPSS stationary tests to the dividend-price ratios of indices in order to test the stationarity of ISE indices. The evidence of a nonstationary price-dividend ratio of the index is considered as an indication of the rational bubble.

While implementing the augmented Dickey-Fuller unit root test, we investigated three different models of price-dividend ratio time series for all indices. The first model donot have a constant term, the second model has a constant term and the last model has both constant and linear trend terms. On the other hand we also implemented two models for the KPSS test: model with constant term and the model with constant term and linear trend. The results of the models are summarized in Table 3.

The augmented Dickey-Fuller test results presented in Table 3 show that the null hypothesis of unit root in price-dividend ratio cannot be rejected for all indices except InvTrst index for the models without a constant term and with a constant term and linear trend in the full sample period. On the other hand, the null hypothesis of unit root is rejected for the N-All, N-100, N-30 N-Serv and InvTrst indices when we implement the model with a constant term. This result is also supported by the KPSS test. Considering the robustness of the KPSS test relative to the augmented Dickey-Fuller test, the results of the KPSS model with a constant and linear trend becomes important with the rejection of the stationarity in most of the indices. The nonstationary price-dividend ratios of N-All, N-100, N-30 and N-Fin are indicative for the existence of rational bubbles in ISE.

The analysis results of the first subperiod are stronger. The null hypothesis of unit root in price-dividend ratios cannot be rejected in all indices except InvTrst index in all three models. The results of the KPSS tests are also consistent with the augmented Dickey-Fuller tests when the model with constant term is applied. The rejection of stationarity in all indices, except InvTrst index, can be considered as the evidence of the presence of rational bubbles in March 1998 – October 2000.

The results obtained from the second subperiod are harder to be interpreted. When we implement the augmented Dickey-Fuller test to the models with a constant term, and a constant term and linear trend, the null hypothesis of unit root in price-dividend ratios are rejected for all indices except N-Fin index. However the results of the model without constant term cannot reject the null hypothesis of all indices except InvTrst. The results of the KPSS tests are also controversial in March 2001 – December 2006 subperiod. It can be seen that the null hypothesis of stationary price-divided time series is rejected for all indices except for N-Serv and InvTrst indices when we implement the model with constant term. On the other hand, when we include the linear trend, stationarity is rejected for only N-30 and InvTrst indices. As an overall result, we can say that there is the evidence of unit root and nonstationarity in all indices in at least one model. So we can conclude that there is some evidence of the existence of rational bubbles also in the second subperiod.

Table 2. Summary Statistics of Monthly P_t, D_t and P_t/D_t Data

Variables	Index	March 1998 – December 2006			March 1998 – October 2000			March 2001 – December 2006		
		Mean	Standard Deviation	JB p-value	Mean	Standard Deviation	JB p-value	Mean	Standard Deviation	JB p-value
Monthly Close Level of Price Index P_t	N-All	15992.48	11241.97	0.0001	7608.37	5081.86	0.1295	20243.85	11236.10	0.0156
	N-100	16617.27	11550.52	0.0002	8013.83	5397.88	0.1323	20972.29	11520.56	0.0177
	N-30	21023.86	14703.02	0.0003	9930.28	6776.53	0.1392	26626.95	14615.83	0.0203
	N-Ind	13568.35	8976.21	0.0039	5854.25	3832.73	0.1277	17485.95	8360.18	0.0345
	N-Serv	10113.20	5180.01	0.0018	7857.84	4169.38	0.0925	11411.48	5262.81	0.0207
	N-Fin	23855.48	18737.63	0.0000	10712.40	7470.64	0.1306	30500.07	19394.18	0.0102
	InvTrst	9701.55	6287.18	0.0085	4935.75	3617.92	0.1023	12121.57	6045.22	0.0333
Dividends D_t	N-All	261.66	231.85	0.0000	100.30	14.20	0.0000	344.98	246.92	0.0052
	N-100	268.62	244.17	0.0000	103.17	15.74	0.0041	354.02	262.35	0.0056
	N-30	319.41	314.06	0.0000	120.22	28.58	0.8833	422.65	343.32	0.0068
	N-Ind	387.67	386.74	0.0000	81.24	16.04	0.0245	544.02	392.97	0.0029
	N-Serv	122.64	81.42	0.0000	83.57	13.71	0.4387	143.28	93.38	0.0039
	N-Fin	227.75	215.64	0.0000	139.89	39.87	0.2232	275.08	251.46	0.0111
	InvTrst	561.60	535.84	0.0005	557.26	738.01	0.0446	536.31	381.72	0.0979
Price – Dividend ratio P_t/D_t	N-All	70.48	30.81	0.0000	75.67	48.18	0.1302	66.88	17.53	0.0000
	N-100	72.84	32.00	0.0004	76.63	48.00	0.1344	69.88	20.93	0.0000
	N-30	84.87	41.95	0.0073	82.32	53.00	0.1505	84.52	36.21	0.0019
	N-Ind	48.90	29.36	0.0000	59.74	41.89	0.0651	38.44	12.98	0.0000
	N-Serv	95.80	46.52	0.0000	98.49	63.62	0.0477	94.50	37.53	0.0014
	N-Fin	157.21	128.47	0.0000	86.49	69.42	0.0994	190.92	139.00	0.0000
	InvTrst	19538.14	200550.1	0.0000	29.31	28.71	0.0000	29572.12	246787.5	0.0000

Table 3. Unit Root and Stationary Test Results of Price-Dividend Ratio

Index	Augmented Dickey-Fuller Test[a]						KPSS Test[b]			
	Model with no constant term		Model with constant term		Model with constant term and linear trend		Model with constant term		Model with constant term and linear trend	
	t-Statistic	L[c]	t-Statistic	L[c]	t-Statistic	L[c]	LM statistic[d]	B[f]	LM statistic[e]	B[f]
PANEL A: March 1998 – December 2006										
N-All	-1.0527	0	-2.6382*	0	-2.7161	0	0.1893	8	0.1392*	8
N-100	-1.0811	0	-2.7180*	0	-2.8030	0	0.2023	8	0.1535**	8
N-30	-1.0997	1	-3.0733**	0	-3.1270	0	0.2288	8	0.1993**	8
N-Ind	-1.3284	0	-2.4217	0	-2.7892	0	0.3926*	8	0.0825	8
N-Serv	-1.1930	0	-2.8701*	0	-2.8888	0	0.1252	8	0.1126	8
N-Fin	-1.5253	0	-2.4817	0	-2.4250	0	0.2400	8	0.2247***	8
InvTrst	-10.1977***	0	-10.2472***	0	-10.2247***	0	0.1065	1	0.0705	2
PANEL B: March 1998 – October 2000										
N-All	-0.3151	0	-1.1109	0	-1.7778	0	0.4908**	5	0.1227*	4
N-100	-0.3253	0	-1.1638	0	-1.8594	0	0.4963**	5	0.1220*	4
N-30	-0.3942	0	-1.2445	0	-2.2895	0	0.5011**	5	0.1415*	4
N-Ind	-0.5429	0	-1.3391	0	-1.4227	0	0.4679**	4	0.0920	4
N-Serv	-0.6286	0	-1.4022	0	-2.4528	8	0.4432*	5	0.0902	4
N-Fin	-0.5882	0	-2.1126	5	-2.1430	5	0.5589**	4	0.1618**	4
InvTrst	-2.1276**	0	-3.2061**	0	-3.2942*	0	0.1464	3	0.1218*	2
PANEL C: March 2001 – December 2006										
N-All	-1.1261	1	-3.6468***	0	-4.5994***	0	0.7548***	5	0.0625	4
N-100	-1.1289	1	-3.2589**	0	-4.1577***	0	0.7266**	5	0.0835	5
N-30	-1.2094	1	-3.0428**	0	-3.8858**	0	0.6637**	6	0.1254*	5
N-Ind	-1.3504	1	-4.0098***	0	-4.6033***	0	0.5845**	5	0.1141	4
N-Serv	-0.8739	2	-3.3437**	1	-3.6964**	1	0.2596	5	0.0878	5
N-Fin	-1.2907	0	-2.1011	0	-2.7205	0	0.4853**	6	0.1047	6
InvTrst	-8.3063***	0	-8.3669***	0	-8.6609***	0	0.3165	0	0.1233*	1

[a] Null hypothesis of augmented Dickey-Fuller unit root test: Ho = price-dividend ratio of the index has a unit root,
[b] Null hypothesis of KPSS test: Ho = price-dividend ratio is stationary,
[c] L=Lag length is based on Schwartz info criterion,
[d] Asymptotic critical values: 1% level = 0.739 , 5% level = 0.463, 10% level = 0.347,
[e] Asymptotic critical values: 1% level = 0.216 , 5% level = 0.146, 10% level = 0.119,
[f] B=Bandwidth:Newey-West using Barlett kernel,
* Null hypothesis is rejected at 1% level,
** Null hypothesis is rejected at 5% level,
*** Null hypothesis is rejected at 1% level.

Table 4. Summary Statistics of Monthly Δd_t, r_t and $\left(d_t - p_t\right)$ Data

Variables	Index	March 1998 – December 2006			March 1998 – October 2000			March 2001 – December 2006		
		Mean	Standard Deviation	JB p-value	Mean	Standard Deviation	JB p-value	Mean	Standard Deviation	JB p-value
Panel A: First logarithmic difference of dividends Δd_t	N-All	0.0245	0.1285	0.0000	0.0141	0.1237	0.0000	0.0302	0.1337	0.0000
	N-100	0.0243	0.1323	0.0000	0.0139	0.1255	0.0000	0.0302	0.1385	0.0000
	N-30	0.0258	0.1862	0.0000	0.0158	0.1653	0.0000	0.0316	0.1996	0.0000
	N-Ind	0.0275	0.1701	0.0000	0.0196	0.0641	0.0000	0.0322	0.2042	0.0000
	N-Serv	0.0156	0.1751	0.0000	0.0025	0.1322	0.0000	0.0223	0.1955	0.0000
	N-Fin	0.0237	0.2174	0.0000	0.0091	0.2694	0.0000	0.0314	0.1961	0.0000
	InvTrst	0.0143	1.5600	0.0000	0.0755	0.5720	0.0000	0.0151	1.8607	0.0000
Panel B: Logarithm of total return index r_t	N-All	0.0252	0.1496	0.0000	0.0311	0.2053	0.2420	0.0237	0.1165	0.0687
	N-100	0.0249	0.1530	0.0000	0.0314	0.2096	0.3366	0.0229	0.1197	0.0843
	N-30	0.0254	0.1554	0.0000	0.0329	0.2132	0.4622	0.0221	0.1214	0.0902
	N-Ind	0.0261	0.1381	0.0000	0.0330	0.1948	0.1220	0.0250	0.1048	0.0025
	N-Serv	0.0183	0.1422	0.0000	0.0156	0.1894	0.3550	0.0196	0.1152	0.0304
	N-Fin	0.0260	0.1666	0.0002	0.0322	0.2209	0.4158	0.0239	0.1342	0.2592
	InvTrst	0.0243	0.1781	0.0001	0.0358	0.2486	0.7915	0.0240	0.1350	0.0442
Panel C: Dividend return $d_t - p_t$	N-All	-4.1656	0.4293	0.7481	-4.1163	0.6703	0.2784	-4.1713	0.2516	0.7331
	N-100	-4.1953	0.4389	0.7961	-4.1358	0.6595	0.2883	-4.2057	0.2864	0.8270
	N-30	-4.3186	0.5054	0.2679	-4.2023	0.6631	0.2849	-4.3531	0.4087	0.3002
	N-Ind	-3.7640	0.4737	0.0015	-4.0794	0.5837	0.5373	-3.5987	0.3185	0.3254
	N-Serv	-4.4551	0.4636	0.6616	-4.3587	0.6267	0.4326	-4.4769	0.3770	0.3040
	N-Fin	-4.7595	0.8003	0.6369	-4.1374	0.8251	0.2573	-5.0426	0.6241	0.0746
	InvTrst	-3.2897	1.6477	0.0000	-2.9794	0.9498	0.5827	-3.4972	1.8727	0.0000

Table 5. Augmented Dickey-Fuller Unit Root Test Results of Loglinear Model

Index	Model with no constant						Model with constant term						Model with constant term and linear trend					
	Δd_t		r_t		$d_t - p_t$		Δd_t		r_t		$d_t - p_t$		Δd_t		r_t		$d_t - p_t$	
	t-Statistic	Lag[a]	t-Statistic	Lag[a]	t-Statistic	Lag[a]	t-Statistic	Lag[a]	t-Statistic	Lag[a]	t-Statistic	Lag[a]	t-Statistic	Lag[a]	t-Statistic	Lag[a]	t-Statistic	Lag[a]
	PANEL A: March 1998 – December 2006																	
N-All	-11.9160***	0	-10.0240***	0	-0.2812	0	-12.4296***	0	-10.2591***	0	-2.4275	0	-12.3712***	0	-10.2157***	0	-2.4150	0
N-100	-12.0207***	0	-10.1740***	0	-0.2826	0	-12.5081***	0	-10.4019***	0	-2.4684	0	-12.4535***	0	-10.3599***	0	-2.4640	0
N-30	-11.7639***	0	-10.3772***	0	-0.3489	0	-11.9931***	0	-10.6193***	0	-2.5314	0	-11.9359***	0	-10.5834***	0	-2.5293	0
N-Ind	-12.8783***	0	-9.8759***	0	-0.5144	1	-13.2343***	0	-10.1562***	0	-2.3646	0	-13.1726***	0	-10.1146***	0	-2.8053	0
N-Serv	-10.6738***	0	-10.5770***	0	-0.2157	0	-10.7305***	0	-10.6968***	0	-2.5819*	0	-10.7089***	0	-10.6450***	0	-2.5486	0
N-Fin	-10.0334***	0	-10.0408***	0	-0.2403	0	-10.1519***	0	-10.2506***	0	-1.9076	0	-10.1053****	0	-10.2072***	0	-1.7787	0
InvTrst	-15.3412***	0	-9.5211***	0	-1.5062	1	-15.2692***	0	-9.6327***	0	-5.6775***	0	-15.1942***	0	-9.5958***	0	-5.7565***	0
	PANEL B: March 1998 – October 2000																	
N-All	-7.8538***	1	-4.3358***	0	0.1980	0	-7.5592***	1	-4.3293***	0	-0.9622	0	-7.3001***	1	-4.2552**	0	-2.1204	0
N-100	-6.1593***	0	-4.4664***	0	0.2069	0	-6.1855***	0	-4.4685***	0	-1.0190	0	-6.5242***	1	-4.3932***	0	-2.1518	0
N-30	-5.9194***	0	-4.6274***	0	0.1698	0	-5.8976***	0	-4.6479***	0	-1.0812	0	-6.4917***	0	-4.5800***	0	-2.4975	0
N-Ind	-3.1273***	1	-4.3266***	0	0.1140	0	-3.1079**	1	-4.3176***	0	-1.0446	0	-5.5076***	0	-4.2240**	0	-1.3540	0
N-Serv	-6.8869***	0	-4.0259***	0	0.0854	0	-6.7915***	0	-3.9376***	0	-1.1496	0	-7.1672***	0	-4.0101**	0	-1.5097	0
N-Fin	-7.2860***	0	-4.5220***	0	0.1532	0	-7.2176***	0	-4.5369***	0	-1.0854	0	-8.2455***	0	-4.4547***	0	-2.6371	0
InvTrst	-5.5200***	0	-4.5771***	0	-0.8592	0	-5.5513***	0	-4.5567***	0	-1.6320	0	-5.7743***	9	-4.4529***	0	-2.6195	0
	PANEL C: March 2001 – December 2006																	
N-All	-9.9408***	0	-9.5399***	0	-0.5590	0	-10.5208***	0	-9.9041***	0	-3.1653**	0	-10.4428***	0	-9.8267***	0	-4.0834**	0
N-100	-10.0246***	0	-9.5610***	0	-0.5768	0	-10.5665***	0	-9.8769***	0	-2.8551*	0	-10.4912***	0	-9.8021***	0	-3.8339**	0
N-30	-9.8378***	0	-9.5665***	0	-0.6937	1	-10.0707***	0	-9.8506***	0	-2.4756	0	-9.9988***	0	-9.7761***	0	-3.3445*	0
N-Ind	-10.6810***	0	-9.9059***	0	-0.7406	1	-10.9690***	0	-10.5115***	0	-3.3253**	0	-10.9249***	0	-10.4409***	0	-3.8626**	0
N-Serv	-8.4323***	0	-10.2434***	0	-0.3439	0	-8.4835***	0	-6.5872***	4	-2.4657	0	-8.4674***	0	-6.8294***	4	-2.7032	0
N-Fin	-6.4327***	0	-8.9313***	0	-0.4545	0	-6.5197***	0	-9.1538***	0	-1.4855	0	-6.5644***	0	-9.0860***	0	-2.4433	0
InvTrst	-12.9274***	0	-8.7524***	0	-1.2861	1	-12.8329***	0	-8.9623***	0	-4.9316***	0	-12.7400***	0	-8.9472***	0	-4.9564***	0

[a] Lag length is based on Schwartz info criterion.

* Null hypothesis of augmented Dickey-Fuller unit root test: Ho = variable has a unit root is rejected at 10% level.

** Null hypothesis of augmented Dickey-Fuller unit root test: Ho = variable has a unit root is rejected at 5% level.

*** Null hypothesis of augmented Dickey-Fuller unit root test: Ho = variable has a unit root is rejected at 1% level.

Table 6. KPSS Test Results of Loglinear Model

Index	Model with constant term						Model with constant term and linear trend					
	Δd_t		r_t		$d_t - p_t$		Δd_t		r_t		$d_t - p_t$	
	LM statistic	Bandwidth[c]	LM statistic	Bandwidth[c]	LM statistic	Bandwidth[c]	LM statistic	Bandwidth[c]	LM statistic	Bandwidth[c]	LM statistic	Bandwidth[c]
PANEL A: March 1998 – December 2006												
N-All	0.0954	5	0.0533	1	0.1689	8	0.0707	6	0.0491	1	0.1684**	8
N-100	0.1005	4	0.0546	1	0.1867	8	0.0656	4	0.0495	1	0.1837**	8
N-30	0.0830	3	0.0611	1	0.2234	8	0.0687	3	0.0516	1	0.2200***	8
N-Ind	0.0493	7	0.0532	2	0.4602*	8	0.0483	7	0.0409	2	0.0966	8
N-Serv	0.1314	3	0.0584	4	0.1254	8	0.0498	5	0.0579	4	0.1264*	8
N-Fin	0.1677	2	0.0537	1	0.3453	8	0.0964	1	0.0520	1	0.2602***	8
InvTrst	0.1252	26	0.0565	3	0.2059	7	0.1255*	26	0.0436	3	0.1023	7
PANEL B: March 1998 – October 2000												
N-All	0.3478*	3	0.1467	2	0.4909**	5	0.1468**	9	0.1289*	3	0.1199*	4
N-100	0.3168	3	0.1477	2	0.4965**	5	0.1620**	10	0.1297*	3	0.1171	4
N-30	0.3295	3	0.1560	2	0.4991**	5	0.1359*	9	0.1442*	2	0.1284*	4
N-Ind	0.1143	2	0.1234	2	0.4472*	5	0.1117	2	0.1246*	3	0.1002	4
N-Serv	0.2224	4	0.1967	3	0.4845**	5	0.1242*	6	0.1313*	3	0.0969	4
N-Fin	0.3294	4	0.1479	2	0.4917**	5	0.2656***	15	0.1411*	2	0.1456*	4
InvTrst	0.1951	1	0.1220	3	0.4089*	4	0.0746	3	0.1171	3	0.1471**	4
PANEL C: March 2001 – December 2006												
N-All	0.0700	5	0.0877	7	0.741***	5	0.0689	5	0.0818	7	0.0725	4
N-100	0.0741	3	0.0918	7	0.973***	5	0.0681	3	0.0836	7	0.0960	5
N-30	0.0816	2	0.0897	6	0.183**	6	0.0759	2	0.0824	6	0.1446*	5
N-Ind	0.0864	6	0.0806	8	0.6008**	5	0.0780	7	0.0723	8	0.1230*	5
N-Serv	0.1088	8	0.2100	14	0.2115	6	0.0632	9	0.1088	15	0.0952	5
N-Fin	0.1790	3	0.0826	4	0.6190**	6	0.0999	2	0.0783	5	0.1040	6
InvTrst	0.2224	33	0.1131	3	0.2294	5	0.2193***	33	0.0669	3	0.1463**	5

[a] Asymptotic critical values: 1% level = 0.739 , 5% level = 0.463, 10% level = 0.347.

[b] Asymptotic critical values: 1% level = 0.216 , 5% level = 0.146, 10% level = 0.119.

[c] Bandwidth:Newey-West using Barlett kernel.

* Null hypothesis of KPSS test: Ho = price-dividend ratio of the index is stationary is rejected at 10% level.

** Null hypothesis of KPSS test: Ho = price-dividend ratio of the index is stationary is rejected at 5% level.

*** Null hypothesis of KPSS test: Ho = price-dividend ratio of the index is stationary is rejected at 1% level.

Table 7. Results of Linear Rational Bubble Tests

Metho-dology	Augmented Dickey-Fuller Unit Root test of P_t/D_t			KPSS Stationary test of P_t/D_t		Augmented Dickey-Fuller Unit Root test of Δd_t, r_t and $(d_t - p_t)$			KPSS Stationary test of Δd_t, r_t and $(d_t - p_t)$	
Model	no constant	constant term	constant and linear trends	constant term	constant and linear trends	no constant	constant term	constant and linear trends	constant term	constant and linear trends
Index	PANEL A: March 1998 – December 2006									
N-All	*B*	¤	*B*	¤	*B*	*B*	*B*	*B*	¤	*B*
N-100	*B*	¤	*B*	¤	*B*	*B*	*B*	*B*	¤	*B*
N-30	*B*	¤	*B*	¤	*B*	*B*	*B*	*B*	¤	*B*
N-Ind	*B*	*B*	*B*	*B*	¤	*B*	*B*	*B*	*B*	¤
N-Serv	*B*	¤	*B*	¤	¤	*B*	¤	*B*	¤	*B*
N-Fin	*B*	*B*	*B*	¤	*B*	*B*	*B*	*B*	¤	*B*
InvTrst	¤	¤	¤	¤	¤	*B*	¤	¤	¤	.
	PANEL B: March 1998 – October 2000									
N-All	*B*	*B*	*B*	*B*	*B*	*B*	*B*	*B*	.	.
N-100	*B*	*B*	*B*	*B*	*B*	*B*	*B*	*B*	*B*	.
N-30	*B*	*B*	*B*	*B*	*B*	*B*	*B*	*B*	*B*	.
N-Ind	*B*	*B*	*B*	*B*	¤	*B*	*B*	*B*	*B*	.
N-Serv	*B*	*B*	*B*	*B*	¤	*B*	*B*	*B*	*B*	.
N-Fin	*B*	*B*	*B*	*B*	*B*	*B*	*B*	*B*	*B*	.
InvTrst	¤	¤	¤	¤	*B*	*B*	*B*	*B*	*B*	*B*
	PANEL C: March 2001 – December 2006									
N-All	*B*	¤	¤	*B*	¤	*B*	¤	¤	*B*	¤
N-100	*B*	¤	¤	*B*	¤	*B*	¤	¤	*B*	¤
N-30	*B*	¤	¤	*B*	*B*	*B*	*B*	¤	*B*	*B*
N-Ind	*B*	¤	¤	*B*	¤	*B*	¤	¤	*B*	*B*
N-Serv	*B*	¤	¤	¤	¤	*B*	*B*	*B*	¤	¤
N-Fin	*B*	*B*	*B*	*B*	¤	*B*	*B*	*B*	*B*	¤
InvTrst	¤	¤	¤	¤	*B*	*B*	¤	¤	¤	.

¤: Evidence of the presence of the nonexistence of rational bubbles,
B: Evidence of the presence of the existence of rational bubbles.

.: The condition of stationary Δd_t and stationary r_t does not hold.

Lardic and Priso (2004) also implemented unit root tests to the price-dividend ratios of the stock market indices of France, Italy, UK, Belgium, Spain, Canada, Australia and Germany. The results are in favor of accepting the existence of rational bubbles for most of the countries. Our results are also parallel to their findings.

The possibility of time-varying discount rates requires another methodology of rational bubble testing for getting more dependable evidence. We also tested the loglinear model of Craine (1993) which is described in the equation (20) for this purpose. The summary statistics of the variables which are tested in loglinear methodology is presented in Table 4.

The test results of the loglinear model are summarized in Table 5 and Table 6. According to the test methodology, if the Δd_t and r_t are stationary and $(d_t - p_t)$ is unit root, then this is consistent with the presence of the rational bubbles in the market.

The augmented Dickey-Fuller test results in the full period present the evidence of the existence of rational bubbles in all indices when the model with no constant term is employed. The Δd_t and r_t series of all indices reject the null hypothesis of unit root at 1% significance level. However the null hypothesis cannot be rejected for $(d_t - p_t)$ time series of all indices, indicating the dividend returns are not stationary, therefore the rational bubbles are present in all indices. On the other hand, the models which implement constant terms, also support the existence of rational bubbles in all indices except N-Serv and InvTrst indices. When the model with constant term and linear trend is implemented, we cannot reach the evidence of rational bubbles for only InvTrst index.

The first subperiod of March 1998 – October 2000 presents strong evidence of the existence of rational bubbles in all indices when we employ augmented Dickey-Fuller test. The Δd_t and r_t series of all indices reject the null hypothesis of unit root at 1% significance level for all models. On the other hand the null hypothesis cannot be rejected for $(d_t - p_t)$ time series of all indices. However the results reject the existence of rational bubbles for N-All, N-100, N-Ind and InvTrst indices when the model with constant term, and constant term and linear trend are implemented in March 2001 – December 2006.

On the other hand, when we implement KPSS test, we get the evidence of the existence of rational bubbles in all indices except InvTrst index in full period. The presence of the rational bubbles is also supported by the KPSS tests in the first subperiod for all indices except for N-All index. The general structure of the existence of the rational bubbles continued to be accepted in the second subperiod for all indices except for N-Serv and InvTrst indices.

The results of both tests which implement different models are summarized in Table 7. As a general result, it can be seen that there is the evidence of the presence of rational bubbles in all indices in at least one model. We also have the evidence of the existence of rational bubbles in both subperiods. The evidence of the presence of rational bubbles in the indices is stronger when the loglinear model test results are analysed. This difference can be attributed to the time-varying discount rates.

6.2. Empirical Findings of Bilinear Unit Root Model

Following Charemza, Lifshits and Makarova (2005) we also implemented a two stage test procedure in testing rational bubbles by bilinear unit root methodology. In the first stage we implemented the Leybourne type augmented Dickey-Fuller unit root and KPSS stationary tests and in the second stage the unit root bilinearity is tested. We utilized Gauss 7.0 package program and Blini 1.03 software[10] for performing the Leybourne type augmented Dickey-Fuller, KPSS and Bilineer unit root tests.

Daily returns of the indices of full period (2nd March 1998-29th December 2006) and two subperiods (2nd March 1998–31st October 2000 and 1st March 2001–29th December 2006) are computed by taking the first logarithmic differences of dividend adjusted daily close values of the indices. All index returns are further adjusted according to their best convenient generalized autoregressive conditional heteroscdasticity (GARCH) models in order to eliminate the GARCH effects on the bilinear test procedure. The adjustment process is implemented as follows. In the first step, the conditional variance series of each index are generated by implementing the most significant GARCH model to the index return data. In the second step, conditional variance series are utilized for computing the correction coefficients of each index. In the third step, logarithmic returns of each index are divided into their correction factors and adjusted returns are generated. The correction factor is computed by using the following formula (see Cajueiro and Tabak, 2005 and Charemza, Lifshits and Makarova, 2005):

$$CF_t = {h_t^{1/2}} \Big/ {mean\left[h_t^{1/2}\right]} \tag{31}$$

where, CF_t is the correction factor, h_t is the conditional variance, $mean[\cdot]$ is the average operator. We utilized E-views 4 in order to estimate the GARCH models and generate the adjusted returns. The summary statistics of the adjusted returns are presented in Table 8.

The logarithmic price levels that are used to perform the linear unit root and linear stationarity tests are derived by the inclusion of the GARCH adjusted returns on the previous index values starting from the first day index value of $log100 = 4.6052$.

The null hypothesis of the Leybourne type augmented Dickey-Fuller test is the variable is unit root. However the null hypothesis of the KPSS test is the variable is stationary. Charemza and Syczewska (1998) state that the critical values of each test for testing their null hypotheses are not sufficient to perform a joint test for investigating the stationarity and calculated the required critical values for a joint test. We also implemented these critical values in the first stage of the bilinear tests. The test results are presented in Table 9.

The summarized results of Leybourne type augmented Dickey-Fuller test in Table 9 show that the null hypothesis of unit root cannot be rejected for all indices in all periods. The unit root feature of indices is also supported by the results of KPSS test. According to the test results, the null hypothesis of stationarity is rejected at 1% significance level for all indices in the full period and both subperiods.

---

[10] See Charemza and Makarova (2002) for Bilini software.

Table 8. Summary Statistics of Daily Adjusted Returns

Index	Mean	Standard Deviation	Skewness	Kurtosis	JB	JB p-value	GARCH(p,q)*
	PANEL A: 2nd March 1998 – 29th December 2006						
N-All	0.0013	0.0266	-0.2884	4.6623	281.0824	0.0000	GARCH(2,2)
N-100	0.0012	0.0276	-0.2424	4.5583	241.8154	0.0000	GARCH(2,2)
N-30	0.0012	0.0289	-0.1249	4.4226	189.4100	0.0000	GARCH(2,2)
N-Ind	0.0013	0.0241	-0.4847	4.9135	417.7506	0.0000	GARCH(3,3)
N-Serv	0.0009	0.0263	-0.2217	4.8768	337.6314	0.0000	GARCH(1,1)
N-Fin	0.0014	0.0304	-0.1367	4.6084	241.6727	0.0000	GARCH(3,3)
InvTrst	0.0010	0.02681	-0.2827	5.7055	693.6062	0.0000	GARCH(7,7)
	PANEL B: 2nd March 1998 –31st October 2000						
N-All	0.0019	0.0337	-0.2122	4.0796	36.4985	0.0000	GARCH(2,2)
N-100	0.0020	0.0347	-0.1519	3.9569	27.3397	0.0000	GARCH(2,2)
N-30	0.0020	0.0366	-0.0499	3.8963	22.0631	0.0000	GARCH(1,1)
N-Ind	0.0018	0.0303	-0.4117	4.1201	52.4218	0.0000	GARCH(1,1)
N-Serv	0.0014	0.0331	0.1021	4.2310	42.2367	0.0000	GARCH(1,1)
N-Fin	0.0022	0.0377	-0.0475	3.8092	18.0074	0.0001	GARCH(3,3)
InvTrst	0.0199	0.3812	-0.3558	5.1997	144.9334	0.0000	GARCH(5,5)
	PANEL C: 1st March 2001 – 29th December 2006						
N-All	0.0012	0.0225	-0.2164	4.7788	202.1985	0.0000	GARCH(4,4)
N-100	0.0012	0.0272	-0.2126	7.0920	1021.143	0.0000	GARCH(1,1)
N-30	0.0015	0.0272	-0.0635	5.0375	251.4396	0.0000	GARCH(2,2)
N-Ind	0.0011	0.0219	-0.0977	4.4181	123.6354	0.0000	GARCH(2,2)
N-Serv	0.0011	0.0255	-0.1442	4.3472	114.5117	0.0000	GARCH(2,2)
N-Fin	0.0013	0.0241	-0.0928	5.0117	246.2325	0.0000	GARCH(3,3)
InvTrst	0.0018	0.0255	-0.0193	3.8912	48.0100	0.0000	GARCH(5,5)

* The GARCH model which is estimated in order to calculate the correction factor for adjusting the returns for conditional heteroscedasticity.

Table 9. Unit Root Test Results of Logaritmic Price Levels of Indices Derived from the GARCH Adjusted Returns

Index	Leybourne type Augmented Dickey-Fuller Unit Root Test*				KPSS Stationarity Test**		
	t-value	Sign.***	Max. Augm.	Forward/ Backward	Max. t-value	Sign.***	Length of Autocorrelation
	PANEL A: 2nd March 1998 – 29th December 2006						
N-All	-0.1133	¤	45	Forward	162.806	+++	0
N-100	-0.3231	¤	45	Forward	160.104	+++	0
N-30	-0.1748	¤	45	Forward	162.347	+++	0
N-Ind	0.0328	¤	45	Forward	175.559	+++	0
N-Serv	-0.2324	¤	45	Forward	102.922	+++	0
N-Fin	-0.2969	¤	45	Forward	155.144	+++	0
InvTrst	-0.7248	¤	45	Forward	168.452	+++	0

Table 9. (Continued)

Index	Leybourne type Augmented Dickey-Fuller Unit Root Test*				KPSS Stationarity Test**		
	t-value	Sign.***		t-value	Sign.***		t-value
	PANEL B: 2nd March 1998 –31st October 2000						
N-All	-1.0255	¤	45	Forward	51.5183	+++	0
N-100	-0.9807	¤	45	Forward	52.5159	+++	0
N-30	-0.9882	¤	45	Forward	53.5033	+++	0
N-Ind	-0.8743	¤	45	Forward	50.6005	+++	0
N-Serv	-0.9990	¤	45	Backward	47.7679	+++	0
N-Fin	-1.0422	¤	45	Forward	54.9112	+++	0
InvTrst	-0.6661	¤	45	Forward	48.5948	+++	0
	PANEL C: 1st March 2001 – 29th December 2006						
N-All	-0.3308	¤	45	Backward	139.9020	+++	0
N-100	-0.8745	¤	45	Backward	136.7002	+++	0
N-30	-0.0081	¤	45	Forward	129.2950	+++	0
N-Ind	0.2845	¤	45	Forward	127.2264	+++	0
N-Serv	-0.3977	¤	45	Forward	132.5169	+++	0
N-Fin	-0.6577	¤	45	Backward	137.6130	+++	0
InvTrst	-0.0076	¤	45	Forward	139.7303	+++	0

* Null hypothesis of augmented Dickey-Fuller unit root test: Ho = variable is unit root.
** Null hypothesis of KPSS stationarity test: Ho= variable is stationary.
*** ¤ the null hypothesis cannot be rejected, +++: the null hypothesis is rejected at 1% significance level.

The strong evidence about the nonstationarity of all index returns provided from two linear unit root tests satisfy the initial condition for testing the bilinear structure of the unit root. In the second stage of the test, the significance of the b coefficient, the bilinear term, in equation (26) is tested. The results of the bilinear unit root test are summarized in Table 10.

The bilinear test results presented in Panel A of Table 10 show that the null hypothesis of insignificant bilinear coefficient or, no rational bubble is rejected for all indices. These results can be interpreted as important evidence in favor of the existence of the rational bubbles in ISE. The test results also show that the bilinear coefficients of ISE National-All, ISE National-100, ISE National-30, ISE National-Industrials, ISE National-Financials and ISE Investment Trusts Indices are statistically significant at 1% level in the full period. However the test results of ISE National-Services reject the insignificant bilinear coefficient at 5% level.

The results of the subperiods are different than the full period. The test results of the first subperiod 2nd March 1998 –31st October 2000 are presented in the Panel B of Table 10. The evidence of the presence of rational bubbles can be seen in this pre financial crisis period when we analyse ISE National-All Shares, ISE National-100 and ISE National-30 indices. The null hypothesis of no bilinear term is rejected at 5% significant level for these indices. This can be interpreted as the evidence of the existence of rational bubbles in ISE in this subperiod. The test results of ISE National-Industrials, ISE National-Financials and ISE Investment Trusts also support this evidence. However the result of ISE National-Services index is controversial. According to the test results we cannot reject the insignificance of the bilinear term for the indices, except ISE National-Services index.

The analysis of the 1st March 2001–29th December 2006 period also presents different results than the results of the full period. In this sub period, the indices which represent the general market, namely ISE National-All Shares, ISE National-100 and ISE National-30 indices, have statistically significant bilinear terms. Thus we can say that the unit root bilinearity is a general characteristic for the whole market and the rational bubbles exist in all three periods. However, in the second sub period, we cannot see the evidence of the presence of rational bubbles in ISE National-Industrials, ISE National-Services and ISE Investment Trusts indices.

Table 10. Bilinear Test Results of GARCH Adjusted Returns

Index	B-max	Significance[a]	Max. Aug.
PANEL A: 2nd March 1998 – 29th December 2006			
N-All	2.9986	+++	5
N-100	2.9149	+++	5
N-30	2.5543	+++	5
N-Ind	3.0439	+++	5
N-Serv	1.8430	++	1
N-Fin	2.4523	+++	5
InvTrst	2.5658	+++	3
PANEL B: 2nd March 1998 –31st October 2000			
N-All	2.2092	++	1
N-100	1.9246	++	4
N-30	1.9729	++	4
N-Ind	2.6742	+++	1
N-Serv	0.5723	¤	6
N-Fin	1.5310	+	4
InvTrst	1.6042	+	3
PANEL C: 1st March 2001 – 29th December 2006			
N-All	2.1000	++	4
N-100	1.9698	++	1
N-30	1.9165	++	1
N-Ind	-1.0429	¤	10
N-Serv	1.0772	¤	1
N-Fin	1.4874	+	4
InvTrst	0.9207	¤	6

[a] +++: Significant at 1% level,
++: Significant at 5% level,
+: Significant at 10% level,
¤: Statistically insignificant.

As an overall result, we found the evidence of the existence of rational bubbles in the indices which have great representative features in ISE, such as ISE National-All Shares, ISE National-100 and ISE National-30 indices in all sample periods. These results are parallel to the previous findings for different stock markets. For example Capelle-Blanchard and Raymond (2004) analyzed the presence of bubbles in French, German, Japanese, UK and US stock markets from 1973 to 2002. They also could not reject the existence of bubbles in these markets. Similar results also come from the analysis of Lardic and Priso (2004) in France, Italy, UK, Belgium, Spain, Canada, Australia and Germany stock markets. The results are also in favor of accepting the existence of rational bubbles for most of the countries.

7. Conclusion

The detection of the divergence between fundamental value and market prices has important aspects on the investors who are trading in the stock market and as well as the whole economy. The importance of the possible presence of the bubbles in stock prices attracted the academic interest in this area and result in a great number of research with different bubble test methods which are still continuously developing.

We investigated the presence of rational bubbles in ISE between 1998-2006 by implementing linear and nonlinear unit root tests to the monthly and daily data of ISE National-All, ISE National-100, ISE National-30, ISE National-Industrials, ISE National-Services, ISE National-Financials and ISE Investment Trusts indices.

Considering the possible effects of the financial crises in the Turkish economy in November 2000 and February 2001, we decided to exclude these periods from our analysis. Thus we implemented our analysis to the full period of March 1998-November 2006 as well as two subperiods of March 1998-October 2000 and March 2001-December 2006.

In the first stage, we applied linear unit root test procedures to ISE monthly data. The first test is based on implementing augmented Dickey-Fuller unit root and KPSS stationarity tests to the price-dividend ratio of the indices which are stated above. The results are in favor of the presence of rational bubbles in all indices for at least one model in the full period and both sub periods. Considering the weakness of this classical test, a further test which enables time-varying discount rates is implemented to the data. The augmented Dickey-Fuller and KPSS test results of the loglinear model also support the previous results. We reach the track of the existence of rational bubbles in all indices when we apply augmented Dickey-Fuller test, however the results of KPSS tests are in favor of the nonexistence of rational bubbles in N-Serv index in the full period and the second subperiod. The potential weaknesses of linear test methods as well as the advantages of nonlinear models motivated to use the bilinear test method in detecting rational bubbles in ISE as a second stage.

When the test results of nonlinear models are considered, the evidence is in favor of the existence of rational bubbles in all indices in the full period. But the results of the sub periods are contradictory for some indices. In the first and second sub periods we cannot accept unit root bilinearity for ISE-National Services index. The results also reject the significance of the bilinear term for ISE-National Industrials and ISE Investment Trusts indices in the second sub period.

Comparing this evidence with the evidence of linear tests, we are inclined to favor nonlinear unit root test results in this research. Because there is an important number of previous evidence of nonlinear structure of financial time series and the bilinear test procedure is considered to be robust in capturing the sudden and unexpected changes in the time series. Thus we can conclude that as a general structure, the market prices diverge from the fundamental values and so rational bubbles present in ISE but this structure can change according to the sample periods and sector indices that are under the investigation.

References

Abreu, B.D. & Brunnermeier, M.K. (2003). Bubbles and Crashes, *Econometrica,* 71, 173-204.

Blanchard, O.J. & Watson M. (1982). Bubbles, Rational Expectations and Financial Markets. In P. Watchtel (Ed.), *Crises in the Economic and the Financial Structure,* (295-315) Lexington: Lexington Books.

Bohl, M. T. (2003). Periodically Collapsing Bubbles in the US Stock Market?, *International Review of Economics and Finance,* 2, 385-397.

Boucher, C. (2003). Testing for Rational Bubbles with Time Varying Risk Premium and Non-Linear Cointegration: Evidence from the US and French Stock Markets, www.univ-orleans.fr/deg/GDRecomofi/ Activ/boucher_nice.pdf, 20.08.2006.

Brooks, C. & Katsaris, A. (2003). Rational Speculative Bubbles: An Empirical Investigation of the London Stock Exchange, *Bulletin of Economic Research,* 55, 319-346.

Brunnermeier, M. K. (2001). *Asset Pricing Under Asymmetric Information: Bubbles, Crashes, Technical Analysis, and Herding,* Oxford: Oxford University Press.

Cajueiro, D.O. & Benjamin, M.T. (2005). Testing for Rational Bubbles in Banking Indices, Phsyca, 366, 365-376.

Campbell, J. & Shiller, R. J. (1987). Cointegration and Tests of Present Value Models, *Journal of Political Economy,* 95, 1062-1088.

Campbell, J. & Shiller, R. J. (1988). The Dividend Price Ratio and Expectations of Future Dividends and Discount Factors, *Review of Financial Studies,* 1, 195-227.

Campbell, J. Y., Lo A. W. & MacKinlay A. C. (1997). *The Econometrics of Financial Markets,* Princeton, NJ: Princeton University Press.

Capelle-Blanchard, G. & Raymond, H. (2004). Empirical Evidence on Periodically Collapsing Stock Price Bubbles, *Applied Economic Letters,* 11, 61-69.

Chang, T., Chang, H., Chu H. & Su, C. (2005). Does Rational Bubbles Exist in the Taiwan Stock Market? Evidence from a Nonparametric Cointegration Test, *Economics Bulletin,*3, 1-9.

Charemza, W. W. & Syczewska, E. M. (1998). Joint Application of the Dickey-Fuller and KPSS Tests, *Economic Letters,* 61, 17-21.

Charemza, W.W. & Makarova, S. (2002). *Bilini Version 1.03: Collection of GAUSS Procedures for Linear and Bilinear Unit root Process,* University of Leicester, Mimeo.

Charemza, W. W., Lifshits, M. & Makarova, S. (2005). Conditional Testing for Unit root Bilinearity in Financial Time Series: Some Theoretical and Empirical Results, *Journal of Economic Dynamics and Control,* 29, 63-93.

Craine, R. (1993). Rational Bubbles: A Test, *Journal of Economic Dynamics and Control,* 17, 829-846.

Cunado, J., Gil-Alana, L. A. & de Gracia F. P. (2005). A Test for Rational Bubbles in the NASDAQ Stock Index: A Fractionally Integrated Approach, *Journal of Banking and Finance,* 29, 2633-2654.

De Bondt, W.F.M. & Thaler, R. H. (1985). Does the Stock Market Overreact?, *Journal of Finance,* 40, 793-803.

De Long J., Schleifer, A., Summers, L. & Waldmann J. (1990a). Positive Feedback Investment Strategies and Destabilizing Rational Speculation, *Journal of Finance,45,* 379-396.

De Long J., Schleifer, A., Summers, L. & Waldmann, J. (1990b). Noise Trader Risk in Financial Markets, *Journal of Political Economy,* 98, 703-738.

De Long J., Schleifer, A., Summers, L. & Waldmann, J. (1991). The Survival of Noise Traders in Financial Markets, *Journal of Business,* 64, 1-19.

Dezhbakhsh and Demirguc-Kunt (1990). On the presence of Speculative Bubbles in Stock Prices, *Journal of Financial and Quantitative Analysis,* 25, 101-112.

Diba, B.T. (1990). Bubbles and Stock-Price Volatility. In Dwyer, G.P.Jr & Hafer, R.W. (Eds.) *Stock Market: Bubbles, Volatility and Chaos,* Boston: Kluwer.

Diba, B. T. & Grossman, H. I. (1988a). Explosive Rational Bubbles in Stock Prices?, *American Economic Review,* 78, 520-530.

Diba, B. T. & Grossman, H. I. (1988b). The Theory of Rational Bubbles in Stock Prices, *The Economic Journal,* 98, 746-754.

Evans, G. W. (1991). Pitfalls in Testing for Explosive Bubbles in Asset Prices, *American Economic Review,* 81, 922-930.

Flood, R. P. & Garber, P. (1980). Market Fundamentals versus Price Level Bubbles: The First Tests, *Journal of Political Economy,* 88, 745-770.

Froot, K. & Obstfeld, M. (1991). Intrinsic Bubbles: The Case of Stock Prices, *American Economic Review,* 81, 1189-1214.

Fukuta, Y. (2002). A Test for Rational Bubbles in Stock Bubbles, *Empirical Economics,* 27, 587-600.

Grossman, S. & Shiller, R. (1981). The Determinants of the Variability of Stock Market Prices, *American Economic Review,* 71, 222-227.

Gurkaynak, R. S. (2005). *Econometric Tests of Asset Price Bubbles: Taking Stock,* FEDS Working Paper No. 2005-04.

Hardouvelis, G. A. (1988). Evidence on Stock Market Speculative Bubbles: Japan, The United States and Great Britain, *Federal Reserve Bank of New York Quarterly Review,* Summer, 4- 16.

Hart, O. D. & Kreps, D. M. (1986). Price Destabilizing Speculation, *Journal of Political Economy,* 94, 927-952.

Horvath, M. T. & Watson, M. W. (1995). Testing for Cointegration When Some of the Cointegrating Vectors are Known, *Econometric Theory,* 11, 952-984.

Ikeda, S. & Shibata, A. (1992). Fundamentals-Dependent Bubbles in Stock Prices, *Journal of Monetary Economics,* 16, 353-373.

Kleidon, A. W. (1986). Variance Bounds Tests and Stock Price Valuation Models, *Journal of Political Economy,* 94, 953-1001.

Koustas, Z. & Serletis, A. (2005). Rational Bubbles or Persistent Deviations from Market Fundamentals, *Journal of Banking and Finance,* 29, 2523-2539.

Lamont, O. (1998). Earnings and Expected Returns, *Journal of Finance,* 53, 1563-1587.

Lardic, S. & Priso, A. M. (2004). Rational Stock Price Bubbles: Is There any International Evidence?, *Finance India,* 18, 559-576.

Larsen, E.S. (1997). Theories and Tests for Bubbles, Norges Universitetet, Tromso, www.nfh.uit.no/dok/bubbles%20small.pdf, 20/08/2006.

Lucas, R.E. Jr. (1978). Asset Prices in an Exchange Economy, *Econometrica,* 46,1429-1445.

Peel, D. & Davidson, J. (1998). A Nonlinear Error Correction Mechanism Based on the Bilinear Model, *Economic Letters*, 58, 165-170.

Rappoport, P. & White, E. N. (1993). Was There a Bubble in the 1929 Stock Market?, *The Journal of Economic History,* 53, 549-574.

Rosser, J.B.Jr. (2000). *From Catastrope to Chaos: A General Theory of Economic Discontinuities* (2nd edition). Kluwer Academic.

Siegel, J. J. (2003). What is an Asset Price Bubble? An Operational Definition, *European Financial Management,* 9, 11-24.

Shiller, R. J. (1981). Do Stock Prices Move too much to be Justified by Subsequent Changes in Dividents?, *American Economic Review,* 71, 421-436.

Shleifer, A. & Summers, L. H. (1990). The Noise Trader Approach to Finance, *The Journal of Economic Perspectives,* 4, 19-34.

Taipalus, K. (2006). *Bubbles in the Finnish and US Equities Markets,* Helsinki: Bank of Finland Studies.

Timmermann, A. (1995). Cointegration Tests of Present Value Models with a Time-Varying Discount Factor, *Journal of Applied Econometrics,* 10, 17-31.

Tirole, J. (1982). On the Possibility of Speculation Under Rational Expectations, Econometrica, 50, 1163-1181.

Tirole, J. (1985). *Asset Bubbles and Overlapping Generations, Econometrica,* 53, 1499-1527.

Van Norden, S. & Schaller, R. (1993). The Predictability of Stock Market Regime: Evidence from the Toronto Stock Exchange, *Review of Economics and Statistics,* 75, 505-510.

West, K. D. (1987). A Specification Test for Speculative Bubbles, *Quarterly Journal of Economics,* 102, 553-580.

In: Global Stock Exchanges: Stability, Interrelationships... ISBN: 978-1-60692-184-5
Editor: Paolo B. Cassedes

Chapter 3

LEARNING TO LIVE WITH THE FLOAT: TURKEY'S EXPERIENCE 2001-2003*

Faruk Selçuk[1†] ***and Oya Pinar Ardic***[2‡]
[1]Department of Economics, Bilkent University,
Bilkent 06800, Ankara, Turkey
[2]Bogazici University, Department of Economics,
Bebek 34342, Istanbul, Turkey

Abstract

The conduct of policy under floating exchange rates is becoming an increasingly important concern for developing countries. The challenge facing the central banks is to contain the volatility of the exchange rate while achieving low inflation and stimulating output growth. As a complement, the governments must implement sound policies to bring the fiscal and legal environments close to those of the advanced economies so as to enhance long-term economic growth. One recent example of an emerging economy that confronts this challenge is Turkey with a history of high inflation and a collapse of a fixed exchange rate based stabilization program that resulted in a market-forced devaluation. After a review of the literature, this chapter analyzes the developments in the foreign exchange market in Turkey in light of the Central Bank's policies during the floating exchange rate system between February 2001 and November 2003. The results indicate that the Central Bank had been successful in containing volatility and reducing the average inflation rate. However, the accumulated risks in the economy, such as the extreme appreciation of the currency and high real interest rates make the system vulnerable to adverse shocks.

Keywords: exchange rate systems, emerging markets, financial volatility

JEL No: C32, E31, E58, E65, F31

---

*A version of this chapter was also published in *International Finance and Monetary Policy*, edited by Gleb P. Severov published by Nova Science Publishers, Inc. It was submitted for appropriate modifications in an effort to encourage wider dissemination of research.

†E-mail address: faruk@bilkent.edu.tr, http://www.bilkent.edu.tr/~faruk, Tel: +90 (532) 294 8796, Fax: +1 (208) 694 3196.

‡E-mail address: pinar.ardic@boun.edu.tr, http://www.econ.boun.edu.tr/ardic. Corresponding Author. Tel: +90 (212) 359 7650, Fax: +90 (212) 287 24 53.

1 Introduction

The choice of an exchange rate regime under free capital mobility has become an important concern for the emerging market economies. The Asian crisis in 1997-1998 and the turmoil in Brazil, Russia, Turkey and Argentina afterwards have played a crucial part in raising this question. Furthermore, the increasing degree of globalization has sped up the international integration of capital markets, augmenting the difficulty of policy conduct for the developing economies.

The crises in the international capital markets that had affected the emerging economies since the last decade of the twentieth century had adverse impacts especially on the countries that have some form of pegged exchange rate regimes. Since then, the policy discussions on the choice of exchange rate regimes have been in favor of corner solutions, namely hard pegs and free floats. The intermediate regimes, or soft pegs, have lost their attractiveness to a certain extent. Tavlas (2003) argues that the increase in the international flows of capital is the factor that made the management of exchange rate difficult. In addition, the unpredictable reversal of capital flows and contagion as the other two sources besides the expansion of capital flows that had led to the departure from the intermediate foreign exchange rate regimes.

Even if a country declares that the exchange rate regime is a “free float”, it should be expected that the country will not remain indifferent to wide fluctuations in the exchange rates, a behavior which Calvo and Reinhart (2002) call the “fear of floating.” Fischer (2001) argues that the “fear of floating” is understandable. He points out that although the soft pegs are unsustainable for countries that experience high capital mobility, there still exists a range of flexible exchange rate arrangements. The excluded arrangements from his “acceptable regimes” are certain forms of fixed, adjustable peg, and narrow band exchange rate systems. In these excluded regimes, the government is committed to defending a particular value of the exchange rate, or a narrow range of exchange rates without any required institutional commitment, although the country is open to international capital flows. Thus, free and managed floats, as well as currency unions, currency boards, and dollarization (or Euroization) are acceptable in this “bipolar view” as long as the country backs the system with necessary institutional changes. On the other hand, as the recent Argentine experience shows, the absence of mechanisms other than the nominal exchange rate to create flexibility in the system to absorb negative shocks can lead to a severe crisis under a currency board.

The majority of the emerging market economies still suffer the “fear of floating” although the consensus is that soft pegs are not sustainable for a long period of time, and hard pegs have harmful effects on economic performance when there is lack of sufficient flexibility. The question, then, is the following: Is it possible for an emerging economy to conduct a monetary policy to contain the volatility in the exchange rate and to achieve success in lowering (and/or controlling) inflation and in enhancing output growth under a floating exchange rate regime?

In order to provide a partial answer to this question from an emerging country experience, this chapter analyzes the developments in the foreign exchange market in light of the Central Bank’s policies during the floating exchange rate system in Turkey between February 2001 and November 2003. The main finding is that the Central Bank had been successful in containing volatility and reducing the average inflation rate while there was a surge in output growth. However, the accumulated risks in the economy, such as the extreme appreciation of the currency and high real interest rates makes the country vulnerable to adverse shocks.

The rest of this chapter is organized as follows. The next section reviews the exchange rate regimes and policies, and discusses the implications for the emerging market economies. The third section provides an account of the recent experiences of the Turkish economy. The empirical analysis is presented in Section 4. Section 5 concludes.

2 Exchange Rate Regimes and Policy in Emerging Market Economies

The volatility of the exchange rate is a crucial issue for an emerging economy due to liability dollarization and the sensitivity of domestic prices to fluctuations in the exchange rate. It has important implications on domestic prices and the inflation rate, interest rates, and investment. Thus, containing the volatility of the exchange rate is a crucial aspect of enhancing stability, and the choice of the exchange rate system is a critical issue in this respect.[1]

Exchange rate regimes range from free floats to hard pegs, of which free floats put no restrictions on monetary policy but has the problem of volatility while hard pegs reduce the damages of volatility at the expense of the abandonment of monetary policy as a tool. Soft pegs lie between these two extreme cases, and have served as a tool for stabilization in developing economies. Thus, there is a trade-off between exchange rate volatility and the ability to use monetary policy. For expositional purposes, a summary of the types of exchange rate systems are summarized below.[2,3]

- *Free Float* Under a free float regime, the value of the exchange rate is determined by the demand and supply in the market, and the monetary authority does not intervene for the purpose of affecting the value of the exchange rate. Thus, the exchange rate does not restrict macroeconomic policies. Australia, Canada, Chile, Colombia, Japan, the United Kingdom, and the United States are examples of countries using free float.

- *Managed Float* Other than the intervention of the monetary authority to contain volatility or to correct the long run misalignment of the exchange rate, there is no specific exchange rate target, and macroeconomic policies are not restricted that much by efforts to set the value of the exchange rate. Algeria had a managed float as of the end of 2001.

[1]See Minella *et al.* (2003) for a recent account of monetary policy under exchange rate volatility in Brazil. Calderon and Schmidt-Hebbel (2003) provide an analysis of macroeconomic policies in Latin America. Both studies stress the importance of the credibility of the Central Banks in inflation targeting, exchange rate volatility, and the ability to conduct counter-cyclical policies.

[2]For more details, see Tavlas (2003) who provides a review of exchange rate regimes. His summary emphasizes the choice of an exchange rate regime for an emerging economy. He suggests inflation targeting along with managed float for emerging market economies.

[3]The country examples for each type of exchange rate system are taken from Bubula and Otker-Robe (2002) who use the recent IMF de facto classification of exchange rates (in effect since 1998) to compile historical data (pre-1998) for the classification of exchange rate systems. Before 1998, IMF classifications were based on official announcements by each country (de jure classification). The classification is as of the end of 2001.

- *Soft Pegs* Under a soft peg, there is a particular exchange rate target, and the monetary authority conducts policy to achieve it. Types of soft pegs include adjustable pegs where the target rate might seldom be altered if the target differs from the equilibrium exchange rate and capital controls are used to support the system, and crawling pegs where there is a set path for the exchange rate and the target rate is adjusted frequently. Bolivia, Costa Rica and Israel were among the countries that had some form of a soft peg by the end of 2001.

- *Fixed Exchange Rates* Under a fixed exchange rate system, the monetary authority fixes the value of the domestic currency against a foreign currency or a basket of foreign currencies. Malaysia adopted a fixed exchange rate regime in 1998.

- *Currency Boards* Under this system, which restricts the conduct of monetary policy, the local currency is convertible to the anchor currency on demand at a preset (by law) fixed exchange rate, and this is guaranteed by backing the domestic monetary base with the foreign currency. In Argentina, a currency board system was in effect between 1991-2002.

- *Dollarization (or Euroization)* The country adopts US dollars (or euros) as the official currency. The examples of countries that have adopted US dollars as their official currency include Panama, Ecuador, and El Salvador.

- *Monetary Union* This is an agreement by a group of countries to adopt a common currency and to have a common central bank to conduct monetary policy for the whole group. Monetary policy can no longer be used for the needs of individual members of the group. The Euro area is an example of a monetary union.

The choice of an exchange rate regime has long been a concern for economists. See, for example, Mundell (1961), McKinnon (1963), and Kenen (1969). Obstfeld and Rogoff (1995) argue that a fixed exchange rate has costs in terms of developing and maintaining credibility, and that the exchange rate should not be the target of the monetary policy, but rather can be used as an indicator. The alternative to fixed exchange rates as a tool for reducing inflation and exchange rate volatility is to establish sound monetary institutions. Reinhart (2000) and Calvo and Reinhart (2002) state that although there seems to be an observed shift in the world toward floating exchange rate regimes, the "fear of floating" is pervasive, and in practice, except for a few developed nations, the countries do conduct policies to affect their exchange rates.

Most emerging market economies are characterized by economic problems including high inflation, and current account deficits. The majority of the domestic debt in these countries is denominated in terms of a foreign currency (usually the US dollar), elevating the importance of having a stable exchange rate. In addition, there is evidence that the pass-through from exchange rates to prices is higher in emerging economies (Calvo and Reinhart, 2001). Thus, some form of a peg appears to be the most attractive exchange rate regime. Furthermore, by restricting the use of monetary policy, pegged regimes have been used as a tool in developing countries to enhance the credibility of the monetary authority in stabilizing the economy.

Until recently, soft pegs were desirable, and were widely adopted by the developing economies, in many cases as a part of a stabilization program. The crises of the last decade and a half, however, resulted in a departure away from pegged exchange rates, which is basically attributable to the increased integration of the international capital markets. The concept of the "impossible (or unholy) trinity" provides an explanation for this phenomenon. This concept states that it is impossible for a country to have fixed exchange rates, capital mobility, and monetary policy as a tool for domestic goals at the same time. Soft pegs can be thought of as a means for having fixed exchange rates and domestic monetary policy for a country with capital mobility (Fischer, 2001). However, in a world with increased openness of capital accounts, responding to domestic and external shocks that shift the equilibrium exchange rate has become increasingly difficult, and such countries have been objects of speculative attacks. The Asian crisis of the 1997-1998 is the major example of this phenomenon when Malaysia imposed capital controls in order to control the exchange rate. But, although capital controls under such situations can provide some short term relief, they are ineffective in the long term.

The preference for the pegged systems by the developing economies stems from the idea that pegged systems implicitly call for fiscal discipline under capital mobility, since bad policies by the government would lead to the worsening of the external balance, eventually forcing the abandoning of the peg. In practice, however, this fiscal discipline is not observed since the eventual outcome, devaluation, may come long afterwards leaving the authorities very little incentive to take the necessary fiscal measures. As put forth by Tornell and Velasco (2000), flexible exchange rate regimes, on the other hand, provide an incentive for the authorities to enhance fiscal discipline since the costs of bad policies are immediate. Examples of crises due to insufficient fiscal discipline under pegged systems include the Mexican crisis of 1994, the Asian crisis of 1997, the Brazilian crisis of 1999 and the Turkish crisis of 2001. Argentina can also be included in this list since one of the major reasons for the collapse of the currency board regime was the lack of fiscal discipline in local governments.

The case against the currency boards was demonstrated by the dramatic collapse of the Argentine economy in 2001. While labor market rigidity and lack of fiscal discipline were the two main factors contributing to this collapse, perhaps the most important reason was the wrong choice for the anchor currency that lead to the loss of international competitiveness. The lesson of the collapse of the Argentine currency board is that the use of a proper peg, fiscal sustainability, and credibility are crucial for success while over the long term maintaining the peg comes at high costs. Also, fiscal sustainability not only means reducing primary spending or raising taxes, but also conducting policies to correct the mismatch between debt composition and output composition in terms of tradables versus non-tradables. [4]

Eichengreen (2001) provides an account of the 2001 crises in Argentina and Turkey. Although Argentina and Turkey had differences in terms of the underlying inflation history, and the timing and the type of the exchange rate regime used in their stabilization programs (currency board in Argentina, crawling peg in Turkey), the two countries shared

[4]See Calvo *et al.* (2003) for more on the collapse of the Currency Board in Argentina. In addition to the points outlined in this paragraph, Calvo *et al.* (2003) emphasize the role of liability dollarization besides the smaller share of tradables in output relative to the share of non-tradables in the effects of a sudden stop of capital flows.

many aspects such as experiencing an extended period of depressed growth followed by a short-lived boom after the initiation of the stabilization program, increased exports and imports, need for capital inflows to finance the increased imports, and efforts to privatize the state enterprises, to strengthen the banking system and to balance public sector accounts. However, in both Argentina and Turkey, incomplete fiscal consolidation and lack of political support for reduced public spending still continued to be problems. In addition, the increase in domestic demand proved to be temporary, and once the problem of competitiveness that arose from the exchange rate anchor was added, financing the current account became difficult, and a one-time adjustment of the exchange rate was necessary to improve competitiveness. But, this would diminish the stability of the banking system in both countries as the banks had large foreign currency liabilities. Furthermore, it would hurt the credibility of the policy-makers. Thus, short-term foreign liabilities and rollover risk increased as maturities shortened. Both economies became vulnerable to deteriorating external conditions, and eventually were not able to avoid the crises.

According to Eichengreen (2001) there are eight lessons of the crises in Argentina and Turkey. First, exchange-rate based stabilizations are risky as exit from a peg is difficult. Second, the existence of large short-term debt creates fears of crisis. Third, debt swaps only delay the problems, they do not provide a solution. Fourth, fiscal stability requires reduced public spending, which in turn implies reduced aggregate demand and growth. The decline in growth decreases the tax base, and thus the tax revenues, worsening the fiscal position. Therefore, engineering fiscal consolidation while maintaining output growth is difficult. Fifth, under circumstances in which market-based solutions are not viable, it is not easy to overcome the problem of moral hazard in international lending, and thus the international financial institutions found themselves bailing out both countries in fears of a more widespread crisis. Sixth, in both countries, the governments adopted fiscal and financial reforms to catalyze private lending in the aftermath of the crises, and the international financial institutions provided necessary funds in the meantime, until the markets react. However, market reaction was delayed as investors waited for evidence of commitment to stabilization policies. Seventh, as the Argentine case shows, there are limitations to private contingent lines since the collateral bonds were limited in supply as a result of the debt swap prior to the crisis. Thus, the governments may have a tendency to think it unlikely to ever be drawing those lines. Eighth, and last, it is difficult to get the private sector involved in the bail out as the market is unwilling to hold new claims after a crisis. Thus, Eichengreen (2001) claims that there is still much to be done in terms of formulating policies to prevent and to resolve the crises.

The common features of the crises that the emerging markets have experienced since the 1990s are the collapse of some form of pegged exchange rate regime and an accompanying sudden stop of capital inflows. These crises resulted in a sharp currency depreciation, a decline in the stock market, and contraction in output in the short run. Cespedes *et al.* (2000) model a small open economy that has liability dollarization, [5] sticky wages, and where the net worth of domestic entrepreneurs play a crucial role in capital flows to the economy, and find that flexible exchange rates help the adjustment process in the immediate aftermath of a financial crisis which results in a large depreciation and sudden stop. A high

[5]See Cespedes *et al.* (2000), Cavallo *et al.* (2002), Allen *et al.* (2002), Calvo *et al.* (2003) and the references therein for details on the magnifying effects of liability dollarization on the emerging market financial crises.

degree of liability dollarization acts as a magnifier of external shocks through balance sheet effects, which diminishes the risk premium of the country and lead to the reversal of capital inflows. Allen *et al.* (2002) also consider the balance sheet effects of the emerging market crises, and discuss how liability dollarization can eventually trigger the crisis. They stress the importance of the maturity and the denomination of domestic debt, and claim that the solution to the problems of currency and maturity mismatches are limited.

Cavallo *et al.* (2002) also model this phenomenon, and claim that the sudden stop of capital inflows and output contraction are related to the degree of liability dollarization in the economy. They find that the cause of the overshooting of the exchange rate is the existence of large foreign currency denominated debt stock and the need for hedging open foreign currency positions after the collapse of the peg. Exchange rate overshooting, together with large foreign currency debt create balance sheet effects and result in a decline in the stock market, leading to a contraction in output. Then, Cavallo *et al.* (2002) evaluate the cost of the crisis in a country with a high degree of liability dollarization. Exchange rate overshooting and the decline in the stock market force the investors to leave the economy. However, this induces further depreciation of the exchange rate and the fall in the stock market, creating a cycle which results in large, adverse wealth effects for the economy. Their findings indicate, contrary to the findings of Cespedes *et al.* (2000), that if the authorities maintain the peg for at least a temporary period in the immediate aftermath of the crisis, they can reduce overshooting and its negative wealth effects, but at the expense of additional output contractions in the short run. The mechanism that ensures this is the presence of margin constraints imposed on the domestic economy.

In order to analyze alternative exchange rate regimes and monetary policy options for an emerging market economy that experiences shocks to world interest rates and terms of trade, and is subject to risk premia in external financing, Devereux and Lane (2003) calibrate a model and find that financial distortions do not have a major impact on alternative policy options. They conclude that liability dollarization does not necessarily make fixed exchange rates desirable for macroeconomic stabilization, but the degree of pass-through in import prices has important consequences for price stabilization.

Mussa *et al.* (2000) consider the effects of increased capital mobility and integration of developing economies into world markets on the exchange rate regimes of the advanced economies as well as of the developing and transition economies. For developing economies that are closely integrated to the world economy, they conclude that maintaining pegged exchange rates have become difficult, and more flexible exchange rate regimes have become more desirable. In order for an emerging market country to opt for a form of hard peg, it needs to have established institutional structures and sufficient policy discipline to support the peg.

Putting special emphasis on the Turkish experience, Alper and Yılmaz (2003) argue that the best choice for the exchange rate regime for a developing economy with capital mobility is a floating system, supporting the conclusions of Mussa *et al.* (2000). A floating system would provide immediate costs to the governments that do not undertake serious fiscal measures. In addition, Alper and Yılmaz (2003) claim that as the foreign exchange risk will be transferred to the investors from the Central Bank under a free float, this would reduce the volume of short term capital flows and reduce the risk of speculative attacks (see also the arguments put forth by Eichengreen and Hausmann (1999) below for reducing the moral hazard problem). Further, if there is significant dollarization in the economy, the depreciation of the domestic currency implies a redistribution with undesirable political consequences, forcing the government to achieve fiscal discipline.

The high degree of currency substitution is another problem inherent in emerging market economies which has important consequences for the conduct of monetary policy and the implementation of stabilization programs, as currency substitution makes the use of monetary policy more difficult in fighting inflation since the demand for domestic money becomes unstable. Selçuk (2003) provides empirical evidence that the degree of currency substitution in emerging economies in the European Union periphery is indeed high. Domaç and Bahmani-Oskooee (2002) study the effects of currency substitution on inflation dynamics in Turkey. They find that the higher the degree of currency substitution is, the lower the monetary base will be, and thus, the fiscal authority needs to raise the administered prices in order to compensate for the decline in inflation tax. In the meantime, the domestic currency depreciates with the increases in the degree of currency substitution. Thus, the monetary authority would experience credibility problems more under a flexible exchange regime than it would under fixed exchange rates. In conclusion, Domaç and Bahmani-Oskooee (2002) indicate the emergence of inflation targeting as a suitable policy as it could limit the degree of currency substitution through leading to a higher exchange rate volatility than price volatility.

Eichengreen and Hausmann (1999) consider three problems that most emerging market economies suffer - moral hazard, original sin, and commitment problems - and examine the implications of exchange rate regimes in providing solutions to them. The bailing out of a troubled emerging market economy by the international financial institutions gives the investors incentives to take on excessive risks since they do not face the full risk of their investments. This creates moral hazard problem in international lending. Eichengreen and Hausmann (1999) argue that the solution is to require the private sector to share part of the burden of the bail-out. Pegged exchange rates in this case are undesirable as they reinforce the moral hazard problem, while flexible exchange rated are preferred as they limit short-term capital inflows.

The incompleteness in financial markets in emerging market countries may result in the inability of the country to borrow in terms of domestic currency in international markets and/or to borrow long-term domestically in terms of domestic currency. This "original sin" problem leads to currency mismatch where borrowing is in terms of foreign currency while revenues are in terms of domestic currency, and to maturity mismatch where liabilities are short-term and revenues are generated by long-term contracts. Eichengreen and Hausmann (1999) claim that dollarization (or euroization) is the best choice if original sin is the problem because flexible exchange rates cause bankruptcies by increasing the degree of currency mismatch and hard pegs cause defaults on short-term debt by increasing the degree of maturity mismatch.

The third problem Eichengreen and Hausmann (1999) consider for emerging markets is the commitment problem, which arises due to weak institutions that address commitment issues. Financial transactions are not self-enforcing by nature of being intertemporal, and in order to ensure commitment and enforce financial contracts, the economy needs to strengthen its financial infrastructure. Eichengreen and Hausmann (1999) argue that, in this case, both flexible and fixed exchange rates would increase financial fragility. Thus, taking these three problems into consideration, they suggest two options for emerging market economies. The first option is to dollarize while the second is to build well-structured domestic markets in which long-term domestic currency denominated instruments are traded. The second option, they state, takes longer and is harder, and therefore, most emerging market economies may rather choose to dollarize.[6]

Whether emerging market economies should float and whether they should adopt inflation targeting is considered by Eichengreen (2002). Under inflation targeting, the primary goal of monetary policy is price stabilization, and this goal and the policy tools are openly communicated to the public. Once the commitment to stable prices is institutionalized, credibility of the monetary authority would improve, leaving it room for pursuing policy to achieve the target. Eichengreen (2002) concludes that inflation targeting is not infeasible but complicated for emerging markets due to openness, liability dollarization, and lack of credibility. Openness adds to the challenge as it makes the economy vulnerable to external shocks, and the presence of liability dollarization would lead the monetary authority to refrain from movements in the exchange rate. However, when the economy is less open, the degree of liability dollarization is not very high, and credibility is easier to construct, inflation targeting would be attractive.

Domaç and Mendoza (2002) investigate whether the policy makers in emerging market economies should take into account the movements in exchange rates under inflation targeting. Although the primary goal under inflation targeting is the stability of prices, emerging economies would also be willing to contain the shocks to exchange rates in order to enhance stability. On the other hand, too much intervention in foreign exchange may alter inflation target as the primary goal. They suggest that policies aimed at containing the volatility of the exchange rate, but not affecting its level, can be useful under inflation targeting as they would reduce the adverse effects of exchange rate shocks on inflation and financial stability.

3 Turkish Economy: An Overview

This section provides an overview of the economic developments in Turkey, leading to the collapse of the most recent fixed exchange rate based stabilization program. The year 1980 had been the beginning of the period of liberalization and integration of the Turkish economy to the world economy. The structural change and reform plan of 1980 called for abandoning the barriers to trade, adopting export-led growth strategy, reducing the controls on foreign exchange, transition to the flexible exchange regime, lifting the controls on interest rates, easing bureaucracy, subsidizing foreign capital, and adopting price mechanism were among the main economic reforms introduced in this period. In the immediate aftermath of the implementation of this program, the economy experienced high output growth, low inflation and a healthy balance of payments situation.

The period since the late 1980s is characterized by increasing inflation and several stabilization programs. Nominal anchoring and monetary tightening were used in these programs without any serious effort to reduce the public sector borrowing requirement. In 1989, the capital account was liberalized and high nominal interest rate and low depreci-

[6]The conclusion of Eichengreen and Hausmann (1999) (supporting a form of hard peg) agrees with Calvo and Reinhart (2001) who suggest that some form of a peg is attractive for emerging economies.

ation rate were used to attract short term foreign capital to roll-over the public debt. By the end of 1993, the fiscal and external deficits were viewed by the market participants as no longer sustainable. These developments led to the crisis of April 1994. The stabilization program adopted after the crisis was not pursued vigorously and eventually abandoned (Ertuğrul and Selçuk, 2002).

The next stabilization attempt was in 1999 when the Russian crisis of 1998, the general elections and the earthquakes of 1999 deteriorated the fiscal balance. In December of 1999, a stand-by agreement was signed with the IMF with the crawling peg regime being the major disinflation tool.[7] The initial phase of this program was successful in reducing the interest rates and slowing down inflation which in turn led to increased consumption of consumer durables. However, the overvaluation of the exchange rate and lower real interest rates led to increased imports of consumption goods as well as intermediate goods. Increased world oil prices and the depreciation of the euro against the US dollar were the developments in the international markets that had adverse effects on the trade balance.

On the fiscal side, the program failed to achieve its targets which led the IMF and the World Bank to postpone the release of funds in the second half of 2000. In the meantime, inefficiencies and increased risk in the banking sector resulted in increased interest rates and reduced confidence in the financial markets. The slow pace of the government in undertaking the necessary steps to solve the financial problems of the state-owned banks and to implement other reforms, the lack of consensus and action in terms of privatization, the record levels of the current account deficit due to appreciation and negative domestic real interest rates, the deterioration of relations between Turkey and the European Union, and political instability are among the factors that contributed in this reduced confidence. In addition, the history of unsuccessful stabilization programs made it more difficult for the authorities to build up credibility, and the inability to deal with the fundamental problems of the economy resulted in an erosion of credibility.

There was a short-lived crisis in November 2000 which started with the inability of a commercial bank with a risky position to borrow from the money market. In two days, the overnight interest rates increased while the international investors started to get out. In order not to give up the parity, the Central Bank had to use its reserves to meet the increased demand for foreign currency. Later, to restore confidence in the program, the Central Bank had announced that such an action would not be repeated. However this only increased the interest rates. In December 2000, the IMF supplied extra funds, which provided temporary relief. There was short-term capital inflow to the economy for a while, and the reserves of the Central Bank returned to their pre-crisis level. Nevertheless, there were still concerns about the developments in the economy. In the end, the adverse political developments of February 2001 triggered another crisis and led the Central Bank to finally abandon the parity.

This last crisis, on February 19, 2001, was triggered by domestic political issues and led to an 18% drop in the stock market and the loss of approximately one-third of the total official reserves of the Central Bank in one day (USD 7.5 billion). When the Central Bank refused to provide Turkish Lira (TRL) liquidity to the two state banks that were not able to meet their obligations or other banks the following day, the banks were forced to

[7]The percentage change of the Turkish lira against a basket of euro and the US dollar was fixed.

give up USD 6 billion foreign exchange buying contracts with the Central Bank. The daily average overnight interest rates shot up to (simple annual) 2000 percent on February 20, and 4000 percent on February 21.[8] The government could not resist and dropped its exchange rate controls early February 22 and the TRL/USD exchange rate went up 40% in one week. Monthly inflation was 10% and 14% in March and April of 2001 respectively. The government prepared a new letter of intent to the IMF, emphasizing a major overhaul in the banking system and a promise of further acceleration of structural reforms outlined in the earlier letters of intent. On May 15, 2001, the IMF approved this revision of Turkey's three-year Stand-By arrangement by USD 8 billion with an understanding that the country moved into a floating exchange rate regime, and would stick to this policy.

Following the crisis, the challenge for the Central Bank was to re-establish confidence and contain volatility in financial markets while pursuing an implicit inflation targeting policy in a free floating exchange rate system. It was a challenge in the sense that the country had a long history of high inflation, and had never experienced a free float. Nominal exchange rates almost always increased in line with high inflation. The recent collapse of the fixed exchange rate based stabilization program further eroded the credibility of the Central Bank and led economic agents to think that any policy announcement by the authorities is not credible.[9]

4 Policy Under Floating Exchange Rate Regime in Turkey

In the aftermath of February 2001, the Central Bank of Turkey repeatedly stressed that it would stick to the floating exchange rate regime, and the volatility of the nominal exchange rate will be a concern rather than its level or direction. Meanwhile, an implicit inflation targeting policy would be pursued by controlling the monetary aggregates and setting an indicative interest rate (CBT, 2002, 2003).

In order to control the volatility of the exchange rate, the Central Bank conducted several buying and selling auctions. During the early stages of the float, between March 29, 2001 and November 30, 2001, all interventions were in the form of selling auctions, and the Central Bank sold a sum of USD 6,553 million. All other episodes of preannounced interventions had been in the form of buying auctions, the first one running from April 4 through June 6, 2002, and the second which started on May 5, 2003 and ended on October 22, 2003. The total amount bought back in these auctions were USD 6,447.3 million. The Bank also directly intervened in the market four times between May 12 and July 18, 2003 buying USD 2,083 million.[10] Thus, since the immediate aftermath of the float, the Central

[8]These are *weighted average* interest rates. The highest realized overnight interest rates during these two days were 2300 and 6200 percent (simple annual).

[9]Gençay and Selçuk (2006) provide an anecdotal story of the February 2001 crisis in Turkey. For a detailed account of the recent developments in the Turkish economy from different perspectives, see Ertuğrul and Selçuk (2002), Metin-Özcan *et al.* (2001), Öniş and Rubin (2003) and references therein. A series of articles in Kibritçioğlu *et al.* (2002) provides a detailed analysis of inflation dynamics and disinflation efforts in Turkey. For earlier studies, see Metin (1995) and Lim and Papi (1997). More recent studies are Celasun *et al.* (2003) and Domaç and Bahmani-Oskooee (2002).

[10]There were three direct interventions in 2002 (one buying and two selling). However, the amounts involved in these interventions as well as the amounts involved in two direct buying interventions in September 10-25, 2003 are not known.

Table 1: Granger causality probabilities. Sample period: March 13, 2001 - October 30, 2003 (667 business days). The rows show equations. The reported probabilities are probabilities that the column variable does not Granger cause the row variable.

	Return	Volatility	Interest Rate	Buying Auction	Selling Auction
Return	0.00	0.13	0.56	0.19	0.00
Volatility	0.00	0.00	0.00	0.46	0.00
Interest Rate	0.09	0.00	0.89	0.10	0.46
Buying Auction	0.89	0.95	0.25	0.00	1.00
Selling Auction	0.04	0.06	0.18	0.96	0.00

Bank had sold USD 6,553 million, and bought at least USD 8,530 million. One crucial aspect of the Central Bank policies since May 2003 is that, the level and the direction of the exchange rate seem to have become the target of the policies rather than its volatility, implying a possible deviation from the free float. There were arguments that recent buying auctions, along with two direct buying interventions in September 2003 were a response to the nominal (and real) appreciation of the Turkish lira during the float period.

In this part, we extend the analysis conducted by Selçuk (2005), employing a larger sample size. In addition, we look at the developments in the foreign exchange market during two separate periods. In our analysis, a five variable VAR system is estimated using daily data in order to investigate the interaction among the exchange rate, its volatility, and the Central Bank policies. The variables in the system are the TRL/USD exchange rate return (log difference, percent), the absolute value of the exchange rate return as a measure of volatility (percent), the change in the Central Bank overnight interest rates (simple annual, percent), the daily total amount bought by the Central Bank in USD buying auctions and the amount sold by the Central Bank in USD selling auctions (million USD). To assess a possible change in the direction of the policy in recent months, the VAR system is estimated for the whole sample, between March 2001 and October 2003, and also for the two sub-samples, pre-May 2003 and post-May 2003, a possible break point reflecting an implicit change in exchange rate policy of the Central Bank.

The VAR model for the whole sample is estimated by using a constant term and 7 lags as indicated by Sims' Likelihood Ratio (LR) test (Sims, 1980) for the period between March 13, 2001 - October 30, 2003 (667 business days).[11] Adjusted R-squares lie between 0.04 (change in the interest rate equation) and 0.79 (buying auctions equation). The results of the Granger causality tests indicate that exchange rate return and selling auctions cause volatility of the exchange rate at 1% level of significance. Exchange rate return and selling auctions, and changes in the interest rate and volatility of the exchange rate exhibit feedback at 5% and 1% levels of significance respectively. See Table 1 for the results of Granger causality tests.

Figure 1 plots the response of exchange rate return to shocks to different variables in the system, along with 95 percent bootstrap confidence intervals. Normally, one would

[11] We excluded the first 8 business days of the floating regime period to avoid any "start-off" effects. As shown by Selçuk (2004a), after a large shock in a financial market, the cumulative number of aftershocks increases at an exponential rate and converges after a certain period of time. These aftershocks, which are not part of the normal system, may cause some bias in our estimations if they are not excluded.

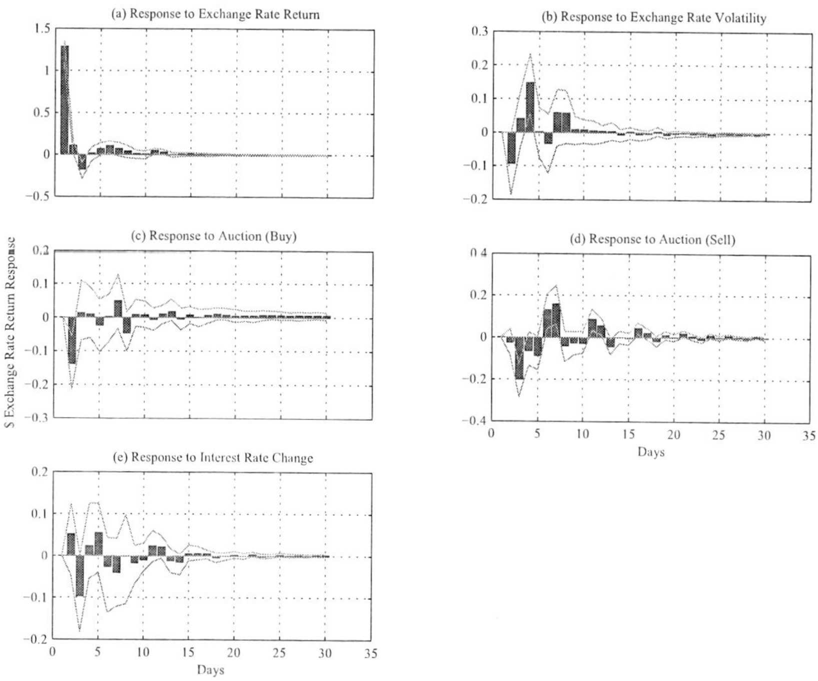

Figure 1: TRL/USD daily exchange rate return (log difference) response to shocks to different variables in the system. (a) Response to a shock (1.36 percent increase) in TRL/USD daily exchange rate return. (b) Response to a shock (1.06 percent increase) in TRL/USD daily volatility (absolute return). (c) Response to a shock (21 Million USD increase) in Central Bank USD buying auction. (d) Response to a shock (30 Million USD increase) in Central Bank selling auction. (e) Response to a shock (0.60 percent increase) in change in overnight interest rates. 95 percent bootstrap confidence intervals are plotted as straight lines. Sample period: March 13, 2001 - October 30, 2003 (667 business days).

expect the response of exchange rate return to shocks to Central Bank buying auctions to be positive since there is an increase in overall demand for the foreign currency. The results, however, indicate that this response is negative and statistically significant for one period. On the other hand, the response of the exchange rate return to a shock in selling auction is negative, as expected, for the first four periods. However, the response is reversed afterward and the overall response is very close to zero. The response of the exchange rate return to a shock to the change in interest rate is not statistically significant. Thus, it is possible to conclude that the Central Bank policies in the form of buying and selling auctions and changes in interest rate did not influence the direction (log return) of the exchange rates. In passing, we also note that a shock to the volatility of the exchange rate does not have any effect on the exchange rate return.

The response of exchange rate volatility to different shocks in the system is plotted in Figure 2. Panel (a) shows that an unexpected increase in exchange rate return increases volatility, and this impact prevails for several periods. Notice that the symmetric nature of the impulse response function implies that a fall in the foreign exchange rate return reduces volatility. However, the symmetric response of volatility to the shocks to the exchange rate

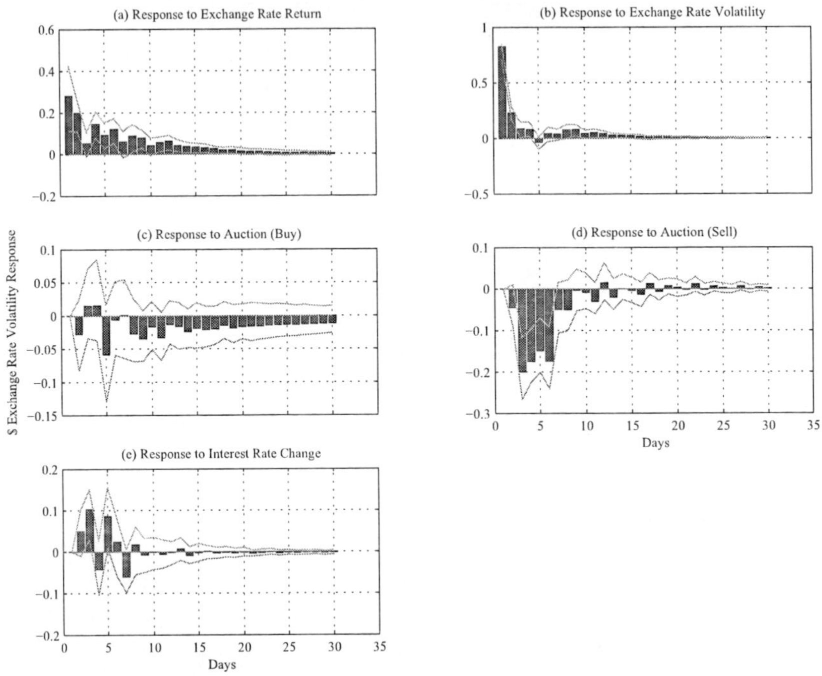

Figure 2: TRL/USD daily exchange rate volatility response to shocks to different variables in the system. (a) Response to a shock (1.36 percent increase) in TRL/USD daily exchange rate return. (b) Response to a shock (1.06 percent increase) in TRL/USD daily volatility (absolute return). (c) Response to a shock (21 Million USD increase) in Central Bank USD buying auction. (d) Response to a shock (30 million USD increase) in Central Bank selling auction. (e) Response to a shock (0.60 percent increase) in change in overnight interest rates. 95 percent bootstrap confidence intervals are plotted as straight lines. Sample period: March 13, 2001 - October 30, 2003 (667 business days).

return is not warranted. In an asymmetric stochastic volatility framework, Selçuk (2004b) shows that there is strong positive correlation between the shocks to the foreign exchange rate return at time t and the shocks to volatility (defined as the standard deviation of the exchange rate return) at time $t + 1$ during the floating exchange rate system in Turkey. However, Selçuk (2004b) implies that the response of volatility is actually asymmetric: the same magnitude of shocks to the exchange rate return cause different effects on the volatility, depending on the sign of shocks.

Response of volatility to selling auction is negative and statistically significant, implying the Central Bank is able to reduce volatility through selling auctions while buying auctions do not seem to influence volatility. In addition, unexpected increases in the interest rate raise volatility, which makes it possible to say that unexpected interest rate cuts reduce the volatility of the exchange rate. These findings are in line with the Central Bank's argument that its policies are not aimed at the level or the direction of the exchange rate but rather the goal is to contain volatility.[12]

[12]The full estimation results in this section are not reported. They are available from the authors.

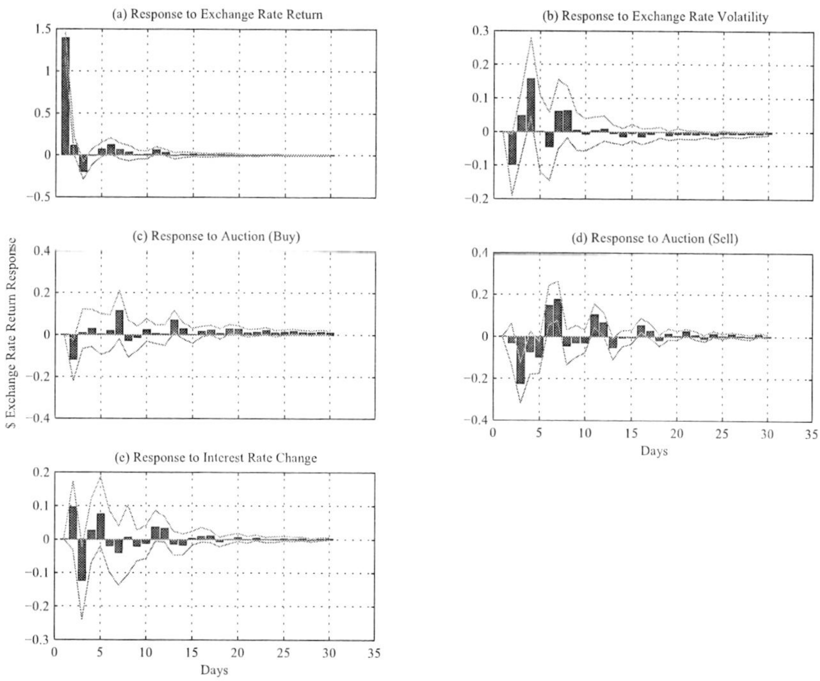

Figure 3: TRL/USD daily exchange rate return (log difference) response to shocks to different variables in the system. (a) Response to a shock (1.48 percent increase) in TRL/USD daily exchange rate return. (b) Response to a shock (1.15 percent increase) in TRL/USD daily volatility (absolute return). (c) Response to a shock in Central Bank USD buying (6 Million USD increase) auction. (d) Response to a shock (33 Million USD increase) in Central Bank selling auction. (e) Response to a shock (0.60 percent increase) in change in overnight interest rates. 95 percent bootstrap confidence intervals are plotted as straight lines. Sample period: March 13, 2001 - April 30, 2003 (538 business days).

The period before May 2003 is also investigated by means of the same five variable VAR system. The system is estimated using 11 lags as indicated by the likelihood ratio tests. Adjusted R-squares for this system lie in the range of 0.03, for the change in the interest rate equation, and 0.45, for selling auctions equation. Granger causality tests indicate that, as in the previous case, exchange rate return and selling auctions cause volatility of the exchange rate at 1% level of significance. Changes in the interest rate and volatility exhibit feedback at 1% level of significance. However, the feedback between selling auctions and exchange rate return is no longer observed: selling auctions cause exchange rate return at 1% significance level. Table 2 reports the results of Granger causality tests. This causality should be interpreted with impluse responses below before reaching a conclusion on the Central Bank policies.

Figure 3 depicts the impulse responses of the exchange rate return to various shocks in the system. These are analogous to the responses of the exchange rate return when the last part of the sample is also included. Similar arguments can be put forth for the responses of volatility to different shocks in the system by observing Figure 4. Thus, one may conclude that the Central Bank's policies from the start of the float until May 2003 targeted volatility

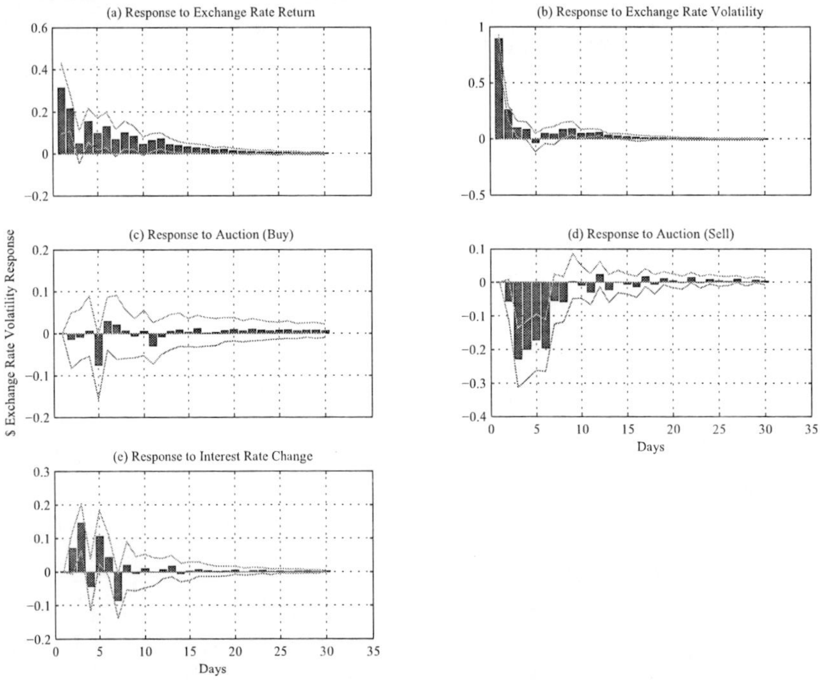

Figure 4: TRL/USD daily exchange rate volatility response to shocks to different variables in the system. (a) Response to a shock (1.48 percent increase) in TRL/USD daily exchange rate return. (b) Response to a shock (1.15 percent increase) in TRL/USD daily volatility (absolute return). (c) Response to a shock (6 Million USD increase) in Central Bank USD buying auction. (d) Response to a shock (33 Million USD increase) in Central Bank selling auction. (e) Response to a shock (0.60 percent increase) in change in overnight interest rates. 95 percent bootstrap confidence intervals are plotted as straight lines. Sample period: March 13, 2001 - April 30, 2003 (538 business days).

rather than the direction or the level of the exchange rate.

The VAR model is estimated using four lags as indicated by the likelihood ratio test for the post-May 2003 period as well.[13] Adjusted R-squares range from 0.04 (change in the interest rate equation) to 0.48 (buying auctions equation). Granger causality tests indicate that exchange rate volatility and buying auctions cause exchange rate return at 5% and 1% significance levels respectively. The results of Granger causality tests are reported in Table 3.

In the period after May 2003, we observe that the response of the exchange rate return to a shock to buying auctions is negative (see Figure 5). Thus, this again confirms that the buying auctions of the Central Bank did not influence the exchange rate positively. This contradicts the claim that the Central Bank was actually intervening in the market to affect the direction of the exchange rate upwards. Even if the bank had such an intention, it was not successful. Panel (d) of Figure 5 depicts the effects of an unexpected increase in the interest

[13]This model includes four variables: exchange rate return, exchange rate volatility, buying auctions, and changes in overnight interest rates. The bank conducted only buying actions during the period.

Table 2: Granger causality probabilities. Sample period: March 13, 2001 - April 30, 2003 (538 business days). The reported probabilities are probabilities that the column variable does not Granger cause the row variable.

	Return	Volatility	Interest Rate	Buying Auction	Selling Auction
Return	0.00	0.26	0.34	0.13	0.00
Volatility	0.01	0.00	0.00	0.53	0.00
Interest Rate	0.16	0.00	0.62	0.98	0.46
Buying Auction	0.44	0.82	0.67	0.00	1.00
Selling Auction	0.08	0.12	0.18	0.92	0.00

Table 3: Granger causality probabilities. Sample period: May 1, 2003 - October 30, 2003 (129 business days). The reported probabilities are probabilities that the column variable does not Granger cause the row variable.

	Return	Volatility	Interest Rate	Buying Auction
Return	0.17	0.02	0.60	0.00
Volatility	0.06	0.10	0.06	0.38
Interest Rate	0.17	0.53	0.84	0.01
Buying Auction	0.35	0.60	0.19	0.00

rate on the exchange rate. The initial impact is negative and statistically significant. Most of the positive responses in the following period are not statistically significant. The response of the exchange rate return to interest rate changes during this period is stronger and more immediate than what it was before May 2003. Previously, we found that the response was either not statistically significant (for the entire sample) or significant after one period (pre-May 2003). Here, the first period response is negative and statistically significant. That is, the exchange rate return responds positively (depreciation) to an unexpected interest rate cut. Finally, Figure 6 shows that impulse responses of the volatility to shocks to different variables after May, 2003 are not statistically significant, except a positive response to a positive shock to the exchange rate return. This indicates that the return-volatility relation is still strong in the foreign exchange market in Turkey.

The results of the VAR analysis indicate that the Central Bank policies were aimed at controlling the volatility of the exchange rate since the beginning of the float, but not to influence the level or the direction of the exchange rate. Contrary to the claims that the Central Bank had been responding to the direction of the exchange rate since May 2003, the results indicate that the policies affected volatility rather than the exchange rate itself. Even if the Central Bank implicitly aimed at the level of the exchange rates in recent months, there is no statistical evidence to determine such a policy change from the sample information.

The results in this part are in line with previous findings. Selçuk (2005) estimated the same model with a shorter sample from the free float period and found similar results. Domaç and Mendoza (2002) estimated an Exponential GARCH model using daily data on foreign exchange intervention in Turkey and Mexico. Using a smaller sample (February 2001 - May 2002), they showed that both the amount and frequency of foreign exchange intervention decreased the volatility of the exchange rates in Turkey. Domaç and Mendoza

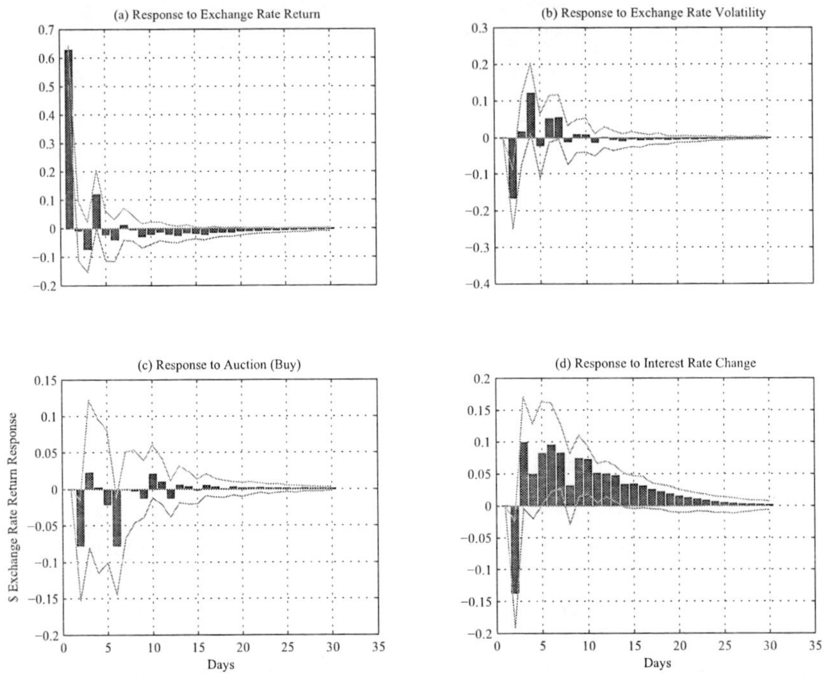

Figure 5: TRL/USD daily exchange rate return (log difference) response to shocks to different variables in the system. (a) Response to a shock (0.70 percent) in TRL/USD daily exchange rate return. (b) Response to a shock (0.43 percent increase) in TRL/USD daily volatility (absolute return). (c) Response to a shock (27 Million USD increase) in Central Bank USD buying auction. (d) Response to a shock (0.58 percent increase) in change in overnight interest rates. 95 percent bootstrap confidence intervals are plotted as straight lines. Sample period: May 1, 2003 - October 30, 2003 (There was no selling auction during this period). (129 business days).

(2002) reported that their results also imply that sale operations are effective in influencing the exchange rate and its volatility, while purchase operations are found to be statistically insignificant in affecting the exchange rate and its volatility. Finally, Selçuk (2004b) shows, in an asymmetric stochastic volatility framework, that there is strong positive correlation between the shocks to the foreign exchange rate return at time t and the shocks to volatility (defined as the standard deviation of the exchange rate return) at time $t+1$ during the floating exchange rate system in Turkey. We also found that shocks to the return and shocks to the volatility are indeed positively related. This finding itself implies that even if the Central Bank aimed at reducing volatility, the bank was in favor of nominal appreciations as compared to nominal depreciations since these two have opposite effects on the volatility.

5 Accumulated Risks

Although the Central Bank has been successful in containing the volatility of the exchange rates, the economy is not free from significant risks. Among these, the record level of real appreciation of the domestic currency and the total public debt with high real interest rates

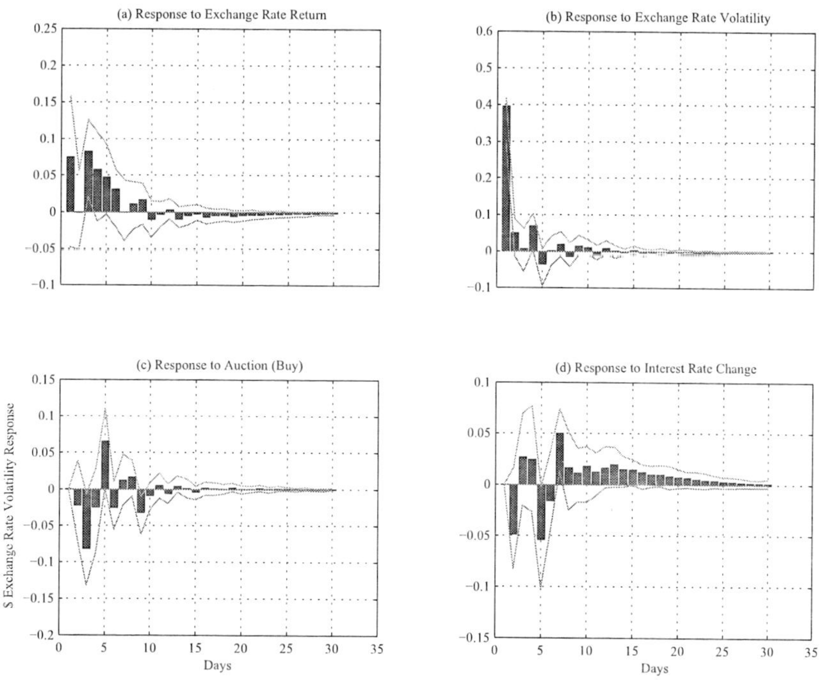

Figure 6: TRL/USD daily exchange rate volatility response to shocks to different variables in the system. (a) Response to a shock (0.70 percent increase) in TRL/USD daily exchange rate return. (b) Response to a shock (0.43 percent increase) in TRL/USD daily volatility (absolute return). (c) Response to a shock (27 Million USD increase) in Central Bank USD buying auction. (d) Response to a shock (0.58 percent increase) in change in overnight interest rates. 95 percent bootstrap confidence intervals are plotted as straight lines. Sample period: May 1, 2003 - October 30, 2003 (There was no selling auction during this period). (129 business days).

are the most important ones.

According to two real effective exchange rate indices published by the Central Bank, the overall real appreciation of the Turkish lira during the float (March 2001 - October 2003) is in between 26 and 34 percent. This appreciation is not as a result of the initial large depreciation (overshooting) in February 2001. The current level of both indices indicate that the real appreciation is in between 28 and 42 percent as compared to 1995 which was a "normal" year in terms of the real exchange rate level. However, the economy did not register a large current account deficit: it is expected to be around 3 percent of GDP in 2003. The record level of the real appreciation may be explained in part by the productivity increase in tradeable goods sector (the so-called "Balassa-Samuelson effect"). Labor productivity in private manufacturing industry increased 20 percent between 2001 and 2003 (second quarter). In addition, there was a fall in hourly nominal wages (in USD terms) during the same period. As a result, the unit wage index fell 30 percent as compared to 2000. This development partially explains why the competitiveness of the country did not suffer much from the record level of real appreciation. However, both the productivity growth and the fall in unit wages (in USD terms) seem to have slowed down during the second half of 2003. As a result, there might be a higher than expected current account deficit in 2004, unless the government takes further actions to increase the productivity and to contain the current account deficit.

Another reason behind the appreciation seems to be an external factor. Ardic and Selçuk (2006) report that the change in the spread between emerging market bonds and US treasury bills is a significant variable in explaining the TRL/USD dynamics. Particularly, they find that a decrease in the spread causes a decrease in TRL/USD while an increase is followed by a nominal depreciation of the Turkish lira. Currently, this spread is at its historical lows and the cycle is expected to reverse following an increase in interest rates in developed markets and a "flight-to-quality". Therefore, another risk for the Turkish economy is a reversal of foreign capital flows. This development, along with an increasing current account deficit, signals that there might be an upward pressure on the nominal exchange rates in year 2004.

One positive consequence of the appreciation manifested itself on inflation rates: During the float, monthly inflation rates went down from an average of 4 percent to and average of less than 1 percent. For a country with a long history of high inflation, this development is considered as a big success. Selçuk (2005) reports that the exchange rate pass through in Turkey is around 35 to 50 percent. Consequently, a slow down in nominal exchange rate depreciation would result in a smaller inflation. Similarly, nominal appreciation would have some deflationary effect on prices. Although it is a free floating exchange rate regime, the positive correlation between the exchange rate and price level may cause a bias in the Central Bank's approach to the developments in the exchange rate market. In other words, the Bank would favor exchange rate appreciations in its policy design since it also follows an implicit inflation targeting policy. If the risks with the current account deficit and its finance are realized, there would be an upward pressure on prices, and consequently an increase in inflation. This potential risk is possibly one reason why both indicative interest rates determined by the Central Bank and the market determined interest rates remain high in the economy. If the real interest rates are stalled at their current level (around 15 percent), the economy faces a much higher risk in another front: public debt rollover and an unsustainable fiscal position.

Table 5 gives the recent history of the public debt in Turkey.[14] It shows that the total public debt, as a percentage of the Gross National Product (GNP), doubled during the last 5 years. Particularly, the increase in total domestic debt is alarming: it was 21.9 percent of GNP in 1998 while it is 57.7 percent in 2003. What is more, foreign exchange (FX) denominated or FX linked component of the domestic debt is also increasing: it was just 7 percent of the total domestic debt in 1998 while it is now 23 percent. The public foreign debt stock, on the other hand, increased from USD 52 billion in 1998 to USD 89.8 billion in 2003, reaching 46 percent of GNP. Foreign public debt and FX denominated/linked component of the domestic debt together (USD 118 billion) is 60 percent of GNP which implies that a nominal depreciation of the domestic currency would increase the foreign debt burden of the country on impact. This concern might be another contributing factor in viewing real appreciations as a positive development from the policy makers' point of view.

Even if we assume that the country would face no difficulties in rolling over the existing

[14]These figures reflect the "gross" public debt of the central government in Turkey. For a detailed debt sustainability analysis, net public debt figures should be calculated. That is, the net foreign assets of the Central Bank and the other public sector should be included in the foreign debt calculation. Similarly, the rest of the public sector and the public deposits should be included in domestic debt figures.

Table 4: Public Debt in Turkey. Source: The Central Bank and the Treasury.

Public Debt (Billion USD)	1998	1999	2000	2001	2002	2003*
Domestic	37.1	42.4	54.2	84.9	91.7	120.8
Foreign	52.0	52.7	61.2	70.1	85.4	89.8
Total	89.1	95.1	115.4	155	177.1	210.6
% of GNP						
Domestic	21.9	29.3	29.0	69.2	54.8	57.7
Foreign	25.3	28.3	30.4	48.7	47.1	46.1
Total	47.2	57.6	59.4	117.9	101.9	103.8

*As of September 2003.

foreign debt, the domestic debt situation is very fragile. In its simplest form, sustainable fiscal policy condition requires that the total debt as a percentage of the total income should not be increasing forever. That is, the following equation should not be positive under the fiscal policy of a country

$$\Delta\beta = (r - g)\beta - x \qquad (1)$$

where β is the debt-income ratio, r is the real interest rate, g is the real growth rate of the economy, and x is the primary surplus (non-interest budget surplus). If the current path of the fiscal policy implies that the change in debt-income ratio ($\Delta\beta$) will be positive, the policy is said to be unsustainable, i.e., the fiscal policy at some point must change.

If we assume a 5 percent real growth and a 15 percent real interest rate, the current domestic debt/income ratio (58 percent) implies that the required primary surplus to keep the domestic debt/income ratio constant is 5.8 percent of GDP. So far, the Turkish government is keen to give this much primary surplus. However, an adverse shock to the system may increase the real interest rate while decreasing the growth rate and worsen the fiscal position. For example, if the real interest rate-real growth differential ($r - g$) increases from its assumed level of 10 percent to 15 percent (2-3 percentage point increase in real interest rate and 2-3 percent decrease in the growth rate), the required primary surplus would increase to 9 percent. Given the fact that the government is currently operating at the limit (in terms of tax revenues and public expenditures), it would be extremely unlikely to obtain a 9 percent primary surplus. In this case, some other policy options to put the fiscal policy into a sustainable path may come into effect in the economy. Otherwise, Anne Kruger, First Deputy Managing Director of IMF, warns that even an IMF assistance could not be helpful:

> Suppose, for instance, that the debt is truly unsustainable and that, for whatever reason, a government fails to introduce economic reforms of the kind needed to rebalance the economy. It is difficult to see how, in such circumstances, a program of Fund financial assistance could help. If the structure of the existing debt does not change, the total amount that a country can repay will not change. It is bound to be less than that needed to service the debt. Additional lending from the Fund will simply displace private debt and, in practice, increase the size of the 'haircut' that private creditors will, eventually, have to accept (Krueger, 2003).

In sum, the high real appreciation during the float along with a recently slowed down productivity in manufacturing industry may result in a large current account deficit in Turkey. This development, coupled with external financing difficulties, may lead to an upward correction in nominal exchange rates. This risk increases the risk premium of the country, and prevents the Central Bank from cutting interest rates further down because of the higher inflation risk. High real interest rates, on the other hand, make the fiscal position of the government very fragile.

6 Conclusion

The choice of an exchange rate regime under high capital mobility has become an important concern for the emerging market economies, especially after the Asian crisis, and the subsequent ones in Brazil, Russia, Turkey and Argentina. Furthermore, the increasing degree of globalization in the world has sped up the international integration of capital markets, augmenting the difficulty of policy conduct for the developing economies.

Recent policy discussions on the choice of exchange rate regimes have been in support of corner solutions, namely hard pegs and floats. In the aftermath of the February 2001 crisis, Turkey has let the Turkish lira float, and the policies of the Central Bank since then have been aimed at controlling the volatility of the exchange rate rather than targeting its level or direction while trying to lower the inflation rate.

This chapter has analyzed the developments in the foreign exchange market in light of the Central Bank's policies during the floating exchange rate system in Turkey between 2001-2004. The main finding is that the Central Bank had been successful in containing volatility and reducing the average inflation rate. The estimation results show that the Central Bank did not target the level nor the direction of the exchange rate, and was successful in containing volatility. Despite the arguments that the Central Bank policies after May 2003 were aimed at preventing the appreciation of the Turkish lira, the results of the empirical analysis indicate no evidence to support this claim.

It is important to note, however, that the accumulated risks in the economy, such as the extreme appreciation of the currency and high real interest rates along with large debt burden suggest that the economy is fragile. More drastic economic policies to restructure the economy would lessen the negative impact of unexpected adverse shocks.

References

Allen, M., Rosenberg, C., Keller, C., Setser, B., and Roubini, N. (2002). A balance sheet approach to financial crisis. *IMF Working Paper,* WP/02/210.

Alper, C. E. and Yılmaz, K. (2003). Domestic needs for foreign finance and exchange rate choice in developing countries with special reference to the Turkish experience. *Turkish Studies*, **4**, 67–91.

Ardic, O. and Selçuk, F. (2006). The dynamics of a newly floating exchange rate: the Turkish case. *Applied Economics*, **38**, 931–941.

Bubula, A. and Otker-Robe, I. (2002). The evolution of exchange rates since 1990: Evidence from de facto policies. *IMF Working Paper,* WP/02/155.

Calderon, C. and Schmidt-Hebbel, K. (2003). Macroeconomic policies and performance in Latin America. *Journal of International Money and Finance*, **22**, 895–923.

Calvo, G. A. and Reinhart, C. M. (2001). Fixing for your life. *Brookings Trade Forum 2000. Policy Challenges for the Next Millennium,* edited by S. Collins and D. Rodrik. Washington DC: Brookings Institution.

Calvo, G. A. and Reinhart, C. M. (2002). Fear of floating. *The Quarterly Journal of Economics*, **117**, 379–408.

Calvo, G. A., Izquierdo, A., and Talvi, E. (2003). Sudden stops, the real exchange rate, and fiscal sustainability: Argentina's lessons. *NBER Working Paper,* WP9828.

Cavallo, M., Kisselev, K., Perri, F., and Roubini, N. (2002). Exchange rate overshooting and the costs of floating. *Mimeo,* New York University.

CBT (2002). Monetary policy and exchange rate policy in 2002 and prospective developments. *The Central Bank of the Republic of Turkey. Basic Policy Readings.* http://www.tcmb.gov.tr.

CBT (2003). General framework of the monetary and exchange rate policy in 2003. *The Central Bank of the Republic of Turkey. Basic Policy Readings.* http://www.tcmb.gov.tr.

Celasun, O., Gelos, R. G., and Prati, A. (2003). Would "cold turkey" work in Turkey? *IMF Working Paper,* WP/03/49.

Cespedes, L. F., Chang, R., and Velasco, A. (2000). Balance sheets and exchange rate policy. *NBER Working Paper,* WP7840.

Devereux, M. B. and Lane, P. R. (2003). Exchange rates and monetary policy in emerging market economies. *Mimeo,* http://http://www.arts.ubc.ca/econ/devereux/hkimr.pdf.

Domaç, İ. and Bahmani-Oskooee, M. (2002). On the link between dollarization and inflation: evidence from Turkey. *The Central Bank of the Republic of Turkey, Discussion Paper.*

Domaç, İ. and Mendoza, A. (2002). Is there room for forex interventions under inflation targeting framework? Evidence from Mexico and Turkey. *The Central Bank of the Republic of Turkey, Discussion Paper.*

Eichengreen, B. (2001). Crisis prevention and management: Any new lessons from Argentina and Turkey? *Background paper written for the World Banks Global Development Finance 2002,* University of California, Berkeley.

Eichengreen, B. (2002). Can emerging markets float? Should they inflation target? *Mimeo,* University of California, Berkeley.

Eichengreen, B. and Hausmann, R. (1999). Exchange rates and financial fragility. *NBER Working Paper,* WP7418.

Ertuğrul, A. and Selçuk, F. (2002). Turkish economy: 1980-2001. *Inflation and Disinflation in Turkey,* edited by A. Kibritçioğlu, L. Rittenberg and F. Selçuk. Aldershot: Ashgate Publishing Company.

Fischer, S. (2001). Exchange rate regimes: Is the bipolar view correct? *Journal of Economic Perspectives*, **15**, 3–24.

Gençay, R. and Selçuk, F. (2006). Overnight borrowing, interest rates and extreme value theory. *European Economic Review*, **50**, 547–563.

Kenen, P. B. (1969). The theory of optimum currency areas: An eclectic view. *Monetary Problems of the International Economy,* edited by R. A. Mundell and A. K. Swoboda. Chicago: University of Chicago Press.

Kibritçioğlu, A., Rittenberg, L., and Selçuk, F. (2002). *Inflation and Disinflation in Turkey*. Edited by A. Kibritçioğlu, L. Rittenberg and F. Selçuk, Ashgate Publishing Company, Aldershot.

Krueger, A. O. (2003). The difference is in the debt: Crisis resolution in Latin America. *Luncheon Address,* Latin America Conference on Sector Reform, Stanford Center for International Development, Stanford, CA. November 14, 2003.

Lim, C. H. and Papi, L. (1997). An econometric analysis of determinants of inflation in Turkey. *IMF Working Paper,* WP/97/170.

McKinnon, R. I. (1963). Optimum currency areas. *American Economic Review*, **53**, 717–725.

Metin, K. (1995). An integrated analysis of Turkish inflation. *Oxford Bulletin of Economics and Statistics*, **57**, 513–531.

Metin-Özcan, K., Voyvoda, E., and Yeldan, A. E. (2001). Dynamics of macroeconomic adjustment in a globalized developing economy: growth, accumulation and distribution, Turkey 1969-1999. *Revue Canadienne d'Etudes du Developpement*, **22**, 219–253.

Minella, A., Freitas, P. S., Goldfajn, I., and Muinhos, M. K. (2003). Inflation targeting in Brazil: constructing credibility under exchange rate volatility. *Journal of International Money and Finance*, **22**, 1015–1040.

Mundell, R. A. (1961). A theory of optimum currency areas. *American Economic Review*, **51**, 657–665.

Mussa, M., Masson, P., Swoboda, A., Jadresic, E., Mauro, P., and Berg, A. (2000). Exchange rate regimes in and increasingly integrated world economy. *IMF Occasional Paper,* No:193.

Obstfeld, M. and Rogoff, K. (1995). The mirage of fixed exchange rates. *Journal of Economic Perspectives*, **9**, 73–96.

Öniş, Z. and Rubin, B. (2003). *Turkish Economy in Crisis*. Edited by Ziya Öniş and B. Rubin, Frank Cass & Co., London.

Reinhart, C. M. (2000). The mirage of floating exchange rates. *American Economic Review Papers and Proceedings*, **90**, 65–70.

Selçuk, F. (2003). Currency substitution: new evidence from emerging economies. *Economics Letters*, **78**, 219–224.

Selçuk, F. (2004a). Financial earthquakes, aftershocks and scaling in emerging stock markets. *Physica A*, **333**, 306–316.

Selçuk, F. (2004b). Free float and stochastic volatility: the experience of a small open economy. *Physica A*, **342**, 693–700.

Selçuk, F. (2005). The policy challenge at floating exchange rates: Turkey's recent experience. *Open Economies Review*, **16**, 295–312.

Sims, C. A. (1980). Macroeconomics and reality. *Econometrica*, **48**, 1–48.

Tavlas, G. (2003). The economics of exchange rate regimes: A review essay. *The World Economy*, **26**, 1215–1246.

Tornell, A. and Velasco, A. (2000). Fixed versus floating exchange rates: Which provide more fiscal discipline? *Journal of Monetary Economics*, **45**, 399–436.

In: Global Stock Exchanges: Stability, Interrelationships... ISBN: 978-60692-184-5
Editor: Paolo B. Cassedes

Chapter 4

GLOBALIZATION AND STOCK MARKET STABILITY*

Nidal Rashid Sabri
College of Economics, Birzeit University, Birzeit, Palestine

Introduction

The globalization of the world stock markets is the one of the new significant development occurred during the last decade. Various factors contributed to the globalization of financial organizations including: First, advancement of technology and remote access which have been utilized in the stock trading. Second: Emerging of international financial institutions, which offer financial services regardless of the geographical and jurisdictions boarders. Third: Introducing new trends of liberalization and removing restrictions on foreign ownership, trading and cross border transactions. Fourth: the movement occurred in the world stock markets towards regional integration of stock exchanges, clearing and settlements organizations, and other financial institutions.

Accordingly, the world stock markets are moving so rapidly towards globalization. The concept of globalization simply means the free movement of goods, technology, labor and capital flow. Our main concern is related to the globalization of capital flow through the world stock trading. The globalization of financial sector means the integration of the local financial system to international financial systems and institutions through cross borders financial transactions, products, and instruments. The globalization phenomenon may be a blessing which is embraced by the majority of economic experts due to the expected benefits of such economic opening. Many experts believe that globalization may bring market to more efficiency, lowering its risk due to the possibility of diversifications, more convenience, and using arbitrage in a relevant way. On the other side, many believe that globalization may harm the interests of some groups of society, such as farmers, labors, and small-scale industries.

* A version of this chapter was also published in *Stability of International Stock Markets,* by Nidal Rashid Sabri published by Nova Science Publishers, Inc. It was submitted for appropriate modifications in an effort to encourage wider dissemination of research.

Major Aspects of Stock Market Globalization

Considering the present practices and the expected trends, it may be stated that the world stock market is heading toward globalization. The world market globalization concept has three major aspects as shown in Table 5-1: The first aspect is liberalization of international stock markets. The second aspect of the stock market globalization is related to integration of the world stock markets, including regional integration of stock exchanges, clearing and settlement agencies, regional Integration of related laws and regulations, and adopting international principles and regulations. The adopted international principles includes international general accepted accounting and disclosure requirements, audit principles and standards, cross boarders financial transactions accepted principles. The third aspect is related to internationalizing the stock trading including: cross listing of corporations on other stock exchanges, global public offerings in more than one jurisdiction, cross boarders' transactions and settlements, internet stock trading and consultation, alternative stock trading systems, increasing linkages between stock markets, International mutual fund investment. Some of these aspects were discussed in previous chapters, while the remaining issues will be investigated throughout the rest of this chapter.

Table 5-1. Major Aspects of Stock Market Globalization

Major Aspects	Practices
Liberalization of stock trading	Removing restrictions imposed on foreign ownership Attracting foreign investors to invest in national stock exchanges Permitting foreign investors for direct investments
Integration of stock markets	Regional integration of stock exchanges and settlement agencies Regional integration of related laws and regulations Harmonization of international accounting standards and disclosure requirements Adopting International trading and corporate laws, regulations and practices
Internationalizing of stock trading	Cross boarders transactions and cross boarders settlements Internet stock trading and consultations Alternative stock trading systems Global public offerings in more than jurisdictions Increasing of foreign trading in national stock exchanges Cross (Dual) listed firms in national and foreign exchanges Introducing international mutual funds

Liberalization of Stock Trading

The liberalizations of stock markets may take various forms as in the world stock markets, including: removing restrictions imposed on foreign ownership, attracting foreign investors to invest in the national stock exchanges and increasing the share of foreign trading in the stock trading to permit direct investments by foreign investors. As a result, the liberalization concept of world stock markets has been materialized through the following aspects:

First: The majority of the world stock exchanges adopted regulatory changes in the last decade, most of which are favorable towards the liberalization of stock market trading and operating financial institutions. The number of countries that introduced changes to release their investments laws and cash flow mechanism, and to encourage foreign investments including direct foreign investments has increased significantly; reaching to 102 countries in 2004 issuing about 234 regulatory changes in favor of foreign investments as shown in Table 5-2 (UNCTAD, 2006).

Second: Out of the fifty two emerging stock markets states, thirty five states have removed the ceiling of ownership for listed stocks up to 100% of the total equities by the end of 1998. The other seventeen states removed the restrictions on foreign ownership partially, such as Brazil: 49%, Trinidad and Tobago: 30%, India 24%, Korea: 39%, Philippines: 40%, Taiwan: 30%, Thailand: 49%, Russia: 9%- 25%, Ghana: 74, Jordan: 50%, Saudi Arabia 25%, Tunisia: 49.9%, and Zimbabwe: 40% (IFC, 1999). In addition, most of the European countries have no foreign ownership restrictions, such as Austria, Denmark, Belgium, Luxemburg, Greece, Germany, Ireland, UK, Sweden, Netherlands and Italy.

Third: The majority of the world emerging and developed countries witnessed and concluded bilateral, multilateral, and international investment agreements to encourage foreign investments and cash flows cross borders. In 2002, eighty-two bilateral investments treaties were concluded by seventy-six countries. This is also applied to double taxation treaties, in 2002; sixty-eight double taxation treaties were concluded by seventy-six countries as reported by the UN World Investment report (UNCTAD, 2003).

The liberalization of financial markets includes removing restrictions on foreign ownership of local corporations, permitting foreign investments in local companies, increasing the national investors from emerging countries holdings foreign equities in developed markets. Liberalization of stock markets was received and interpreted as a positive signal in the development of global stock markets, which may lead to various advantages, such as: reducing the cost of equity capital (Bekaert and Harvey (2000), and Miller (1999). Increasing investments opportunities (Henry, 2000). Increasing liquidity, reducing risk, increasing diversification, and increasing the investor base (Hargis, 2000; and Jayaraman, et al. 1993).

However, in spite of the previously mentioned advantages of the world stock markets' liberalization, various serious barriers, and disadvantages had existed and had been attached to the concept of liberalization of the world stock markets, which is facing the flow of funds between countries. These legal barriers and economic disadvantages are summarized as follows:

First: There are direct legal constrains imposed by governmental laws or individual listed corporations, as well as indirect barriers such as capital gains income tax.

Second: There are various related laws of controlling local exchange rates and transferring of funds outside the borders that still exist in many jurisdictions in the world economy.

Table 5-2. National Regulatory changes for Foreign Investments between 1991- 2004

	1991	1998	2002	2004
Number of countries introduced changes in their investments regimes	35	60	70	102
Number of regulatory changes favorable to Foreign investments	80	136	234	234

Source: UNCTAD, 2006.

Third: Liberalization may harm the national economy because it is expected that liberalization of stock markets in countries with weak currency might damage the economy in case of negative equity flows. Torre et al. (2002) suggested that developing countries who are seeking financial globalization should have a strong currency or should not be fearful of floating their home currencies against other currencies and should have a strong institutional framework.

Fourth: barriers of direct foreign trading are still imposed either by the corporate laws or stock exchanges' laws in most of the Middle Eastern countries, some of the Latin American countries and South Asia countries. However, in some countries, the restrictions on foreign investments are imposed by the individual corporation's bylaw, and not by the governmental laws as in Switzerland, Finland and Thailand (Stulz and Wasserfallen, 1995). Other restrictions of ownership may be imposed only in specific sectors such as the financial sector as in Brazil, Russia, and Sir Lanka. In other countries there are special shares that are issued for local residents, and other shares issue for foreign investors. For example, a company in Switzerland may issue as a part of its own capital bearer shares, registered shares and restricted shares with different vote rights (Gardiol et al. 1997).

Fifth: liberalization may increase the stock markets' volatility and volatility spillovers amongst stock markets that may harm the economies of emerging countries as reported by Levine and Zervos (1998) who found that stock markets have become larger, more liquid, more volatile, and more integrated as a result of stock markets liberalization of sixteen emerging stock markets. Lauridsen (1998) found that financial liberalization contributed to the meltdown of financial crisis in Thailand. Kim and Rogers (1995) found that the stock volatility spillovers have increased since the liberalization of Korean stock exchange. Kawakatsu and Morey (1999) stated that liberalization does not seem to improve the efficiency of emerging stock markets

Sixth: Liberalization may lead to incomplete integration: In majority of the developing countries, the liberalization of financial regulation may lead to incomplete integration and increase volatility of capital flows (World Bank, 2001, 70-71).

Seventh: Liberalization means high competitions facing financial systems from international financial institutions including international stock exchanges. This situation may put a pressure on the local financial institutions, and thus lead to instability of local stock markets and other local financial systems. The IMF report (2000) concluded that emerging market assets remain heavily dependent upon mature markets' developments considering investors' risk tolerance.

Eight: Fewer policy instruments: Liberalizations of the related rules regarding financial systems leave governments, especially in developing countries, with less monetary and controllable measures to cope with emergencies and financial crisis. This is because liberalization of financial regulations leads to transferring a substantial part of government power to the market mechanism, which is usually uncontrollable in the case of emergencies or during unstable periods of trading.

Integration of the World Stock Markets

The integration of international stock markets may be considered as the most significant change in the global capital market. Financial markets and institutions are moving towards a globally integrated economy. This includes stock markets, banks, and other financial intermediates in both developed and emerging markets. Integration increases substantially over time, especially since 1995, when these differentials began shrinking, and by mid-1998, six months before the official date for EMU launch, stock markets in EMU member states seem to be almost fully integrated. The average saving in the cost of capital from integration in Europe over the period 1992-1998 is estimated at around 2% (Hardouvelis et al. 1999).

However, the integration of emerging stock markets may still not be materialized according to IMF and the World Bank reports. The IMF, Global financial stability report, (2003) indicated that the local securities markets remain highly segmented in most of emerging regions, and number of measures would have to be undertaken to fully develop integrated markets. Other studies found that integrations are still incomplete regarding to the world stock markets even within economic integrated regions such as the EC region. For example, St John (2001) reported that while the EUs' success in monetary integration has been impressive due to the introduction of Euro as a single currency and establishing the European central bank, there is one area that remains incomplete which is the integration of EU equity markets. In addition, Agenor (2003) argues that the benefits of financial integration for small open developing countries are mostly long term, while risks can be significant in the short-run. Thus, there is a need for careful preparation to ensure that short-run costs do not lead to policy reversals. This situation can be noticed in case of developed economies because increased integration of financial markets may be considered as a risk factor and may reduce expected gains from international diversification (Shawky et al. 1997).

In addition, there are no generally accepted measurements of stock market integrations. Nevertheless, there are various aspects which indicate to what extent the world stock market is moving towards global and regional integrations. These aspects include: adopting international principles and regulations, adopting harmonized accounting standards and disclosure requirements, increasing linkages of the world Stock market indices, and regional integration of stock exchanges.

Adopting International Principles

One of the most recent aspects of integration of the world stock market is the adoption of various principles and standards issued and stated by the international and regional commissions, federations, and associations. Such international standards and principles are supposed to reduce diversity of the world stock markets' laws and practices and to increase the level of integration and improve coordination among the world stock markets regulators.

Recently, several institutions recommended the international standards and principles as shown in Table No, 5-3. These groups include global and regional commissions of securities, global and regional federations of stock exchanges, global and regional associations of corporate governance associations.

Table 5-3. Summary of the world organizations and commissions, which have effects on the world stock markets

Major Organizations	Examples of Organizations	Contributions
World Securities Commissions	IOSCO	Statement of objectives and principles Technical reports and public instructions Resolutions concerning major issues Multilateral memorandum of understanding
Regional commissions	Forum of European Securities Commissions	Recommendations, coordination in developing regulations
World Federations	(WFE) World Stock Exchanges	Stock Market principles Best practices for clearing and settlements
Regional Federations	Euro-Asia stock exchanges federations	Stock Market principles Best practices for clearing and settlements
World Corporate associations	OECD	Principles of corporate governance Best practices
	ICGN	Corporate governance guidelines Voting rights principles
	Commonwealth Association for corporate governance	Guidelines and recommendations

First group: the IOSCO commission: It is the worlds' recognized body of the government regulatory commissions. The IOSCO contributions in concurrence with the practices and laws of stock trading ascertained in various aspects: First: It issued 46 resolutions from 1983 to 2003 covering various issues such as clearing and settlements, coordination between cash and derivatives' markets, cross- borders transactions and disclosures standards. Second: It issued 30 principles concerning securities regulations. Third: It issued more than one hundred documentations regarding principles, standards regulations, surveys, and reports about almost all aspects of stock trading. Fourth: It issued multilateral memorandum of understanding among its members, as a response to the increasing international activity in the securities and derivatives markets, and to meet the need of cooperation and consultation amongst IOSCO Members (IOSCO, 2002a and 2002b).

Second: New various regional securities commissions were emerged recently by regional securities commissions: in order to coordinate between the national securities commissions. The Forum of European Securities Commissions and the Committee of European securities regulators are examples of these organizations. In addition, the emerging of the World Federation of Exchanges, it is the world federation of the stock exchanges, located in Paris. It includes 54 exchanges, 22 affiliates, and 35 bourses from all over the world, which forms about 97 % of world stock market capitalization. It issued stock marketing principles and good practices, related surveys of trading practices, regulations, enforcement, trading halts, and other topics (WFE, 2004). The WFE adopted fifteen market principles of stock trading including organization and operation, access to market, listing and disclosure of trading financial products, trading, clearing and settlements, business conducts, investor protection, and transparency. It requires from its members an obligation to adopt their trading activities based on the suggested principles as rapidly as is feasible (WFE, 2002).

Third; there are now various regional stock exchanges which have established recently, and have significant impact on the world stock marketing concerning trading practices, jurisdictions, and interrelationships among stock exchanges. These federations of exchanges include South Asian Federation of Exchanges, Federation of Euro-Asian Exchanges, East Asian and Oceanic stock exchange federation, Union of Arab Exchanges, Ibero-American Federation of Stock Exchanges, and the Federation of European stock Exchanges.

Most of these regional federations issue recommendations and standards to be adopted by their members of stock exchanges. For example the Euro-Asia stock exchanges federations stated 28 best practices to enhance the stock exchanges in transition countries into alignment with global standards. The related best practices include regulating of stock exchanges, institutional framework, operation of stock exchanges, clearing, settlement, custody and registration, issuers listing rules and ongoing disclosures (FEAS, 2000)

Fourth: There are many world and regional corporate governance organizations are now existed in the world economy. This group includes the organization for Economic Co-operation and Development, which issued principles of corporate governance (OECD, 1999) International Corporate Governance Network which issued statements on global corporate governance principles (ICGN, 1999) and statements on global implementation of share voting principles (ICGN, 2000). The Commonwealth Association for corporate governance which issued guidelines and principles in 1997 regarding corporate governance ethics (CACG, 1999).

Adopting Accounting Standards and Disclosure Requirements

Today, the majority of the world jurisdictions adopt harmonized accounting standards and disclosures requirements. The need for generally accepted international accounting standards and disclosures requirements exists in various situations of stock trading, including:

1. Listing or dual listing requirements for secondary stock markets in home stock exchange or in foreign stock exchanges.
2. Primary stock market of international and local public offerings.
3. Annual financial reports of the listed firms in local and international stock markets.
4. Interim reports of listed firms in stock exchanges.
5. The reporting of other disclosure requirements and material changes.

The harmonized accounting standards and disclosures requirements became reality due to the willingness of the related regulators, and the efforts of various international bodies. There are three bodies, which play a critical role in the harmonization and the internationalization of the world accounting standards and other disclosure requirements of stock marketing activities, including the international public offering requirements, the cross listed firms in the case of first listing requirements, and for annual and interim reporting. These major bodies are:

First: the International Accounting Standard Board: This is a generally accepted accounting standards setting body located in London that aims to develop a unified single high quality accounting standards for preparing financial statements of business firms to be applicable and acceptable all over the world. It was established in June, 1973 by the accounting official agencies of nine countries, namely: Australia, Canada, France, Germany, Japan, Mexico, Netherlands, UK, and USA. Today, more than one hundred countries are members with two million accountants. It works in cooperation with the IFAC, IOSCO, Word Bank, UNCTAD, Bank for International Settlements and other national accounting standards boards such as the FASB of USA, ASB of Japan, ASB of UK, and CNC of France. This accounting body was known as the international accounting standards committee during the period from 1973 to 2001, which became known thereafter as the international accounting standards board. It issued the generally accepted international standards named as IASs, then IFRSs for preparing financial statements. About 41 IAS standards were issued from1973 to 2002 (IASC, 2002) and thereafter issued 5 IFRS statements up to 2004. The most recent accounting standards being issued by the IASB were related to business combinations and insurance contracts.

Second: The IFAC, which is the professional accounting national organizations are organized in a federation known as international federation of accountants since 1977. It is located in New York and includes 118 states, 158 organizations and 2.5 million accountants. It works through specialized committees such as public sector, management accounting auditing, ethics and education committees. It published 36 standards regarding ethics and auditing in computerized environment and designated from 100 to 1000 (IFAC, 2000). It also issues international accounting practice statements, international public sector accounting standards and auditing practice statements.

Third: the IOSCO issued various resolutions concerning adopting international accounting standards and auditing, these are:

1. Adoptation of a resolution concerning international standards in auditing (IOSCO Resolution, 1992).
2. Adoptation of a resolution concerning accounting standards IAS 7, and asked its members to prepare cash flow statements in their home jurisdictions according to IAS 7 (IOSCO resolution, 1993).
3. Adoptation of a resolution regarding accepting the International accounting standards for preparing financial statements of listed corporations (IOSCO resolution, 2000).
4. Adoptation of international disclosures standards for cross-border offerings and initial listings.

As a result, the international accounting standards and other disclosure requirements received wide recognition and acceptance in the last few years. Various significant steps have just been implemented recently, which lead to almost harmonized international accounting standards and other disclosures requirements, which may be summarized as following:

- Issuing international disclosure standards for cross-border offering and initial listing for foreign issuers in 1998 by the international organization of securities committees of (IOSCO, 1998) It requires information about directors, selected financial data, capitalization and indebtedness, reasons for the offer and risk factor, history and development of the company, business overview operating results, liquidity and capital resources, trend information, share ownership, major shareholders, related party transactions, plan of distribution, markets, selling shareholders, dilution, expenses of the issue, share capital, memorandum and articles of association.
- A resolution on IASC standards was issued by the IOSCO in 2000. It stated that the Presidents' committee recommended that IOSCO members permit incoming multinational issuers to use the 30 IASC standards to prepare their financial statements for cross boarder offerings and listing with special treatments related to reconciliation, disclosure and interpretation (IOSCO Resolution, 2000). In a survey conducted about the disclosure requirements of 43 stock exchanges indicated that the stock exchanges require on average about 80% of the IOSCO recommended disclosures for listing. In addition, the highest conformity with IOSCO benchmark was for disclosures of financial results. The stock exchanges are now more closely interested in disclosures policies and practices than five years ago in 1998. In addition, about two third of participated stock exchanges implemented changes in disclosures rules during 2001 and 2002 (Frost, 2003).
- The European commission accepted that all listed companies in the European stock markets to apply the international accounting standards issued by the IASB no later than 2005. In addition, Australia which is one of establishing countries of IASB, and one of seven setters attached to the IASB will accept IFRSs as the national accounting standards starting the beginning of 2005. In addition, many developing countries accepted the IASB as their national accounting standards during the last decade such as Malaysia, Malta, Kuwait, Cyprus, Oman, and Thailand.
- Many jurisdictions adopted the international disclosure standards (IDS) stated by the IOSCO. In a survey about the implementation of international disclosures standards, it indicated that 16 jurisdictions out of 17 members were either accepting documents from foreign firms based on IDSs or they have taken steps in this regard. Eight jurisdictions, namely: Australia, Belgium, Germany, Hong Kong, Japan, Luxembourg, Netherlands, and Switzerland indicated that they permit foreign firms to use IDSs without the necessity of changing their laws and rules (IOSCO, 2000). In addition, the SEC of USA permits in some cases foreign issuers to comply with IDSs for non-financial requirements as alternative to US disclosures requirements (Karmel, 2001).

Finally, it may be stated that not like other related laws and regulations of stock trading, the accounting and other disclosures requirements may be in the final process of harmonization at least for standards of preparing financial statements of listed corporations in the world stock exchanges. With the exceptions of the US, Japan, and Canada stock markets, which require reconciliation according to their national accounting standards issued by their own financial reporting standards boards. However, for the US stock market there is an extensive debate to accept the IASB standards, besides the US FASB standards at least for foreign firms that are listed in the US stock markets, instead of keeping foreign listed securities using the form of ADR alternative. The SEC issued recently a concept release about the possibility of accepting international accounting standards in American stock markets.

Regional Integration of Stock Exchanges

Various experiences were implemented or were under debate regarding the integration of national and regional stock exchanges, considering different forms of integrations such as direct mergers, group alliances, group associations, and through cross network connections. Recently, there are many proposals, studies and reports related to integrate stock markets nationally or regionally. Some of these ideas have been implemented such as national and regional integrations including horizontal and vertical merges. For example, the experience of unifying the local stock exchanges in one major national stock exchange happened in Spain and Italy as well as margining of some European stock exchanges under incorporated legal entity and merging cash and derivative markets have undergone.

Some of the benefits of national or regional integration of the stock market exchanges are increasing liquidity in one market, removing jurisdictions' obstacles, diversifications of risk, when products from a geographical area are listed in one integrated stock exchange, and thus reducing the cost of trading. The integration processes among stock market exchanges may have the benefit of economies of scale, reconcile legal differences and trading mechanism and platforms, harmonize clearing and settlement systems attached to the integrated stock exchanges and reduce the home bias practices as well as reduce transactions costs.

For regional stock exchanges integration, three experiences that have been implemented mainly in the European Economic Area in the last decade may be reported:

First: the merger of Amsterdam, Brussels and Paris stock exchange in one holding company incorporated under Dutch law under the name of Euronext N. V in 2000, after two years and in 2002, followed by other two stock exchanges including the London International Financial Futures and options Exchanges and the Portuguese-Lipson- stock exchange. In spite of the fact that these five stock exchanges work independently through local subsidies, their work is based on unified trading platform and single clearing system. The Euronext stock exchange group is now trading in both cash and derivatives, as well as in secondary and primary markets.

Second: The Nordic exchange alliance was singed in 1998 between Copenhagen and Stockholm stock exchanges to work on a joint trading system and consequently joint trading rules (CSE, 1999). Thereafter, this merger process expanded, and witnessed new mergers in Nordic Baltic area. In 2004 this alliance was named as NOREX alliance and includes seven stock exchanges, four clearing agencies, and three central securities depositories. The Alliance currently consists of the Copenhagen Stock Exchange, Helsinki Stock Exchange, Iceland Stock Exchange, Oslo Börs, Riga Stock Exchange, Stockholmsbörsen and Tallinn Stock Exchange. This means that this alliance has integrated the hall Nordic region and two thirds of the Baltic area (NOREX, 2004).

Third: In 1995, the Euro list system started to operate in all European stock exchanges, Switzerland and Norway, but legally organized as a Belgium stock company. It started with

59 European listed securities that were incorporated in the system. The system aims to create blue chip European companies which can be listed in all European stock exchanges beside their home exchanges using a single set of documents, under the condition that the market capitalization value should not be less than one ECU billion (Licht, 1998).

However, it is not clear where such trend will lead to, or to what extent the integration process will continue, how, and what is the best mechanism of stock market integration. In addition, there are no consent about the advantages of integration process of stock markets as compared to the existed market segmentation and diversification, and whether this is the time to move more and more to new experiences of integration in other regions of the world stock markets.

For example, in spite of the above-mentioned experiences, two paradigms for Europe stock market integrations are proposed: a central European stock exchange or a decentralized national exchange linked through European- wide network (Ramos, 2003). While others such as Noia study (1998) suggested implicit mergers and remote accesses through cross-network externalities that increase the profit of European stock exchanges. Other studies related to regional integration of stock exchanges were conducted to examine, if other regions should follow the same movement occurred in the European stock exchanges integrations. For example, El Serafile and Shahed (2002) reported that there is a need to restructure and privatize the Arab stock exchanges before moving to mergers or alliances or moving ttwords integration of Arab stock exchanges in one Arab stock exchange. Pieper and Vogel (1999) found that the Central American securities markets lack the development and depth to realize the Latin stock market integration, at this point of time.

Internationalization of Stock Markets

Various aspects of stock market internationalization now exist in the world stock markets and will be explored in this chapter, including four major topics. These are: increasing of the foreign trading in the world stock market, increasing the role of international mutual funds, increasing the number and the value of cross listed firms, and the international public offerings by developed and emerging based firms.

Increasing Foreign Share of Stock Trading

One of the major merits of internationalization of the stock markets is increasing the share of foreign trading and ownership in the world stock markets. The share of foreign trading in the world stock trading used to be limited and immaterial. For example, Cooper and Kaplanis (1994) found that in 1987, 100% of stock equities in Sweden, 98% in US, 91% in Italy, 79% in the UK, 75%, in Germany, and 94% in Spain were owned by residents.

However, this situation has been changing rapidly, just during the last decade. There was a significant increase of the traded value of foreign transactions which reached about $ 5,759,353.2 million in 2005. The value of foreign trading in NASDAQ increased from $ 81 billion in 1995 to $ 712 billion, in NYSE, it increased from $ 260 billion in 1995 to $ 1,829 billion in 2006. While the value of foreign trading in London stock exchange increased from $ 627 billions in 1995 to $ 1,829 billion in 2006. The increasing ratio of the value of foreign trading from 1995 to 2006 reached 7292% in Swiss, and up to 1837% in Germany, as presented in Table 5-4. The foreign trading ratio formed about 77% of total traded value of London stock exchange, and 1166% of Swiss stock exchange, this means that the foreign stock trading is about 12 times of domestic stock trading in Swiss exchange (WFE, 2006). In addition, the share of foreign trading including foreign direct investments has been increased significantly because of expanding practices of using the GDR and ARD instruments in both secondary and international public offerings in both USA and European markets. However, the increase of foreign trading ratio to total traded value of the world stock markets may have some disadvantages regarding stock market stability, which may be summarized as follows:

First: foreign investors may look for firms with special merits only, such as large firms. Kang and Stulz (1997) reported that ownership by foreign investors are strongly biased against small firms, while it is biased in favor of large firms, factory firms, and ADRs firms and those with good accounting performance.

Second: There is a serious criticism against the foreign portfolio capital flow, as a short-term rather than long-term investment.

Third: Various studies blamed foreign speculators and the free flow of equity investments in the instability of stock markets in emerging countries. For example, Froot et al. (2001) found that there is sensitivity of local stock prices to foreign fund inflows, which is positive and large. Sarno and Taylor (1999) found that the sudden actual or reversal portfolio flows might have played an important part in the East Asian crisis. The World Bank (2000) stated that the increasing of capital flows might be accompanied by continued high volatility and frequent crises as in 1990s. Singh and Weisse (1998) argued that there is some serious criticism against the portfolio capital flow, as a short-term rather than long term investment, which may lead to various problems such as: economic and financial crises, undermining the existing bank and financial systems.

Table 5-4. Top five markets based on value of foreign stock trading (1995 and 2006) in $ millions

Exchange	1995	2006	Increased Ratio (1995-2006)	Percentage to domestic trading
London	626,862.9	3,295,091.2	526%	77%
NYSE	260,643.4	1,828,614.3	702%	9%
Swiss	17,600.8	1,283,454.3	7292%	1166%
Nasdaq	81,353.0	712,045.8	875%	7%
Deutsche Borse	13,801.5	253,518.0	1837%	10%

Source: WFE, 2006 and 2007.

Increasing the Role of International Mutual Funds

One of the new merits of the internationalization of the world stock markets is increasing the value of mutual funds in the world stock markets and extending it to the emerging economies. There are various international funds and investment firms that play a critical role in the world stock markets, including closed-end funds, mutual open-end funds, insurance companies, pension and provident funds, and hedging funds. The role of such funds is increasing in both developed and emerging markets. In spite of the fact that the majority of the world mutual funds are located in USA and Europe, this phenomenon is extending so rapidly to Asian and emerging economies. The world funds with exception of USA funds increased from 52 to 273 funds, during the period from 1991 to 1998, while the net asset value increased from $ 16 billion to $125 billion for the same period (Kaminsky et al. 2001). The majority of these funds' investments are stocks of firms located mainly in developed countries.

However, reducing risk, through diversification requires holding a variety of portfolios of securities. Accordingly, a substantial part of mutual funds equities are now from emerging markets. The net private portfolio across stock market witnessed high fluctuations during the period from 1995 to 1999 because of Asia financial crises in 1997-1998 (IMF, 2000). The World Bank report (2000) stated that the capital flow of equity portfolio is not able to take full advantage of international portfolio diversification, has unstable structure relation between stock markets and less stable aspects compared to the direct foreign investments flow. Accordingly, increasing linkages of stock markets as a consequence of increasing equity portfolio flows to emerging countries may be considered as a negative aspect, leading to destabilizing of emerging stock markets.

The existed high volatility of equity portfolio flows between stock markets created unstable linkages. Thus, there is serious criticism against the portfolio capital outflow from emerging markets, done by the mutual funds, and is considered only as a short-term rather than long term investment, and mutual fund mangers considering to emerging markets only for a possibility of higher return and run in first opportunity. For example, Grabel (1996) found that international portfolio investments have two negative aspects on developing economies, including the increasing potential risk and macroeconomic instability, which impose constraints on policy autonomy.

This negative aspect may be related to what is known as a home bias practice which means that the majority of mutual funds and local individual investors hold a portfolio of a large share of national equities compared to foreign securities. They include foreign securities only for diversifying purposes and reducing risk or for extra high returns. The home bias concept is related to the fact that equity portfolio is concentrated in local markets and not in international foreign markets in spite of the benefit which may be gained from international diversification. Tesar, (1995) found that there is a strong evidence of a home bias in national investment portfolios despite the potential gains from international diversifications.

Increasing Trading Value of Cross-Listed Firms

The practice of cross listing is the most significant phenomenon that creates linkages among stock exchanges. The idea of cross listing is that a listed firm in a domestic exchange looks for second or more stock exchanges to be listed there simultaneously. The number of dual listed firms has increased significantly during the last decade. Cross listing has started in the late seventies by the large multinational corporations to be listed in two or more of the developed stock exchanges. Today, it is not limited to multinational corporations, but it's extended to many national firms even to firms located in emerging countries. As a consequence of increasing the number and trading size of cross-listed firms in many of stock exchanges, some leading corporations' issues are traded now in foreign stock exchanges almost of the same size or more compared to trading in their home exchanges.

For example, the trading value of the major Dutch corporations' stocks traded in foreign exchanges ranges from 30% to 46% of the total trading value as compared to the traded value of the national stock exchange. The foreign exchanges where the Dutch firms are traded include NYSE, NASDAQ, London, Germany, and Swiss Exchanges (ASE, 2000). The majority of foreign firms listed in second stock exchange have to meet dual requirements of exchanges; other firms which may not meet the second exchange requirements use the so called depository receipts as an alternative for cross listing.

The major factors that have to be considered in selecting the foreign stock exchanges includes cost of trading, accounting requirements and any related laws that protect investors, and other listed requirements. Firms appear less likely to list their shares on foreign stock exchanges with higher disclosure levels than those of their domiciles (Biddle and Saudagaran, 1989). The main obstacle of cross listing is the different requirements of accounting standards that is going to be waved by adopting International Accounting Standards Committee, which will eventually lead to international accounting harmonization, and thus makes cross listing process more beneficial and less costly. Firms which may not meet the second exchange requirements use the so called depository receipts as alternative for cross listing.

There are various possible ways of cross-listed firms including direct cross-listed or using alternative methods, the cross-listed may be second listed in another local stock exchange, or in another foreign exchange, using one currency or multicurrency as presented in Table 5-5. The following section represents a summary of types of cross listed shares.

Table 5-5. Types of cross-listed securities

Types of Cross Listing	Details
Listed in more than local exchanges	Under one jurisdiction One currency, one time, different places in one country
Cross listed in local and foreign exchanges	Under different jurisdictions More than one currency, different times, different places
Dual listed firms with attached derivatives	Derivatives traded under different jurisdiction from the underling shares
Listed in a form of ARD	Foreign security listed in US stock market
Listed in a form of GRD	Global Register depositary shares
Regional listed firm	Euro- listed security in EU stock exchanges

Sabri, 2007.

Direct dual listed firm in local exchanges: in some of the developed countries: there are more than one stock exchange such as in USA, Canada, Japan, Germany and Spain. Accordingly, a firm may have its securities listed in more than national stock exchanges. This process is so simple and has no jurisdictions conflicts, and may be conducted automatically using the same documents for the first listing unless there are some unique or specialized requirements.

Dual listing in national and foreign stock exchange: This occurs using one currency, but under different jurisdictions such as a European firm to be listed in more those European stock exchanges.

Dual listing in national and foreign stock exchanges using different currencies, such as a European firm to be listed in USA stock exchange using the dollar. The majority of dual listed firms are using two or more different currencies.

Cross listed regional base: Such as the Euro lists system, a major European company, may be listed in about 27 European stock markets, under the condition that the securities first are listed in three major stock exchanges. Then it may use the same documents to be listed in all European Stock exchanges.

Dual listing in national and foreign stock exchange with attached derivatives listed in different stock exchange: In most of cases, the dual listed firms have attached derivatives which trade in another national or foreign market or in both markets and thus increase the involved stock exchange for one underling security to more than four stock exchanges.

ADR (American depository Receipts) are negotiable certificates that represent a foreign company and be traded mainly in US stock exchanges. The process of offering and selling the ADR is conducted by specialized depositary houses which are mainly major banks, or specialized depository houses. This instrument was created to avoid that foreign security to be traded without satisfying the listed requirements applied to the national securities, the practice of using deposit receipt as a way of trading foreign security started in the early of twenty century, but it is increasing significantly in the last decade. The demand for depositary receipts is increasing by about 30% annually; it reached about 32 billion shares in 002, with a traded value of $ 550 billion (BNY, 2003). The trading value of Mexican, Argentine, and Chilean stocks that were traded in the US was greater than the total value traded in their respective domestic stock markets during the year 1995. In 1995, 87% of Mexican local stock market indices, 54% of Argentine stock market, 62% of Chilean stock markets, 71% of Brazilian stock markets were available for trading in the form of ADRs in US stock market as found by a study (Hargis, 2000). In addition, about 67% of the foreign listed companies in NYSE were using global depositary receipts method as reported by Martell, (1999). The number of cross listing is expected to increase, due to the competitions among the international stock exchanges, to attract other foreign stocks for dual listing.

Another alternative for cross listing of foreign firms is using what is known as the global depositary registered share. Similar to the American depositary receipts, foreign securities may listed as global depositary receipts which issues by foreign depositary house such as that in Euromarkets. GDRs listed at some European Stock exchanges such as Luxemburg stock exchange. Using of ADR and GDR as alternative mean of cross listing in foreign markets has benefits for both possible investors as well as for listed securities. ADR and GDR both may be used in the process of international public offering in the primary market as well as to be traded in the secondary markets as cross listed securities.

The holder of ADR or GDR has no voting rights, and it has a specific system for trading, pricing, and settlings, and usually traded in foreign currency rather than the national currency. There are various types of depositary receipts including un-sponsored which issues without a formal agreement with the related company; the sponsored form which issues by with the related company. The depositary receipts may be traded inside stock exchange or OTC, and may be used in primary or secondary market, and may be listed by initiating from the foreign company or may be initiated by specialized depositary company.

If we considered the size of the above forms of cross listing it may be concluded that it is increasing and expanding to new markets as presented in Table 5-6. Which shows the number of listed foreign firms in the world stock market as it was in 2002. It's clear that there is a significant increase of cross listing in most of the stock exchanges such as NYSE, NASDAQ, London, Tokyo, Paris, Australian, and Luxembourg as compared to a previous decade. In addition, newly developed stock exchanges have started to admit foreign firms only in the ninnies such as Milan, Madrid, and Lisbon. The top ten stock markets as based on the number of foreign listed firms is classified as developed stock markets, and is accounted for 83% of the number of dual listed firms in the world stock markets. These are: NYSE, London, NASDAQ, Frankfurt, Luxembourg, Paris, Amsterdam, Swiss, Brussels, and Singapore.

The cross-listed firms are extended to emerging stock exchanges such as Johannesburg stock exchange. In addition, in the last decade various major firms from emerging countries listed their stocks in developed stock exchanges. For example, the number of cross listings of Latin American firms in Foreign exchanges increased from 2 in 1989 to 106 in 1999, and the traded value of Latin American firms in US exchanges increased from $ 2,669 million in 1990 to $167,990 million in 1996 (Hargis, 2000). On the other side some emerging stock exchanges started to attract foreign listed stocks from both developed and emerging markets. In addition, the concept of cross listing has expanded to even small stock markets classified as frontier stock exchanges, such as Botswana stock exchange, which includes 9 foreign listed firms (IFSE, 2000).

Table 5-6. Number of Foreign listed Shares in International Stock Exchange in December, 2006

Exchanges	Number	Rank
NYSE	451	1
London	343	2
Nasdaq	321	3
Euronext	256	4
Singapore Exchange	247	5
Luxembourg	224	6
Mexican Exchange	203	7
Deutsche Börse	104	8
Swiss Exchange	92	9
Australian Stock Exchange	78	10
Other stock exchanges	478	
Total foreign listed stocks in 2006	2,789	

Source: WFE, Focus, 2007.

Today, the listed foreign firms form more than the domestic listed firms in some stock exchanges such as Luxembourg stock exchange. It forms 42% of the total listed firms in Zurich, and 40% in Amsterdam (IFSE, 2000). In the Toronto stock exchange, about 189 stocks are cross - listed in the US and other stock markets, which accounted for 78% of the total trade volume, while at the same time the Toronto Stock exchange included 66 foreign listed companies (Ahn et al. 1998). The share of cross-listed stocks in total trade volume in some stock exchange is higher than domestics' shares. For example the trade value of foreign firms listed in London stock exchange has increased up to 58% of the total trade stock value in 1999 (IFSE, 2000). In addition, the majority of the world securities listed in foreign markets is listed in their home exchanges. However, this is changing, many firms listed in foreign securities while not listed in any of their home exchanges. There are many Canadian and European firms listed in NASDAQ without being listed in their home exchanges.

If we look in more details to the geography of the cross listed firms in the world stock markets, we may conclude that these are mainly concentrated in the Northern American and the European stock markets, with less part concerning Latin American, South Africa and some of Asian stock markets. For example the foreign, dual listed firms originated in Netherlands are listed in Europe stock exchanges of about 58 securities, 17 in NASDAQ, 16 in NYEs. The UK dual listed Firms are listed in other European stock exchanges of about 55 securities, other 55 securities listed in NASDAQ, and 46 listed in NYSE. Canadian companies are listed in Europe stock exchanges of about 45, while 40 securities listed in Amex, 165 listed in NASDAQ 165, and 65 listed in NYSE, 65. South African firms are listed in NASDAQ of about 15 securities, in London 55, in Brussels 18, and in Frankfurt 6, (Pagano et al. 2002)

The cross listing processes is attracting various parties. First, the listed firms look for increasing liquidity and broad base for stockholders. Second, the stock exchange looks for foreign firms to be listed with an intention to increase revenues and more competitions to other stock exchanges. Third, there is a benefit for both, the less developed stock markets and the developed markets as well. There is an opportunity to invest in different markets, different securities and different currencies. Fourth, some emerging stock exchanges also try to attract other foreign firms from both developed and emerging firms. In addition, various empirical studies reported other benefits for cross listing concept. For examples, Claessencs (1995) stated that emerging stock markets have provided attractive investment and diversification opportunities for industrial countries, which became increasingly integrated with the world financial market and reduced their costs of capital. Biddle, and Saudagaran study (1991) indicated the benefits of foreign stock listings, including enhancing name recognition among investors and consumers in the foreign country, building ties and images to the foreign financial community, increasing local ownership and increasing employee relations benefits. Tanzer (1991) reported how an American Apple corporation gained publicity in Japan by getting listed in the Tokyo stock Exchange. Baker (1992) reported that the major benefits of foreign listing are to broaden shareholder base. Foerster and Karolyi (1999) found that non US firms listed in US exchanges as ADR (American Depository Receipts) earn cumulative abnormal return of 19% during the year before listing and an additional 1.2% during the listing week, but they lose 14% during the year following the listing, and referred these changes to market segmentation hypothesis and to the expansion of the shareholder base.

In addition, the cross listing concept may be used to create an association between developed and emerging stock markets. Such adventure increases financial and economic ties and expand the association between different geographical regions, creating awareness of the listed corporations and their products. For example, a study conducted by the author (Sabri, 2002) examined the possibility of introducing stocks in both stock exchanges in developing and emerging markets in a neighboring area, which is the Euro-Arab stock markets (Mediterranean region) and found support to the concept of cross listing of foreign companies, to benefit from diversification of investments, reducing risk, and increasing financial and economic ties. However, the study recommended removing restrictions on foreign investments and transfer of funds from the Arab size, and to increase the awareness of companies and investors regarding to the benefit of cross listing, such as diversifying investments and improve risk sharing for both markets.

On the other side, cross listing may have some disadvantages as related to weakening the local stock exchanges and reducing their annual revenues. In addition, it may increase the volatility of underling shares in the home exchange. Other limitations may exist in certain conditions such as increasing the systemic risk in the home stock exchange and may create price fragmentations. In addition, increasing the share of cross listed securities in all over the world may reduce the benefit from the diversification concept of using multi portfolio from cross economies. Various studies examined the impact of cross listings of firms in more than one exchanges on the volatility of underling stock prices. The majority of these studies indicated that the cross listing of firms may increase price volatility. For example, the high price volatility may come from reducing the domestic market liquidity, because the cross listing may divert order flow to the foreign market, therefore may have a negative impact on the domestic stock market (Ramchand and Susmel, 1998; and Domowitz et al. 1998).

International Public Offerings

Besides the cross listing firms, in which national securities are to be sold in foreign secondary markets, there is a possibility for national firms to sell their issues in foreign primary markets upon establishments or in further issues of capital, or when national private companies go public. The practices, regulations and requirements of international public offering is so varied, and mainly depend on the related laws in both the home and the host countries in which securities are to be sold. Other regional institutions also may have various regulations to organize the international public offerings.

However, there are four possible conditions are used for international public offering: First: private companies decide to go public using foreign markets to get more liquidity or to issue shares in foreign currency. A company's decision to go public may occur for various reasons:

1. Technical reason such as the increase of number of stockholders, many jurisdictions state the maximum number of a private company to fifty members. The moment this number exceeds this level, the company has to go public and switch to become a public corporation.
2. Another reason is related to listing the company in the secondary stock market, and makes the transferability of the capital share easier and liquid.
3. Improving the stock price in the market: This is influenced by the news about the decision of going public and is reflected positively in most cases on the price of the company's share, especially, when it goes public using international offering instead of the local market.
4. Companies select international markets for initial offering rather than local offering look for broader base for investments, and thus lowering cost of offering and capital to enhance the future market price of firm. This enables the company for cheap borrowings and helps to rebalance their account after high investments and growth (Pagano et al. 1998). Another study found that international public offering may be

perceived as of better quality and will be diversified and priced compared to domestic market (Khurshed, 2003). Chaplinsky and Ramchand (2000) reported that global equity offerings expand demand and the benefit is associated with increasing foreign stockholders. Miller (1999) concluded that foreign firms that enter US capital markets raise new equity capital in a public offering and experience a positive change in shareholder wealth. However, not all companies can succeed in international offering, but some sectors are more attractive for foreign investment such as IT and technology sectors. Many European based companies prefer to go public in NASDAQ stock market because of the less costs and relevant requirements.

The process of going public is based on the laws of home, and the market country. However, and generally speaking, the process started by getting the permission from the home country legislation, adjusting the by-laws of the firm, restating the articles of incorporation to fit the corporation status and getting approval of stockholders in a special meeting, and deciding upon the portion or the part of the selling, the selling price, the international offering period, and the closing time and date, and other attached plans for employees or other groups of stockholders. On the other side, certain conditions and requirements should be met regarding the home or market country, especially the audited financial statements and other requirements, permissions and fees.

Second: A public corporation decides to increase its own capital through new subsequent offering by issuing a part of the authorized capital, and decided to offer the share in international market or in both local and foreign markets. The new issue may include a premium in case of par value shares, or based on stated value in case of no- par value shares.

Third: Privatization of public sector: Some countries prefer to implement the privatization process of their state owned companies in international markets. This action may be conducted by some countries that are urgently needed for hard currencies, and or needed to connect their local financial system to international financial systems. In addition, this process aims to attract foreign investors to the national market. However, selling the state enterprises in international markets may not include all types of industries and sectors for political or economic reasons. For example, the Turkish government privatized public banks in international and local markets, through international public offering. The privatization process started with stating the capital value based on special financial statements prepared for this purpose and decided upon the number of outstanding shares, the par value, and the portion to be privatized and to be sold in public offering and the part to be kept for government, employees or other related parties. The period of public offering and the mechanism should consider both laws of home and host countries.

Fourth: In case of establishing a new corporation for the first time through which the initial promoters or investors pay for the expense of underwriting the issuance in foreign markets. The part of capital which should be purchased by the promoters is probably stated by the home country. Many jurisdictions stated that the promoters should cover at least 10% of the new established corporation shares. The ratio between the shares to be sold locally and internationally in the primary market may be stated by promoters. However, in spite of removing the restrictions that are imposed on foreign ownership of the securities, many countries prefer to have the majority of the shares to be owned by national investors, and accordingly, they may request that international public offering should not exceed 49% of the total shares of a newly established corporation.

The international equity offering is one of the most sophisticated procedures compared to other cross border stock trading. Due to the fact that there are lots of contradictory regulations and timetables between the firm's home and host's related rules. In addition, many firms offer their own primary capital or increase it simultaneously in both local and international capital primary markets. Accordingly, this issue has received an attention lately from the related jurisdictions in order to make the related procedures more accurate, efficient, feasible and easy to implement. In addition, there is a need to reconcile the contradicted rules, frameworks, and timetables which organize the offering process from the first proposed step to the final settlements, and the completion of the process including stating the price, dealing commence, underwriting and settlement processes.

The major issue here is the harmonization between the home country legislation where the issuing company is based, and the host country where the public offering takes place. The Forum of European Securities Commissions issued the European passport report to facilitate public offering of securities within the European economic area by adopting the European passport regulations. This includes leaving the full control of the entire set of documents to the home country authority and having an automatic procedures based on a simple notification to the host country where the initial offerings or listing takes place (FESCO, 2000). The FEAS requires that stock exchanges in transition economies lead investors to offer an assessment of the present and the prospective assets, liabilities, financial position, profits and losses, the commercial prospects of the issuer of the securities that have and to be available before the offer (FEAS, 2000). Finally, some jurisdictions stated other rules to control the price issue of the offered security, definitions of public offering, usually related to percentage of free shares to be traded, or required the issuing process to be conducted through specialized investment firm or by the issuer directly.

Conclusion

This chapter explored the major features incorporated in the world stock markets based on the concept of globalization. This book classifies the concept of globalization of the world stock markets into three sub terms including liberalization, internationalization, and integration, and discussed the attached practices for the three major aspects. The liberalization of stock market increases the trading volume of stock markets and liquidity, but may have various negative effects which may be reflected on the stability of the world stock markets. In addition, the linkages between sub-segments of the financial markets also have been increasing, including stock markets, bonds markets, derivatives markets, loans, interest rates and banks, exchange rates and money markets and this is specially when there is a significant increase in the linkage between world stock markets, mainly related to the correlation of stock price movements in high volatility periods.

The positive and adverse effect of the above-mentioned practices such as international public offerings, foreign trading, and cross-listed securities, closed national and international stock price indices and harmonization of accounting and disclosures requirements are not materialized yet. There is a need to indicate what are the effects of the above practices in the world stock markets in the various aspects of information flows between the related parties, the risk factor in both local and host stock markets, the cost of trading in the home and other related markets, the trading volume, price behavior, the volatility of volume and return.

Finally, the phenomenon of globalization is more expanding and going in depth in the world stock markets, but it is still far from being integrated or transferred to a harmonized unified market.

References

Agenor, Pierre-Richard (2003) "Benefits and costs of international financial integration: theory and facts" *World Economy*, 26; 1089-1118.

Ahn, Hee-Joon, Charles Q. Cao, and Hyuk Choe (1998) "decimalization and competition among stock markets: evidence from the Toronto Stock exchange cross-listed securities" *Journal of Financial Markets* 1; 51-87.

ASE, (2000) Amsterdam stock exchange: facts & figures (July, Amsterdam, Netherlands).

Baker, H Kent (1992) "Why US Companies List on the London, Frankfurt and Tokyo Stock Exchanges" *The Journal of International Securities Markets* 6; 219-227.

Bekaert, Geert, and Campbell R. Harvey (2000) "Foreign speculators and emerging equity markets" *Journal of Finance* 55; 565-613.

Biddle, Gary C. and Shahrakh M. Saudagaran (1989) "The effects of financial disclosure levels on firms' choices among alternative foreign stock exchange listings" *Journal of International Financial Management and Accounting* 1; 56-87.

Biddle, Gary C. and Shahrakh M. Saudagaran, (1991) "Foreign stock listings: benefits, costs and the accounting policy dilemma" *Accounting Horizons* 5 (3); 70-81.

BNY (2003) *The global equity investment guide: the case for investing in depositary receipts* (The Bank of New York, NY).

Chaplinsky, Susan and Latha Ramchand (2000) "The Impact of global equity offerings" *Journal of Finance* 55; 2767-2789.

Claessencs, Stijn (1995) "The emergence of equity investment in developing countries: overview" *The World Bank Economic Review* 9 (1); 1-18.

Cooper, I., Kaplanis, E., (1994) "Home bias in equity portfolios, inflation hedging and international capital market equilibrium". *Review of Financial Studies* 7; 45-60.

Domowitz, Ian, Jack Glen, and Ananth Madhavan, (1998) "International cross listing and order flow migration: Evidence from an emerging market" *Journal of Finance* 53; 2001-2028.

CSE (1999) Rules governing issuers of securities listed on the Copenhagen stock exchange (Copenhagen Stock Exchange, Copenhagen, August).

El-Serafile, Healah and Shahira F. Abdel Sahhid (2002) "World stock exchanges are integrating/consolidating/merging: what could be done by Arab Exchange" (Cairo & Alexandria Exchanges, Working Papers No. 2, available on line; www.feas.org/library).

FEAS (2000) Best practices for the development of stock exchanges in transition economies (Federation of Euro- Asian Stock Exchanges).

FESCO (2000) A "European Passport" for issuers (The Forum of European Securities Commissions, France).

Foerster, Stephen R. and Andrew Karolyi (1999) "The effects of market segmentation and investor recognition on asset prices: Evidence from foreign stocks listing in the United States" *Journal of Finance* 54; 981-1013.

Froot, Kenneth A. Paul G. O'Connell and Mark S. Seasholes (2001) "The portfolio flows of international investors" *Journal of Financial Economics* 59 (1); 189-216.

Frost, Carol Ann (2003) *Disclosure Survey* (World Federation of Exchanges, Paris, March).

Gardiol, Lucien, Rajna Gibson-Asner, Nils S. Tuchshmid (1997) "Are Liquidity and Corporate Control Priced by Shareholders? Empirical Evidence from Swiss Dual Class Shares" *Journal of Corporate Finance* 3; 299-323.

Grabel, Ilene (1996) "Marketing the third world: the contradictions of portfolio investment in the global economy" *World Development* 24 (11); 1761-1776.

Hardouvelis, G., D. Malliaroupoulos and R. Priestley (1999). EMU and European stock market integration. (Center Economic Policy Research, Discussion Paper).

Hargis, Kent (2000) "International cross- listing and stock market development in emerging economics" *International Review of Economics and Finance* 9; 101-122.

Henry, Peter Blair (2000) "Stock market liberalization, economic reform, and emerging market equity prices" *Journal of Finance* 55; 529-564.

IASC (2000) *International Accounting Standards IAS 33* (International Accounting Standards Committee, United Kingdom).

IASC (2002) *International Accounting Standards* (International Accounting Standards Committee, United Kingdom).

ICGN (1998) *Global share voting Principles* (International Corporate governance Network, San Francisco).

ICGN (1999) *Statement on global corporate governance network* (International Corporate governance Network, London).

ICGN (2000) *Statement on global of ICGN voting principles* (International Corporate governance Network, London)

IFAC (2000) *IFAC Handbook 1999; Technical Pronouncements* (IFAC, New York).

IFC (1999) *Emerging Stock Markets Fact Book 1999* (International Finance Corporation, Washington D. C.).

IFSE (2000) *International Federation of Stock Exchanges Database* (Paris, September).

IMF (2000) *International capital markets: development, prospects and key policy issues,* World Economic and Financial Surveys, (Washington, September).

IMF (2003) *Global financial stability report, Market Developments and Issues*, International Monetary Fund, March).

IOSCO (1992) A resolution concerning international standards on auditing (International Organization of securities commissions, October).

IOSCO (1993) A resolution concerning accounting standards 7 (International Organization of securities commissions, October).

IOSCO (1998) International disclosure standards for cross-border offerings and initial listings by foreign issuers (International Organization of Securities Commissions September).

IOSCO (2000) Report on Implementation of International Disclosure Standards (International Organization of securities commissions, October).

IOSCO (2002b) A resolution on IASC Standards (International Organization of securities commissions, May).

IOSCO (2002b) *Multilateral memorandum of understanding concerning consultation and cooperation and the exchange of information* (International Organization Of Securities Commissions, May).

Jayaraman N., K. Shastri, K. Tandon (1993) "The impact of international cross listings on risk and return, the evidence from American depository receipts" *Journal of Banking & Finance* 17; 91-103.

Kaminsky, Graciela Laura, Richard K. Lyons and Sergio Schmkler (2001) "Mutual fund investment in Emerging Markets: An overview" *World Bank Economic Review* 14; 315-340.

Kang, Jun- Koo. and Rene M., Stulz, (1997) Why is there a home bias? An analysis of foreign portfolio equity ownership in Japan. *Journal of Financial Economics* 46; 2-28.

Karmel, Roberta (2001) "Will convergence of financial disclosure standards change SEC regulation of foreign issuers" *Brooklyn Journal of International Law* 26; 485- 525.

Kawakatsu, Hiroyuki and Matthew R. Morey (1999) Financial liberalization and stock market efficiency: an empirical examination of nine emerging market countries *Journal of Multinational financial management* 9; 353-371.

Khurshed, Arif (2003) Initial public offerings: does multinational matter?" *Finance Letters* 1; 24-28.

Kim, Sang W., and John H. Rogers (1995) "International stock price spillovers and market liberalization: Evidence from Korea, Japan and United States" *Journal of Empirical Finance* 2 (2); 117-144.

Lauridsen, Laurids (1998) "The Financial Crisis in Thailand: causes, conduct and consequences?" *World Development* 26; 1575-1591.

Levine, Ross and Sara Zervos (1998) Capital Control Liberalization and Stock Market Development, *World Development* 26; 1169-1183

Licht, Amir N. (1998) Regional stock market integration in Europe" (CAER II, Discussion paper No. 21, Harvard Institute for International Development).

Martell, Terrence F., Luis Rodriguez Jr., and Gwendolyn P. Webb (1999) "The Impact of Listing Latin American ADRs on the Risks and Returns of the Underlying Shares" *Global Finance Journal* 10 (2); 147-160.

Miller, Darius P. (1999) "The market reaction to international cross-listings: Evidence from Depositary Receipts" *Journal of Financial Economics* 51; 103-123

Mueller, Gerhard. (1999) "Global financial accounting standards setting at crossroads" *Emerging Issues in International Accounting* (Niagara University, USA); 7-11.

Noia, Carmine Di, (1998) Competition and integration among stock exchanges in Europe: Network Effects, Implicit mergers and remote access (Center of financial Insinuations, University of Pennsylvania).

NORDIX (2004) Press Release: Nordic Integration Continues (NORDIX, available on line www.norex.com/press).

OECD (1999) *Principles of corporate governance* (Organization For Economic Co-operation and Development, France)

Pagano, Marco, Fabio Panetta and Luigi Zingales (1998) "Why do companies go public? An empirical analysis" *Journal of Finance* 53; 2651-2694.

Pagano, Marco, Ailsa A. Roell, and Josef Zechner (2002) "The Geography of Equity Listing: Why do companies List aboard?" *Journal of Finance* 57 (6); 2651-2694.

Pieper, Paul B. and Rober C. Vogel (1999) "Stock market integration in Latin America" (CAER II, Discussion paper No. 21, Harvard Institute for International Development).

Ramchand, L., and R., Susmel (1998). "Volatility and cross correlation across major stock markets" *Journal of Empirical Finance* 5; 397-416.

Ramos, Sofia B. (2003) "Competition between Stock Exchanges: A Survey" (Research No. 77, FAME, International Center for Financial Assets Management and Engineering, Geneva).

Sabri, Nidal Rashid (2002) "Cross listings of stocks among European Arab markets" *Finance India* 16; 205-227.

Sabri, Nidal Rashid (2007) Recent Developments and Stock Market Stability" (Manuscript under publication).

Sarno, Lucio and Mark P. Taylor (1999) "Moral hazard, asset price bubbles, capital flows, and the East Asian crisis: the first tests" *Journal of International Money and Finance*. 18; 647-657.

Shawky, H. A., R., Kuenzel and A. D. Mikhail, (1997) "International portfolio diversification: A synthesis and an update" *Journal of International Financial Markets, Institutions & Money* 7; 303-327.

Singh, Ajit and Bruce Weisse (1998) "emerging stock markets, portfolio capital flows and long- term economic growth micro and macroeconomics perspectives" *World Development* 26; 607-622.

St John, Alexander B. (2001) "The regulation of cross- borders public offerings of securities in the European Union: present and future" *Denver Journal of International Law and Policy* 29 (3); 237-258.

Stulz, Rene M. and Walter Wasserfallen (1995) "Foreign equity investment restrictions, capital flight, and shareholder wealth maximization: theory and evidence" *Review of Financial Studies* 8; 1019-1057.

Tanzer, A. (1991), How Apple Stormed Japan *Fobers* (May, 27) 40-41.

Tesar, Linda L. (1995) "Home bias and high turnover" *Journal of International Money and Finance* 14; 467-492.

Torre, Augusto De La, Eduardo Levy-Yeyati and Sergio L. Schmukler (2002) "Financial globalization: unequal blessings" (The World Bank, Working Paper No. 2903).

UN (2000) *World Investments Report 1999* (United Nations, New York and Geneva).

UNCTAD (2003) *World Investments Report 2003*; FDI Policies for development: National and international Perspectives (United Nations, New York and Geneva).

UNCTAD (2006) *World Investments Report 2006*; FDI Policies for development: National and international Perspectives (United Nations, New York and Geneva).

WFE (2002) *Market Principles* (The World Federation of Exchanges, Paris).

WFE (2004) World Federation of Exchanges: About the organization (Available on line: http://www.world-exchanges.org

WFE, (2006) World Federation of Exchanges Data Base (available on line http://www.world-exchanges.org

WFE, (2007) *Focus* Issue No. 167 (World Federation of Exchanges, Paris, January, 2007.

World Bank (2000) *Global Development Finance 2000* (The World Bank, Washington, D. C).

World Bank (2001) *Global Development Finance 2001* (The World Bank, Washington D. C.).

In: Global Stock Exchanges: Stability, Interrelationships… ISBN: 978-60692-184-5
Editor: Paolo B. Cassedes

Chapter 5

ANALYST ORIGIN AND THEIR FORECASTING QUALITY ON THE LATIN AMERICAN STOCK MARKETS*†

Jean-François Bacmann‡
RMF Investment Management, Quantitative Analysis, Huobstrasse 16, CH-8808 Pfäffikon SZ.
Guido Bolliger#
Olympia Capital Management, Paris, France

Abstract

This paper investigates the relative performance of local, foreign, and expatriate financial analysts on Latin American emerging markets. We measure analysts' relative performance with three dimensions: (1) forecast timeliness, (2) forecast accuracy and (3) impact of forecast revisions on security prices. Our main findings can be summarized as follows. First, there is strong evidence that foreign analysts supply timelier forecasts than their peers. Secondly, analysts working for foreign brokerage houses (i.e., expatriate and foreign ones) produce less biased forecasts than local analysts. Finally, after controlling for analysts' timeliness, we find that foreign financial analysts' upward revisions have a greater impact on stock returns than both followers and local lead analysts forecast revisions. Overall, our results suggest that investors should better rely on the research produced by analysts working for foreign brokerage houses when they invest in Latin American emerging markets.

---

* A version of this chapter was also published in *Economics of Emerging Markets,* edited by Lado Beridze published by Nova Science Publishers, Inc. It was submitted for appropriate modifications in an effort to encourage wider dissemination of research.

† The first version of this article was entitled "Who are the best? Local versus foreign analysts on Latin American stock markets". It was written at a time when Bacmann was affiliated to the University of Neuchâtel and Bolliger to the University of Neuchâtel as well as the International Center FAME. The views expressed in this article are individual views of the authors and do not necessarily reflect their employers' opinions.

‡ Phone: ++4155 417 77 10 . Fax: ++4155 417 77 11. Email: Jean-Francois.Bacmann@rmf.ch

\# Phone: ++331 4953 7426. Fax: ++331 4256 7009. Email: guidobolliger@olympiagroup.com

Keywords: analysts' forecasts, home bias, international diversification, emerging markets, herding behaviour.
JEL Classification: G14, G15, G24

1. Introduction

Past research suggests that geographic proximity is related to information flow. However, the empirical evidence on the impact of geographic proximity on the quality of investors' information is mixed. Brennan and Cao (1997) report that US investors are less informed about foreign market conditions than are local investors. Kang and Stulz (1997) find no evidence that foreign investors outperform in Japan. Using US mutual fund holdings, Coval and Moskowitz (2001) show that investors located near potential investments have significant informational advantages relative to the rest of the market. According to Choe et al. (2000), foreign investors on the Korean market are disadvantaged relative to domestic individual investors. Inversely, Seasholes (2000) reports that foreigners act like informed traders in emerging markets. He finds that foreign investors profits come from trading stocks of large firms with low leverage and liquid shares. Similarly, Grinblatt and Keloharju (2000) exihibit evidence that foreign investors on the Finnish stock market generate superior performance than local investors. It is likely that the previous mixed findings are driven by the information available to the investors. This is why our research does not focus on the relative performance of investors but on the relative performance of analysts located at the upstream side of them.

Research devoted to financial analyst forecast accuracy documents that some groups of analysts display a better forecasting ability than others. Stickel (1992) finds that Institutional Investor All-American analysts provide more accurate earnings forecasts and tend to revise their forecasts more frequently than other analysts. Clement (1999) investigates the origin of financial analysts differential accuracy. He documents a negative relationship between financial analysts relative accuracy and the complexity of their stock portfolio. On the other hand, he shows that analysts' performance improves with their age and that analysts working for big research houses with more resources available, outperform their peers. Agency problems such as corporate financing business conflicts, have also an impact on financial analysts' performance. Lin and McNichols (1999) and Michaely and Womack (1999) show that analysts whose employer is affiliated with a company through an underwriting relationship issue more optimistic forecasts than unaffiliated analysts.

The present paper is directly related to these two streams of research. The objective is to investigate the relative performance of local, expatriate, and foreign analysts on Latin American emerging markets. Local analysts are those who work for local research firms. Expatriate analysts work for foreign brokerage houses but are located in the country. Finally, foreign analysts work for foreign research firms with no local presence. Ex-ante, three main reasons may be at the origin of differential performance across the three groups of analysts: geographical distance, agency problems, and available resources.

Residence may give local and expatriate analysts several advantages compared to foreign ones. First, they may have a better knowledge of the local economy. Local economy has been shown to have a significant impact on emerging stock markets ;see Harvey (1995). Second, they may be more familiar with the institutional context in which the companies evolve. Institutional factors have a significant influence on the properties of financial analyst forecasts; see Hope (2003). Third, they may have a better knowledge of the local culture. Finally, they may have a better human network in the country. This network may give them access to relevant private information. On the other hand, being closer from the analyzed firms, they may be more subject to agency problems such as conflict of interests. Foreign and expatriate analysts usually work for important international research firms. These big research firms have more resources available, they have the financial capacity to attract the best analysts, and their international expertise may help them to better anticipate international macro-economic fluctuations. Overall, if geographic proximity improves the quality of the information available to analysts, local and expatriate analysts should outperform their foreign counterparts. On the other hand, if the quantity of resources available to the analysts, their reputations as well as their expertise are the key determinant of their performance, foreign and expatriate analysts should outperform local ones. Finally, if conflict of interests, caused by tighter investment banking relationships between firms and banks having a local representation, have an important influence on the quality of financial analysts' output in these markets, foreign analysts should outperform both local and expatriate ones.

We conduct our investigation on Latin American markets for two reasons. First, due to geographical considerations, Latin American markets have always presented a great interest for US institutional investors. As a consequence, they create an important demand for financial analysts services on these markets. Second, as underlined by Choe et al. (2002), private information is likely to be more important on emerging stock markets than on developed ones.

We measure analysts' relative performance with three dimensions: (1) forecast timeliness, (2) forecast accuracy and (3) impact of forecast revisions on security prices. Our main findings can be summarized as follows. First, there is strong evidence that foreign analysts supply timelier forecasts than their peers. In particular, we detect a greater number of leaders among foreign analysts than among analysts with local residence. This finding suggests that both local and expatriate analysts have a tendency to revise their earnings forecasts in order to accommodate the opinions of foreign analysts. Secondly, analysts working for foreign brokerage houses (i.e., expatriate and foreign ones) produce less biased forecasts than local analysts. Lead foreign and expatriate analysts produce much more accurate forecasts than other analysts suggesting that leaders have an important informational advantage over other analysts. Finally, after controlling for analysts' timeliness, we find that foreign financial analysts' upward revisions have a greater impact on stock returns than both followers and local lead analysts forecast revisions. This suggests that the market considers forecast revisions provided by foreign leader analysts as being more informative than the revisions provided by their local counterparts.

Our research has important practical implication: investors should better rely on the research produced by analysts working for foreign brokerage houses when they invest in Latin American emerging markets. Moreover, our paper complements previous research in three ways. Firstly, we contribute to the literature on the importance of geography in economics by showing that location has an impact on the quality of the information provided by analysts. If foreign (local) investors rely mostly on foreign and expatriate (local) analysts' research in order to take their investment decisions, our results may explain the superior performance of foreign investors on some markets; see Seasholes (2000) and Grinblatt and Keloharju (2000). Secondly, by showing that analysts' location/affiliation has a significant impact on their forecast accuracy, we contribute to the large amount of literature which investigates the origins of financial analysts' forecasts bias. Thirdly, we complement, and somehow contradict, the recent research which also investigates the impact of analysts' location on forecast accuracy. Malloy (2003), Chang (2003), and Orpurt (2002) document that analysts located closer to the companies they follow make more accurate forecasts than their more distant counterparts. As underlined by Kini et al. (2003), the almost opposite conclusion drawn from our investigation may be due to differences in the industrial structure of the countries examined in these different papers. If, in Latin America, a good understanding of the sectors is a major determinant of forecast accuracy, a foreign (and to some extent an expatriate) analyst who focuses on a sector in multiple countries may have an advantage over a local analyst who focuses on multiple local firms across multiple sectors. Of course, the reverse may be true for other markets. This shows that the conclusions drawn from these studies may not be generalized to all countries.

The paper proceeds as follows. Section 2 presents the data used in this study. Section 3 investigates the relative timeliness of financial analysts. Section 4 tests for differences in forecast accuracy. Section 5 examines the impact of forecast revisions on security prices; and Section 6 concludes.

2. Data and Overview Statistics

The analysts' forecasts[11] are provided by Institutional Broker Estimate System (I/B/E/S) for 7 Latin American emerging markets: Argentina, Brazil, Chile, Colombia, Mexico, Peru and Venezuela. One year earning per share (EPS) forecasts are used from 1993 to 1999. We use the Nelson Directory of Investment Research to classify financial analysts. The Nelson Directory of Investment Research provides the name and the coordinates of each analyst that follows a particular company. Financial analysts who work for local brokerage houses are classified as local, those who work for foreign brokerage houses with residence in the country as classified as expatriate, and those who work for foreign brokerage houses without residence in the country are classified as foreign. Stock prices are extracted from Datastream. To be included in the sample, a forecast should meet the following conditions:

1. Realized EPS has to figure in the I/B/E/S Actual File.
2. The forecast must be issued between the end of previous fiscal year and current year earning reporting date.
3. The forecast must be issued by an analyst listed in the Nelson Directory of Investment Research.
4. The company for which the forecast is issued must be followed by at least 3 analysts of each group during a given year.

The last condition restricts the sample to big and medium-sized companies. The final sample includes 61'209 EPS forecasts. Table 1 shows that local analysts have produced 59% more forecasts than their foreign counterparts and more than twice much forecasts than expatriate analysts. The number of analysts and brokerage houses active on Latin American markets has sensibly increased between 1993 and 1999. This is due to the increasing coverage

[11] Note that we make no distinction between individual analysts and team of analysts.

of the I/B/E/S database but also to the increasing attractiveness of these markets for foreign investors.

Table 1. Summary statistics by year

Year	No. Forecasts			No. Analysts			No. Brokers			No. Stocks
	Local	Foreign	Expatriate	Local	Foreign	Expatriate	Local	Foreign	Expatriate	
1993	1670	783	432	74	56	41	35	18	10	84
1994	4937	2345	2263	114	84	87	49	36	16	208
1995	4999	2526	1989	236	123	122	51	32	20	200
1996	4764	2864	1899	257	163	147	57	37	17	180
1997	5229	3888	2056	245	238	170	56	33	16	212
1998	4508	3694	2141	244	232	175	50	24	15	205
1999	3674	2624	1924	182	176	148	41	19	11	170
Total	29781	18724	12704	719	584	365	93	61	27	351

This table reports yearly statistics for the data. No. Forecasts represents the number of annual earnings forecasts made each year. No. Analyst represents the number of analysts who produced a forecast during the fiscal year t. The total number of analysts who produced an earning forecast during the entire period is indicated in the last row. No. Brokers represents the number of banks (or brokerage companies) for which analysts work each year. The total number of brokers identified during the entire period is indicated in the last row. No. Stocks is the number of firms in the sample. The total number of firms for which forecasts were produced during the period is indicated in the last row.

Table 2. Summary statistics by country

Country	No. Forecasts			No. Analysts			No. Brokers			No. Stocks
	Local	Foreign	Expatriate	Local	Foreign	Expatriate	Local	Foreign	Expatriate	
Argentina	5114	2685	1835	135	215	86	22	36	9	45
Brazil	11897	7238	6349	293	244	191	30	31	19	160
Chile	2224	1530	697	67	150	39	11	25	4	29
Colombia	160	364	174	6	43	15	2	17	2	11
Mexico	12905	7700	3753	242	286	128	21	35	12	82
Peru	651	927	226	27	111	27	7	32	3	17
Venezuela	110	279	97	1	66	15	1	18	2	7

This table reports statistics by country and by industry. *No. Forecasts* represents the number of annual earnings forecasts made each year. *No. Analyst* represents the number of analysts who produced a forecast during the fiscal year *t*. *No. Brokers* represents the number of banks (or brokerage companies) for which analysts work in each country. *No. Stocks* is the number of firms in the sample.

Table 2 shows that most of the forecasts (81%) are concentrated on Brazil and Mexico. In addition, in each country excepting Brazil, foreign analysts tend to be more numerous than local and expatriate ones. However, from Table 1, we see that this finding is reversed at the aggregated level: local analysts are more numerous than foreign ones and the difference between foreign and expatriate is smaller. Thus, foreign analysts tend to follow several different markets while local and expatriate analysts are more focused on specific markets.

Non-tabulated results indicate that the average number of analysts employed by foreign brokerage houses amounts to 7.9 while it amounts to 5.5 for local ones suggesting that, on average, foreign brokerage houses are bigger than local ones. Our sample contains 91 companies out of 351 that have quoted American Depositary Receipts (ADR). Lang et al. (2002) show that non-U.S. companies listed on U.S. exchanges have richer informational environment than other non-U.S. firms. Therefore, we will control for ADR listing in the subsequent analysis.

Table 3 shows that expatriate analysts are the less active ones. On average, they produce a forecast every 77 day while their foreign and local peers do it every 73, respectively 71 day. Similarly, expatriate analysts revise less frequently than their counterparts: on average 1.33 times per firm each year against 1.92 times for foreigners and 2.45 for locals. Although the frequency of forecast revisions gives an insight on the activity of financial analysts, this does not indicate that more active analysts have advantages in collecting and processing information. They may simply change their mind several times to accommodate the opinions of others. Therefore, in the subsequent section, we propose to measure analysts' relative activity with their timeliness.

Table 3. Frequency of forecast issuance and revision

Panel A: number of calendar days elapsed between forecasts				
	Mean	Min	Median	Max
Local analysts	70.63	1.00	59.00	344.00
Foreign analysts	73.00	1.00	59.75	372.00
Expatriate analysts	77.29	1.00	65.75	362.00
Panel B: number of revisions per analyst				
	Mean	Min	Median	Max
Local analysts	2.45	0.00	1.00	50.00
Foreign analysts	1.92	0.00	1.00	19.00
Expatriate analysts	1.33	0.00	1.00	11.00

This table reports summary statistics on financial analysts' activity. Panel A presents statistics about the number of calendar days that separate two consecutive forecasts by analyst for a particular company in a given year. Panel B reports statistics on the number of revisions by analyst for a particular company in a given year.

3. Analysts' Timeliness

3.1. Empirical Design

Cooper, Day and Lewis (2001, thereafter CDL) show that timely analysts' (leaders) forecast revisions provide greater value to investors than other analysts' (followers) forecasts. They argue that timeliness is an important and necessary indicator of financial analysts' relative performance. Using forecast accuracy alone to assess the relative performance of financial analysts can lead to misclassification errors because less informed analysts can improve the accuracy of their forecasts by simply mimicking timely skilled analysts.

The leader to follower ratio (*LFR*) developed by CDL is used to distinguish leaders from followers.[12] This ratio is computed for each analyst/firm/year unit. It is distributed as $F_{(2KH,2KH)}$,[13] where H is the number of other analysts following a particular firm in a given year and K is the total number of forecasts provided by the analyst during the year for that firm. Similar to CDL, analysts having LFR significantly greater than 1 at the 10% level are considered as leaders. Moreover, each analyst is required to produce at least 3 forecasts per year for the firm under consideration. As mentioned CDL, this restriction minimizes the possibility for an analyst to be classified as leader thanks to a single lucky forecast.

In order to test whether a group (local or foreign) tends to lead the other one, we compare the number of local leaders to the foreign ones. However, since the total number of analysts is different between the 2 groups, such a comparison is not directly possible. Thus, the proportion of leaders in a given group g, L_g, is compared to the proportion of analysts in group g in the sample, P_g. In order to determine whether a group of analysts has significantly more (less) leaders than its proportion in the population suggests, we test the following hypothesis:

$$H_0 : L_g = P_g \ vs \ H_1 : L_g \neq P_g .$$

Consequently, the following normally distributed statistic is computed:

$$Time_g = \frac{(L_g - P_g)}{\sqrt{P_g \cdot (1 - P_g)}} \sqrt{N} ,$$

where:

$$L_g = \frac{Number\ of\ leaders\ in\ group\ g}{Total\ number\ of\ leaders},$$

$$P_g = \frac{Number\ of\ analysts\ from\ group\ g}{N},$$

$$N = Total\ number\ of\ analysts .$$

[12] A precise description of the *LFR* computation methodology is given in the Appendix.

[13] CDL derive the distribution of the *LFR* by assuming that the time elapsed between the arrival of two subsequent revisions follows an exponential distribution.

Table 4. Financial analysts' timeliness

Panel A: LFR for Latin America						
	Analysts' origin	No. observations	No. leaders	% leaders	% observations	Difference
		N		L_g	P_g	
Latin America	Local	5599	621	47.7	49.6	-1.9***
	Foreign	3457	444	34.1	30.6	3.5***
	Expatriate	2226	236	18.1	19.7	-1.6***

Panel B: LFR by country						
Country	Analysts' origin	No. observations	No. leaders	% leaders	% observations	Difference
		N		L_g	P_g	
Argentina	Local	938	90	45.9	53.6	-7.7***
	Foreign	476	62	31.6	27.2	4.4***
	Expatriate	337	44	22.4	19.2	3.2***
Brazil	Local	1948	231	44.6	46.5	-1.9***
	Foreign	1247	176	34.0	29.7	4.2***
	Expatriate	998	111	21.4	23.8	-2.4***
Chile	Local	315	26	43.3	48.1	-4.8***
	Foreign	246	29	48.3	37.6	10.8***
	Expatriate	94	5	8.3	14.4	-6.0***
Colombia	Local	4	0	0.0	20.0	-20.0***
	Foreign	12	3	100.0	60.0	40.0***
	Expatriate	4	0	0.0	20.0	-20.0***
Mexico	Local	2323	264	52.6	52.0	0.6
	Foreign	1388	163	32.5	31.0	1.4***
	Expatriate	760	75	14.9	17.0	-2.1***
Peru	Local	65	10	58.8	44.8	14.0***
	Foreign	58	6	35.3	40.0	-4.7
	Expatriate	22	1	5.9	15.2	-9.3***
Venezuela	Local	6	0	0.0	12.8	-12.8***
	Foreign	30	5	100.0	63.8	36.2***
	Expatriate	11	0	0.0	23.4	-23.4***

This table reports the number of analysts identified as leaders as well as the test of the null hypothesis, which is stating that the proportion of leaders in a given group equals the proportion of analysts from the given group in the total sample. The last column represents the difference between the percentage of leaders in a given group, L_g, and the percentage of analysts from the given group, P_g. The significance of this difference is determined by the following normally distributed statistic: $Time_g = \frac{(L_g - P_g)}{\sqrt{P_g \cdot (1 - P_g)}} \cdot \sqrt{N}$.

Panel A reports results for all Latin American markets. Panel B reports results by country
***, **, * denote significance at the 1%, 5%, and 10% levels, respectively.

3.2. Results for Analysts' Timeliness

According to the LFR statistic, 1301 leaders out of 11282 observations are detected. Table 4 shows the breakdown of the leaders according to their origin. The proportions of local and expatriate analysts within the leaders are significantly smaller than their proportions within the full sample.[14] On the other hand, there are more leaders among foreign analysts than their proportion in the sample would suggest. These results indicate that, on average, foreign analysts lead while local and expatriate analysts herd. Analysts with local residence have a tendency to issue their forecasts shortly after foreign analysts and their revisions do not induce other analysts to revise their own forecasts.

Panel B of Table 4 shows the breakdown of the leaders across the different countries. The individual country results are consistent with those obtained for Latin America. The exceptions are Brazil and Peru. In Brazil, the proportion of expatriate analysts identified as leaders is significantly more important than their proportion in the population. The same is true for local analysts in Peru.

In summary, the above results indicate that foreign analysts have a greater tendency to lead than analysts with local residence. This holds at the aggregated level as well as for most of the individual stock markets. The implications of these findings in terms of forecast accuracy and earnings forecasts' informativeness are investigated in the following two sections.

4. Forecast Accuracy

4.1. Empirical Design

Forecast accuracy is the most widely used measure of the quality of an analyst's research. Indeed, the more accurate earnings forecast is, the more accurate the price extracted from any valuation model will be. Forecast accuracy is measured using the average percentage forecast error adjusted for the horizon bias.[15] Analyst i's percentage forecast error at date t is,

$$FE_{ijt} = \frac{FEPS_{it} - EPS}{|EPS|},$$

where:

$FEPS_{it}$ = analyst i's EPS forecast for company j at date t,

EPS = reported earning per share at the end of the forecast horizon.

[14] The inverse is automatically true for foreign leaders.

[15] Prior studies such as Kang, O'Brien and Sivaramkarishnan (1994) show that forecast bias increases with forecast horizon.

In order to correct for the horizon bias, CDL forecast accuracy regression is used. Compared to the matching forecasts methodology used by Stickel (1992), this operation is much less data-consuming and better suited for our study. Each FE_{ijt} is regressed on the length of time from forecast release to earning announcement date. The residuals from this regression are used to measure forecast accuracy. Formally,

$$FE_{ijt} = \alpha + \beta \cdot T + \varepsilon_{ijt}, \tag{1}$$

where:

$T =$ number of days until the earnings announcement date,

$\varepsilon_{ijt} =$ residual forecast error for analyst i on firm j at date t.

The relative accuracy of each group of analysts is computed in three successive steps. First, for a given firm, the average residual forecast error is computed for each analyst,

$$MFE_{ij} = \sum_{t=1}^{K} \left|\varepsilon_{ijt}\right| / K,$$

where:

$MFE_{ij} =$ mean forecast error by analyst i for firm j,

$K =$ number of forecasts issued by analyst i for firm j during a given year.

Second, for each firm/year, individual analysts' mean forecast errors are averaged over all analysts of a given group g,

$$MGFE_{gj} = \sum_{i \in g} MFE_{ij} / N_j^g,$$

where:

$MGFE_{gj} =$ mean group forecast error for firm j,

$N =$ number of analysts from group g following firm j during a given year.

Finally, the mean difference forecast error between 2 groups is computed as

$$MDFE = \sum_{j=1}^{J} \left[MGFE_{Aj} - MGFE_{Bj} \right] / J$$

where J is the number of company/year units. In order to assess whether one group of analysts produces more (less) accurate forecasts than the other, the following hypothesis is tested:

$$H_0 : MDFE = 0 \; vs \; H_1 : MDFE \neq 0 .$$

A parametric mean test, a Wilcoxon sign rank test of equality of medians as well as a non-parametric binomial sign test are performed to test the hypothesis.

4.2. Results for Forecast Accuracy

The slope coefficient of equation (1) equals 0.01 and is significantly different from zero.[16] Emerging market analysts' bias decreases significantly with the distance between forecast release date and earnings announcement date. The intercept is not statistically different from zero.

Hypothesis tests and descriptive statistics for the mean difference forecast errors ($MDFE$) are reported in Table 5. Panels A through C report the difference across each category of analysts for all Latin American countries, for individual countries as well as for different security categories. The distribution of the MDFEs appears to be highly skewed by the presence of some extreme observations. As this may bias the results of the parametric tests, we will only consider the non-parametric results of column 7 and 8 for our analysis and conclusions.

Panel A shows that the median MDFE is positive for the whole sample and each individual countries indicating that local analysts' average forecast error is greater than foreign analysts' one. The Wilcoxon sign rank test and the binomial test reject the null hypothesis of equal forecasting skills at the aggregate level as well as for five of the individual countries. The superior ability of foreign analysts to predict firms earnings does not depend on size. Surprisingly, this superior ability disappears for American Depositary Receipts, which have a richer information environment and are the least distant firms for foreign analysts. Conflicts of interest due to increased investment and commercial banking relationship with foreign banks following U.S. exchange listing may explain this finding.

The results in panel B indicate that, excepting for Venezuela, the average error is greater for local analysts forecasts than for expatriate ones. The difference between both groups of analysts is statistically significant at the Latin American level but only weakly or not significant at the country and security category levels.

As indicated by the results in panel C, no difference between the forecasting skills of expatriate and foreign analysts can be found. As reported, in panel D, there is a strong evidence that leaders produce more accurate forecasts than follower analysts. Their mean forecast error appears to be much smaller than that of follower analysts. This is particularly true for local and foreign leaders for which the null hypothesis is rejected at the 1% level. The leader-follower criterion appears more important than the geographical one. However, no comparison is performed across leaders from each analyst group as the number of firm/year units for which leaders of both types are simultaneously identified is very low. Two important conclusions can be drawn about the behavior of financial analysts on Latin American markets. First, contrary to what has been documented by CDL, leader analysts do not "trade accuracy for timeliness". Indeed, foreign analysts are able to release timelier and more accurate forecasts. Second, follower analysts do not exactly reproduce the earnings per share

---

[16] Results are not shown. They are available on request by the authors.

forecasts issued by leader analysts. Even if their forecast releases closely follow leader analysts' ones, they avoid to reproduce exactly the information released by leader analysts.

Table 5. Financial analysts relative forecast accuracy

Distribution of the Mean Difference Forecast Errors (*MDFE*)									Sign of *MDFE*	
Panel A: Difference in forecast accuracy between local and foreign analysts										
Sample	N	Mean		Stdev	Min	Median		Max	% Local > Foreign	
Latin America	1263	-0.16		7.98	-238.88	0.02	***	62.10	54.95	***
Argentina	191	-0.01		0.88	-9.22	0.02	**	4.59	58.64	***
Brazil	557	-0.55		11.68	-238.88	0.02		47.11	53.68	**
Mexico	332	0.22		3.52	-4.97	0.02		62.10	53.31	
Chili	112	0.11	**	0.50	-1.96	0.03	**	3.31	55.36	
Peru	38	0.23		0.98	-0.42	0.05		5.46	60.53	*
Colombia	21	0.32	*	0.83	-0.38	0.10	**	3.54	71.43	**
Venezuela	12	-0.06		0.43	-1.13	0.02		0.36	50.00	
High Market Value	493	-0.01		6.54	-121.27	0.02	**	62.10	54.56	**
Small Market Value	323	0.16		2.25	-9.22	0.02	*	35.44	53.25	
ADR	277	0.04		0.88	-5.35	0.02		10.51	53.07	
Panel B: Difference in forecast accuracy between local and expatriate analysts										
Sample	N	Mean		Stdev	Min	Median		Max	% Local > Expatriate	
Latin America	1263	0.61	*	12.89	-20.69	0.01	**	402.14	52.26	*
Argentina	191	0.05		0.89	-4.24	0.02		10.27	53.40	
Brazil	557	1.04		18.48	-20.69	0.01		402.14	51.35	
Mexico	332	0.45		7.65	-13.31	0.01		136.34	52.41	
Chili	112	0.08	*	0.46	-0.76	0.00		3.03	50.89	
Peru	38	0.29	*	1.03	-0.65	0.08	*	5.59	60.53	*
Colombia	21	0.24		0.80	-0.36	0.02		3.20	61.90	*
Venezuela	12	-0.09		0.33	-0.75	-0.07		0.55	41.67	
High Market Value	493	0.63		9.60	-3.35	0.00		163.62	49.49	
Small Market Value	323	0.00		2.65	-20.69	0.02		35.23	52.94	
ADR	277	0.05		0.67	-3.61	0.01		6.81	52.71	
Panel C: Difference in forecast accuracy between expatriate and foreign analysts										
Sample	N	Mean		Stdev	Min	Median		Max	% Expatriate > Foreign	
Latin America	1263	-0.77		18.81	-641.02	0.00		19.46	50.75	
Argentina	191	-0.06		1.35	-12.48	0.01		4.41	52.88	
Brazil	557	-1.59		28.10	-641.02	-0.01		19.46	48.29	
Mexico	332	-0.23		4.45	-74.23	0.01		18.11	52.41	
Chili	112	0.03		0.38	-2.58	0.05	**	0.91	58.04	**
Peru	38	-0.06		0.22	-0.45	-0.08	**	0.53	34.21	**
Colombia	21	0.08		0.22	-0.25	0.04		0.50	52.38	
Venezuela	12	0.03		0.47	-1.28	0.10		0.52	66.67	*
High Market Value	493	-0.65	*	8.29	-120.94	0.01		3.71	52.54	

Table 5. Continued

Sample	N	Mean	Stdev	Min	Median		Max	% Expatriate > Foreign	
Small Market Value	323	0.16	1.97	-11.16	0.01		19.46	51.39	
ADR	277	-0.02	0.67	-4.70	0.01		3.71	52.71	
Panel D: Difference in forecast accuracy between leaders and followers									
Sample	N	Mean	Stdev	Min	Median		Max	% Leaders > Followers	
Local Leaders	426	-0.04	1.31	-11.04	-0.05	***	17.08	39.20	***
Foreign Leaders	350	-3.74	70.33	-1315.50	-0.58	***	12.09	40.57	***
Expatriate Leaders	198	0.07	6.13	-40.74	-0.02		73.38	44.95	*

This table presents descriptive statistics as well as hypothesis tests for the Mean Difference in Forecast Errors (*MDFE*). In Panel A, the third column reports the average difference between local analysts' forecast errors and foreign analysts' forecast errors. Column 6 reports the median difference between local analysts' forecast errors and foreign analysts' forecast errors. Column 8 reports the percentage of firm/year units for which the average forecast error of local analysts was greater than the average forecast error of foreign ones. In Panel B, the third column reports the average difference between local analysts' forecast errors and expatriate analysts' forecast errors. Column 6 reports the median difference between local analysts' forecast errors and expatriate analysts' forecast errors. Column 8 reports the percentage of firm/year units for which the average forecast error of local analysts was greater than the average forecast error of expatriate ones. In Panel C, the third column reports the average difference between expatriate analysts' forecast errors and foreign analysts' forecast errors. Column 6 reports the median difference between expatriate analysts' forecast errors and foreign analysts' forecast errors. Column 8 reports the percentage of firm/year units for which the average forecast error of expatriate analysts was greater than the average forecast error of foreign ones. In Panel D, the third column reports the average difference between lead analysts' forecast errors and follower analysts' forecast errors. Column 6 reports the median difference between lead analysts' forecast errors and follower analysts' forecast errors. Column 8 reports the percentage of firm/year units for which the average forecast error of lead analysts was greater than the average forecast error of follower ones. A parametric mean test is performed on column 3 numbers, a Wilcoxon signed rank test of equality of medians is performed on column 6 numbers, and a non-parametric sign test is performed on column 8 numbers. Note that in Panel D, the total number of firm/year units for each group of leader is lower than the number of leaders that has been identified. This is explained by the fact that there can be several leaders for a particular company in a given year.

***, **, * denote significance at the 1%, 5%, and 10% levels, respectively.

Overall, this section shows that foreign analysts foreign analysts have a better ability to analyze Latin American firms' earnings potential than their local peers. There is no significant difference between the performance of foreign and expatriate analysts and only a weak difference between expatriate and local analysts in the favor of expatriate ones. These finding indicate that analysts who work for foreign institutions may have greater resources, expertise and/or talent than their local peers. Finally, timely analysts are the most accurate ones. Consequently, lead analysts do not give up forecast accuracy when releasing more timely forecasts.

5. Impact of Forecast Revisions on Security Prices

5.1. Empirical Design

This section investigates whether one group of analysts' revisions provides more information to investors. The objective is to determine whether the stock price reaction following forecast revisions differs between the different groups of analysts. The reaction around forecast revisions for a given firm is proxied by the cumulative excess return during the forecast release period (days 0 and +1). This cumulative excess return is computed as the difference between the buy-and-hold returns for the firm's common stock and the value-weighted Datastream country index.

The incremental information content of each revision is measured by the scaled distance relative to the consensus forecast.[17] More precisely:

$$FSUR_{ijt} = \frac{FEPS_{ijt} - CF_{jt-1}}{\sigma(CF_{jt-1})}$$

where:

$FSUR_{ijt}$ = forecast surprise following analyst i's revision for firm j at date t,

CF_{jt-1} = consensus EPS forecast for firm j at date $t-1$,

$\sigma(CF_{jt-1})$ = standard deviation of the consensus forecast[18] at date $t-1$.

The consensus forecast is based on the average of the forecasts issued by analysts (excluding analyst i) during the 2 months preceding date t. Each analyst is required to provide at least 3 forecasts per year for the firm and each consensus forecast is required to contain at least 2 individual forecasts.

The impact of forecast revisions on security prices is measured by the following cross-sectional regression equations:

$$CAR_{jt} = \beta_0 + \beta_1 FSUR_{ijt} + \beta_2 LOC_i + \beta_3 FOR_i + \beta_4 LNSIZE_{jt} + \varepsilon_{jt} \quad (2)$$

$$CAR_{jt} = \beta_0 + \beta_1 LOC_i \times FSUR_{ijt} + \beta_2 FOR_i \times FSUR_{ijt} + \beta_3 EXPAT_i \times FSUR_{ijt} + \beta_4 LNSIZE_{jt} + \varepsilon_{jt} \quad (3)$$

$$CAR_{jt} = \beta_0 + \beta_1 FSUR_{ijt} + \beta_2 LOCLEAD_{ij} + \beta_3 FORLEAD_{ij} + \beta_4 EXPATLEAD_{ij} + \beta_5 LNSIZE_{jt} + \varepsilon_{jt} \quad (4)$$

[17] Our results are not sensitive to the choice of the scaling factor.

[18] Similar to Stickel (1992), a standard deviation less than 0.25 is arbitrarily set to 0.25 to mitigate small denominators. Our results are not affected by this operation.

$$CAR_{jt} = \beta_0 + \beta_1 LOCLEAD_{ij} \times FSUR_{ijt} + \beta_2 FORLEAD_{ij} \times FSUR_{ijt} + \beta_3 EXPATLEAD_{ij} \times FSUR_{ijt} + \beta_4 FOL_i \times FSUR_{ijt} + \beta_5 LNSIZE_{jt} + \varepsilon_{jt} \quad (5)$$

where:

CAR_{jt} = cumulative excess return for firm j during the forecast release period (days 0 and +1),

LOC_i = dummy variable set to 1 if analyst i is a local one and 0 otherwise,

FOR_i = dummy variable set to 1 if analyst i is foreign and 0 otherwise,

$LNSIZE_j$ = logarithm of the market value (in USD) of common stock at fiscal year end,

$EXPAT_i$ = dummy variable set to 1 if analyst i is an expatriate and 0 otherwise,

$LOCLEAD_{ij}$ = dummy variable set to 1 if analyst i is a local analyst that has been identified as leader for company j and 0 otherwise,

$FORLEAD_{ij}$ = dummy variable set to 1 if analyst i is a foreign analyst that has been identified as leader for company j and 0 otherwise,

$EXPATLEAD_{ij}$ = dummy variable set to 1 if analyst i is an expatriate analyst that has been identified as leader for company j and 0 otherwise,

FOL_{ij} = dummy variable set to 1 if analyst i has been identified as follower for company j and 0 otherwise,

Equations (2) and (4) measure the abnormal return associated with the different groups of analysts' forecast revisions. Equation (3) and (5) measures the proportion of abnormal return explained by each group of analysts' forecast revisions. The size variable is a proxy for the differences in firms' information environment[19] but also for foreign investors' ownership since they tend to concentrate their investments on high-capitalization liquid firms.

5.2. Results for the Impact of Forecast Revisions on Security Prices

Table 6 reports the mean cumulative abnormal return during the forecast release period. The price reaction depends on the size of the revision. The cumulative abnormal returns display important standard deviations and consequently only the stock returns associated with the bottom 50% sub-sample display statistically significant price reactions. Conversely, other revisions do not impact on prices. This is consistent with Stickel (1992, 1995) who documents a non-linear relation between forecast revisions and price reactions. Therefore, the regressions are restricted to revisions of a given magnitude.

[19] Stickel (1995), among others, reports that buy and sell recommendations induces a greater price reaction for smaller companies than for larger ones.

Results for the cross-sectional regressions (2) and (3) are reported in table 7. First, panel A results indicate that, following downward revisions, there is no difference in the average size of the stock price reaction across groups. On the other hand, following large upward revisions (top 10%), the average cumulative abnormal return is significantly smaller for local analysts than for expatriate ones. The same is true for foreign analysts but the regression coefficient is only marginally significant. Second, results reported in panel B indicate that the stock price reaction following analysts forecast revisions is only significant for expatriate analysts large upward revisions. Unfortunately, the null hypothesis of equality across coefficients cannot be rejected by the F-tests presented in columns 7 through 9.

Table 6. Stock price reactions following forecast surprises

	All FSUR	Bottom 10%	Bottom 50%	Top 50%	Top 10%
Mean (%)	-0.07 **	-0.16	-0.12 **	-0.02	-0.17
Standard deviation (%)	4.39	4.73	4.52	4.27	4.42
N	16699	1670	8352	8347	1670

This table reports some descriptive statistics about the cumulative abnormal returns (CARs) following forecasts' revisions. Cumulative abnormal returns are computed as the difference between the buy-and-hold return for the firm's common stock and the value-weighted Datastream country index during the forecast release period (days 0 and 1). The column All FSUR reports statistics on CARs for all forecast surprise level. Bottom 10% reports CARs for forecast surprises located in the top 10% of the distribution. Bottom 50% reports statistics for CAR's located in the bottom 50% of the distribution. In the column Top 50%, statistics are reported for CAR's located in the top 50% of the distribution. Top 10% reports statistics for CAR's located in the top 10% of the distribution.

***, **, * denote significance at the 1%, 5%, and 10% levels, respectively.

Table 7. Stock price reactions following analyst forecast revisions

Panel A: $CAR_{jt} = \beta_0 + \beta_1 FSUR_{ijt} + \beta_2 LOC_i + \beta_3 FOR_i + \beta_4 LNSIZE_{jt} + \varepsilon_{jt}$

FSUR Cutoff	β_0	β_1	β_2	β_3	β_4	N
Bottom 10%	-0.46	0.09	-0.24	0.02	0.08	1670
	(-0.60)	(0.63)	(-0.77)	(0.05)	(0.88)	
Bottom 50%	-0.59 *	0.07	0.07	0.17	0.06	8352
	(-1.91)	(1.03)	(0.51)	(1.17)	(1.55)	
Top 50%	0.03	-0.04	-0.20	-0.27 **	0.02	8347
	(0.09)	(-0.56)	(-1.57)	(-1.97)	0.58	

Table 7. Continued

Panel B: $CAR_{jt} = \beta_0 + \beta_1 LOC_i \times FSUR_{ijt} + \beta_2 FOR_i \times FSUR_{ijt} + \beta_3 EXPAT_i \times FSUR_{ijt} + \beta_4 LNSIZE_{jt} + \varepsilon_{jt}$

FSUR Cutoff	β_0	β_1	β_2	β_3	β_4	$\beta_1 = \beta_2$	$\beta_1 = \beta_3$	$\beta_2 = \beta_3$	N
Top 10%	1.07	0.20	-0.60 **	-0.52 *	-0.16 *	1670			
	(1.35)	(1.42)	(-2.13)	(-1.68)	(-1.73)				
Bottom 10%	-0.56	0.13	0.05	0.06	0.08	0.40	0.25	0.01	1670
	(-0.76)	(0.86)	(0.30)	(0.35)	(0.87)				
Bottom 50%	-0.50 *	0.13	0.13	0.03	0.06	0.99	0.56	0.02	8352
	(-1.73)	(1.52)	(1.52)	(0.25)	(1.55)				
Top 50%	-0.14	-0.11	-0.03	0.12	0.02	0.42	2.89 *	1.04	8347
	(-0.51)	(-1.25)	(-0.29)	(0.98)	(0.53)				
Top 10%	0.64	0.13	0.22	0.35 **	-0.16	0.46	2.24	0.65	1670
	(0.84)	(0.81)	(1.36)	(1.99)	(-1.74)				

This table presents the coefficients obtained by regressing the cumulative abnormal returns following forecast revisions on the magnitude of the revision, firm size, and dummy variables indicating analysts' status. Revisions are dated within the firm's current fiscal year over the 1993-1999 period. CAR_{jt} is the cumulative abnormal return to security i during the release period (days 0 and +1). $FSUR_{ijt}$ is the forecast surprise following analyst i's revision at date t. $LNSIZE_{jt}$ is the natural logarithm of the market value (in USD) of common stock at fiscal year end. LOC_i is a dummy variable that takes a value of 1 if analyst i is employed by a local brokerage house and 0 otherwise. FOR_i is a dummy variable that takes a value of 1 if analyst i is employed by a foreign brokerage house without local residence and 0 otherwise. $EXPAT_i$ is a dummy variable that takes a value of 1 if analyst i is employed by a foreign brokerage house with local residence and 0 otherwise. All coefficients are multiplied by 100. T-statistics are based on White (1980). For each regression the adjusted R^2 are less than 0.01.

***, **, * denote significance at the 1%, 5%, and 10% levels, respectively.

Table 8 reports the results for the cross-sectional regressions (4) and (5). First, as reported in panel A, the average cumulative return does not differ between leader and follower analysts. Second, as indicated by panel B results, there is a significant market reaction following foreign and expatriate leaders large upward revisions (top 10%). The F-tests indicate that the regression coefficients associated to foreign leaders' revisions are significantly higher than those associated to local leaders and followers' revisions.

Overall, this section shows that there are almost no significant differences in the incremental information contained in financial analysts' forecasts revisions. However, the market seems to consider the forecasts issued by local and, to some extent, by expatriate leaders as being more informative than those issued by other analysts. This is consistent with the view that foreign leaders' revisions have greater information content than other analysts' revisions.

6. Conclusions

Foreign financial analysts' EPS forecasts are more timely than expatriate and local analysts' forecasts. Building on CDL methodology, 1301 leader analysts are identified. Out of these leaders, 444 are foreign. This is significantly greater than the proportion of foreign analysts' forecasts in the sample. Conversely, analysts with local residence display a significant tendency to follow the "crowd".

In terms of forecast accuracy, analysts working for foreign brokerage houses are better at predicting firms' EPS than local analysts. Surprisingly, we detect no significant differences in forecast accuracy for companies with quoted ADRs. This may indicate that foreign and expatriate analysts' superior performance vanishes for companies with richer information environment.

Finally, stock prices react positively to upward forecast revisions released by foreign and expatriate leader analysts. The coefficient associated to foreign leaders forecast surprises is significantly greater than that associated to follower forecast surprises. It is also marginally greater than the coefficient associated to local leaders forecast surprises.

We see that foreign analysts outperform their local peers across all our performance measures. This suggests that residence does not give local financial analysts an advantage relative to their foreign counterparts. The difference between foreign and expatriate analysts' performance is less evident. Foreign analysts outperform their expatriate peers for one out of three performance measures. This suggests that agency problems, due to tighter investment banking relationships between resident analysts' firms and local companies, are not influencing financial analysts' objectivity on Latin American markets. Overall, our results are consistent with better information and greater sophistication on the part of analysts employed by foreign brokerage houses. This superiority may be linked to the superior resources available to analysts who work for important international brokerage houses, to the better international expertise of these analysts, or to their greater talent.

The present results are consistent with better information on the part of foreign investors. Foreigners' portfolio profits on emerging markets, such as those documented by Seasholes (2000), may be driven by the better ability of foreign analysts at analyzing firms' situation for their clients. However, further research is needed to understand which category of investors (foreign or domestic) trade around foreign and local analysts' revisions. Finally, the practical implication of this investigation is that investors should rely more heavily on foreign financial analysts' forecasts than on local ones when they invest in Latin American markets.

Table 8. Stock price reactions following leaders and followers forecast revisions

Panel A: $CAR_{jt} = \beta_0 + \beta_1 FSUR_{ijt} + \beta_2 LOCLEAD_{ij} + \beta_3 FORLEAD_{ij} + \beta_4 EXPATLEAD_{ij} + \beta_5 LNSIZE_{jt} + \varepsilon_{jt}$

FSUR Cutoff	β_0	β_1	β_2	β_3	β_4	β_5	N
Bottom 10%	-0.56	0.09	-0.63	0.52	-0.61	0.09	1670
	(-0.76)	(0.64)	(-1.19)	(0.86)	(-0.59)	(0.92)	
Bottom 50%	-0.48	0.07	-0.24	-0.03	-0.30	0.06	8352
	(-1.66)	(1.05)	(-1.15)	(-0.10)	(-0.72)	(1.57)	
Top 50%	-0.17	-0.03	0.17	-0.33	0.22	0.02	8347
	(-0.62)	(-0.52)	(0.78)	(-1.17)	(0.64)	(0.64)	
Top 10%	0.60	0.20	-0.18	0.78	0.97	-0.16 *	1670
	(0.79)	(1.38)	(-0.40)	(1.24)	(1.23)	(-1.72)	

Panel B: $CAR_{jt} = \beta_0 + \beta_1 LOCLEAD_{ij} \times FSUR_{ijt} + \beta_2 FORLEAD_{ij} \times FSUR_{ijt} + \beta_3 EXPATLEAD_{ij} \times FSUR_{ijt} + \beta_4 FOL_{ij} \times FSUR_{ijt} + \beta_5 LNSIZE_{jt} + \varepsilon_{jt}$

FSUR Cutoff	β_0	β_1	β_2	β_3	β_4	β_5	$\beta_1=\beta_2$	$\beta_1=\beta_3$	$\beta_1=\beta_4$	$\beta_2=\beta_3$	$\beta_2=\beta_4$	$\beta_3=\beta_4$	N
Bottom 10%	-0.55	0.24	0.04	0.46	0.07	0.08	0.26	0.23	0.43	0.77	0.01	1.04	1670
	(-0.75)	(0.76)	(0.14)	(1.05)	(0.51)	(0.86)							
Bottom 50%	-0.50 *	0.26	0.12	0.42	0.05	0.06	0.19	0.14	0.93	0.50	0.07	1.19	8352
	(-1.73)	(1.03)	(0.46)	(1.04)	(0.68)	(1.56)							
Top 50%	-0.14	-0.11	0.33	0.34	-0.05	0.02	1.41	1.32	0.05	0.00	1.64	1.48	8347
	(-0.53)	(-0.45)	(1.11)	(1.26)	(-0.78)	(0.55)							
Top 10%	0.64	0.10	0.88 ***	0.60 **	0.17	-0.16 *	3.60 *	1.35	0.08	0.35	4.41 **	1.44	1670
	(0.85)	(0.37)	(2.80)	(1.96)	(1.18)	(-1.73)							

This table presents the coefficients obtained by regressing the cumulative abnormal returns following forecast revisions on the magnitude of the revision, firm size, and dummy variables indicating analysts' status. Revisions are dated within the firm's current fiscal year over the 1993-1999 period. CAR_{jt} is the cumulative abnormal return to security i during the release period (days 0 and +1). $FSUR_{ijt}$ is the forecast surprise following analyst i's revision at date t. $LNSIZE_{jt}$ is the natural logarithm of the market value (in USD) of common stock at fiscal year end. $LOCLEAD_{ij}$ is a dummy variable that takes a value of 1 if analyst i is a local leader and 0 otherwise. $FORLEAD_{ij}$ is a dummy variable that takes a value of 1 if analyst i is a foreign leader and 0 otherwise. $EXPATLEAD_{ij}$ is a dummy variable that takes a value of 1 if analyst i is an expatriate leader and 0 otherwise. FOL_{ij} is a dummy variable that takes a value of 1 if analyst i is a follower and 0 otherwise. All coefficients are multiplied by 100. T-statistics are based on White (1980). For each regression the adjusted R^2 are less than 0.01.

***, **, * denote significance at the 1%, 5%, and 10% levels respectively.

Appendix

Leader-to-Follower Ratio

The Leader-to-Follower Ratio (LFR) for a particular analyst a who provides forecasts for firm j is expressed a follows:

$$LFR_a^j = \frac{T_{0,a}^j}{T_{1,a}^j}, \tag{6}$$

where T_0 and T_1 are respectively the cumulative lead- and follow time for the K forecasts made by analyst a on firm j during a particular fiscal year. They are defined as follows:

$$T_{0,a}^j = \sum_{k=1}^{K} \sum_{h=1}^{H} t_{jhk}^0 \tag{7}$$

$$T_{1,a}^j = \sum_{k=1}^{K} \sum_{h=1}^{H} t_{jhk}^1 \tag{8}$$

t_{jmk}^0 (t_{jmk}^1) denotes the number of days by which forecast h precedes (follows) the k-th forecast may by analyst a for firm j. H is the number of forecasts made by other analysts that precede and follow the release of the k-th forecast of analyst a. The above figure provides an illustration of the idea underlying the LFR ratio. The forecast issued by analyst a for firm j at date t is denoted as $F_{a,t}^j$.

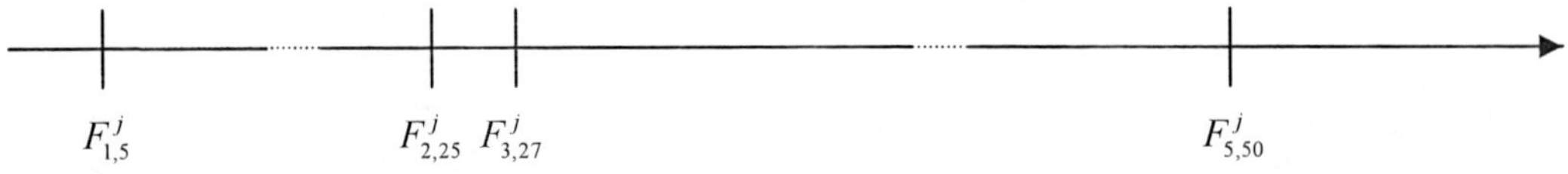

From this example, we see that analyst 2 issues a forecast on day 25. The preceding forecast was issued 20 days before on day 5. The following forecast is released soon afterward, on day 27. Taking into account only these one preceding and one following forecasts, analyst 2's LFR ratio is $\frac{20}{2} = 10$. Analyst 2 would therefore classified as a leader. To the same extent, analyst 3 is a follower analyst. He issues a forecast right after analysts 2 and no one free-rides on its forecast since the next to issue a forecast is analyst 4, only 23 days later. Its LFR would then be $\frac{1}{23} \cong 0.04$.

Acknowledgements

The authors thanks Michel Dubois, Christophe Pérignon, René Stulz, Ernst-Ludvig Von Thadden, and participants at FAME doctoral workshop, 5th Conference of the Swiss Society for Financial Market Research, 2002 FMA European meeting, 2002 EFMA meeting, and 2002 FMA US meeting for their helpful comments.

The authors acknowledge the contribution of Thomson Financial for providing earnings per share forecast data, available through the Institutional Brokers Estimate System. This data has been provided as part of a broad academic program to encourage earnings expectations research.

The authors aknowledge the financial support of the Swiss National Science Fondation (grant nr. 1214-065220).

References

Brennan, M.J. and H.H. Cao, 1997, International portfolio investment flows, *Journal of Finance* 52, 1851-1880.

Brown, L.D., 1997, Analyst forecasting errors: Additional evidence, *Financial Analysts Journal,* November/December, 81-88.

Chang, C., 2002, *Information footholds: Expatriate analysts in an emerging market,* Working Paper, Haas School of Business, U.C. Berkeley.

Choe, H., Kho, B.C. and R.M. Stulz, 2000, *Do domestic investors have more valuable information about individual stocks than foreign investors?,* Working paper, Seoul National University and Ohio State University.

Cooper, R.A., Day, T.E. and C.M. Lewis, 2001, Following the leader: A study of individual analysts' earnings forecasts, *Journal of Financial Economics* 61, 383-416.

Coval, J.D. and T.J. Moskowitz, 2001, The geography of investment: Informed trading and asset prices, *Journal of Political Economy* 109, 811-841.

Grinblatt, M. and M. Keloharju, 2000, The investment behaviour and performance of various investor types: A study of Finland's unique data set, *Journal of Financial Economics* 55, 43-67.

Harvey, C.R., 1995, Predictable risk and returns in emerging markets, *Review of Financial Studies* 8, 773-816.

Hope, O., 2003, *Accounting policy disclosures and analysts' forecasts,* Contemporary Accounting Research, Forthcoming.

Kang, S., O'Brien, J. and K. Sivaramakrishnan, 1994, Analysts' interim earnings forecasts: Evidence on the forecasting process, *Journal of Accounting Research* 32, 103-112.

Kang, J. and R.M. Stulz, 1997, Why is there a home bias? An analysis of foreign portfolio equity ownership in Japan, *Journal of Financial Economics* 46, 2-28.

Kini, O., Shehzad, M., Rebello, M. and A. Venkateswaran, 2003, *On the determinants of international analyst research coverage,* Working Paper, Robinson College of Business, Georgia State University.

Lang, M.H., Lins, K.V. and D. Miller, 2003, ADRs, analysts, and accuracy: Does cross listing in the U.S. improve a firm's information environment and increase market value, *Journal of Accounting Research,* Forthcoming.

Lin, H. and M.F. McNichols, 1998, Underwriting relationships, analysts' earnings forecasts and investment recommendations, *Journal of Accounting and Economics* 25, 101-127.

Malloy, C.J., 2003, The geography of equity analysis, Journal of Finance, Forthcoming.

Michealy, R. and K.L. Womack, 1999, Conflict of interest and the credibility of underwriter analyst recommendations, *Review of Financial Studies* 12, 653-686.

Orpurt, S.F., 2003, *Local asymmetric information advantages: International evidence from analysts' European firm earnings forecasts,* Working Paper, Graduate School of Business, University of Chicago.

Seasholes, M., 2000, *Smart foreign traders in emerging markets,* Working paper, Harvard Business School, Cambridge, M.A.

Stickel, S., 1992, Reputation and performance among security analysts, Journal of Finance 47, 1811-1836.

Stickel, S., 1995, The anatomy of the performance of buy and sell recommendations, *Financial Analysts Journal,* September/October, 25-39.

White, H., 1980, A heteroscedasticity-consistent covariance matrix estimator and a direct test for heteroscedasticity, *Econometrica* 48, 817-838.

In: Global Stock Exchanges: Stability, Interrelationships... ISBN: 978-60692-184-5
Editor: Paolo B. Cassedes

Chapter 6

SARBANES-OXLEY AND THE COMPETITIVE POSITION OF U.S. STOCK MARKETS*

Mark Jickling
Specialist in Public Finance, Government and Finance Division

Abstract

Congress passed the Sarbanes-Oxley Act of 2002 (P.L. 107-204) to remedy weaknesses in accounting and corporate governance exposed by massive fraud at Enron Corp. and other firms. Criticism of the law, which has been fairly widespread among business groups, academics, and accountants, focuses on the costs of compliance, which are said to outweigh the benefits. Several studies and comments have argued that the rising cost of regulation has created incentives for firms to list their shares on foreign markets or to withdraw from the public markets altogether, weakening the international competitive position of U.S. stock exchanges.

Specific evidence cited includes the fact that 24 of the largest 25 initial public stock offerings (IPOs) in 2005 took place on foreign exchanges, and that there has been a boom in the private equity market, where U.S. securities regulation is minimal. This article attempts to put instances like these in context by presenting comparative data on the world's major stock markets over the past decade.

In terms of the number of corporations listing their shares, several foreign markets have shown faster growth than the major U.S. exchanges (the New York Stock Exchange (NYSE) and Nasdaq). However, these increases appear to be fueled primarily by growth in the number of domestic firms listing on their own national markets. While major foreign markets have seen significant declines in foreign listings as a percentage of all listings, U.S. exchanges have not been abandoned by foreign companies in significant numbers.

Perhaps the most common reason for firms to delist, or leave a stock exchange, is a merger with another firm. Lower costs of regulation may be a side benefit of many mergers, but trends in interest rates and stock prices appear to be the primary determinants of merger activity. A rising number of corporate acquisitions result in the acquired firms "going private" — becoming exempt from most regulation — but this trend is also largely driven by economic conditions. Private equity investment has boomed since 2000 because debt financing has been

* This is an edited, reformatted and augmented version of a CRS publication, CRS Report # Rl33796; January 11, 2007.

abundant and relatively cheap, and because institutional investors have sought higher yields than what the stock and bond markets have provided.

Figures on new issues of stock (including IPOs) are volatile, and annual data may be skewed by a few large deals. Certain foreign exchanges have recovered more quickly from the 2000-2002 bear market, but, on the whole, there is little evidence that the U.S. stock market is becoming less attractive to companies seeking to raise capital. When the bond markets are included, the role of the U.S. securities industry in capital formation appears to be as strong as ever.

The data surveyed here suggest that rising regulatory costs have not precipitated any crisis in U.S. markets, and that the outcome of global competition among stock exchanges depends more on fundamental market conditions than on differentials in regulatory costs.

Introduction

The Sarbanes-Oxley Act of 2002 (P.L. 107-204) was enacted in response to massive accounting fraud at Enron and a long list of other U.S. corporations. The law sought to improve — or restore — the effectiveness of the gatekeepers who are supposed to ensure that investors receive accurate information about firms whose securities are traded in public markets. Under Sarbanes-Oxley, corporate executives, directors, auditors, accountants, attorneys, and regulators are all held to more stringent standards of accountability.

Criticism of Sarbanes-Oxley has focused on compliance costs, which to some observers outweigh the benefits of improved governance and regulation.[1] Since direct measurement of those costs and benefits within a single business is impossible, much of the debate has looked to the securities markets, where excessive regulatory costs should be mirrored.

Raising the costs of complying with U.S. securities regulation, as Sarbanes-Oxley unquestionably did, creates incentives both for firms whose securities are listed on U.S. stock markets and for firms weighing the costs and benefits of going public and obtaining such listings.[2] Firms in the first group (including non-U.S. companies) that find compliance costs excessive may choose to delist their shares and become privately held businesses, or list on foreign stock exchanges, where Securities and Exchange Commission (SEC) regulations do not apply. Firms in the second group may decide to avoid SEC regulation by remaining private and seeking funds outside the public securities markets, from private equity investors, for example. They also have the option of going public in a foreign country. If significant numbers of firms have decided since 2002 that the costs of U.S. regulation exceed the benefits of access to U.S. public securities markets (with their traditional advantages of deep liquidity and low transaction costs), some or all of the following would be expected:

- a decrease in the number of firms (domestic and foreign) whose shares are listed on U.S. exchanges, either in absolute terms or relative to foreign stock exchanges;
- an upward trend in delistings, reflecting companies that choose to leave the U.S. public markets; and
- a falling off in the number of new listings on U.S. exchanges, as the initial public offering (IPO) market shrinks or moves offshore.

Several recent comments and studies have cited evidence that U.S. stock markets have indeed become less competitive and have suggested that expensive regulation may be partly to blame.[3] Few would argue that Sarbanes-Oxley (or U.S. regulation in general) is solely responsible for the perceived decline in U.S. markets' competitive position. Other factors include several long-term trends, such as (1) the growth of foreign stock markets, particularly in countries like China and Germany without long traditions of widespread stock ownership; (2) the lowering of legal and regulatory barriers to cross-border investment and trading; and (3) the role of computer technology in reducing communications, information, and transactions costs. However, policy recommendations to address the perceived decline in competitiveness tend to focus on regulatory relief, since there is little Congress or regulators can realistically do to reverse financial globalization or technological progress.

Two facts often put forward are that in 2005, only one of the 25 largest IPOs took place in the United States, and that going-private transactions have reached extremely high levels, both in number and value of deals.[4] In late 2006, Senator Charles Schumer and New York Mayor Michael Bloomberg argued that "while New York remains the dominant global-exchange center, we have been losing ground as the leader in capital formation."[5]

This article attempts to provide a context for evaluating arguments about the competitive position of U.S. stock markets. The tables and charts below present data that illustrate trends in global markets since 1995. The first set of data gives a sense of how the world's stock exchanges rank in size — in other words, where the competition lies. Subsequent tables set out data on new listings and delistings at the major exchanges, and on trends in international listings. Finally, the record in capital formation is examined: how much have firms raised on the major exchanges through IPOs, through follow-up stock offerings. Some data ongoing-private transactions are also presented.

Who are the Competitors?

The World Federation of Exchanges compiles statistics from 51 stock exchanges around the world. At the end of September 2006, the market value of shares listed on these exchanges was about $45.6 trillion, but this was not evenly distributed. There was a top tier of six exchanges, each with more than $3 trillion in market capitalization.[6] Two of these were American (the New York Stock Exchange (NYSE) and Nasdaq), two Japanese (the Tokyo and Osaka Stock Exchanges), and two European (the London Stock Exchange and Euronext).[7] These six accounted for $31.3 trillion in market capitalization, or 70.9% of the total.

There is a second tier of exchanges whose market capitalization fell between $1 trillion and $2 trillion: the Toronto Stock Exchange, the Deutsche Börse, the Hong Kong Exchanges, the BME Spanish Exchanges, and the Swiss Exchange. These five markets combined accounted for $6.7 trillion in market capitalization, nearly the same as the remaining 40 exchanges, which added $6.6 trillion, or 14.4% of the total. Table 1 and Figure 1 set out these figures.

All 51 markets are competitors, but when we think of global competition as framed by Senator Schumer and Mayor Bloomberg — a struggle to become (or remain) the world's financial capital — it makes sense to focus on the top tier, without ignoring the possibility that the second tier markets may rise to the level of global competitors, either through growth of the domestic corporate sector, merger with other exchanges, or cost-saving innovation. Indirect evidence for this assumption is provided by the recent behavior of the NYSE and Nasdaq, which have responded to competitive pressures by pursuing mergers with Euronext and the London Stock Exchange, respectively. This article will present data on the top tier markets, and on the second tier where it seems appropriate.

Table 1. Market Capitalization of Domestic Shares: September 2006

Exchange	Market Capitalization ($ in trillions)	Percent of Total
New York Stock Exchange	14.37	31.55
Tokyo Stock Exchange	4.42	9.70
Nasdaq	3.67	8.06
London Stock Exchange	3.44	7.55
Euronext	3.36	7.38
Osaka Stock Exchange	3.04	6.67
Subtotal	32.30	70.91
Toronto Stock Exchange	1.64	3.60
Deutsche Börse	1.43	3.14
Hong Kong Exchanges	1.36	2.99
BME Spanish Exchanges	1.15	2.52
Swiss Exchange	1.11	2.44
Subtotal	38.99	85.60
World Total	45.55	100.00

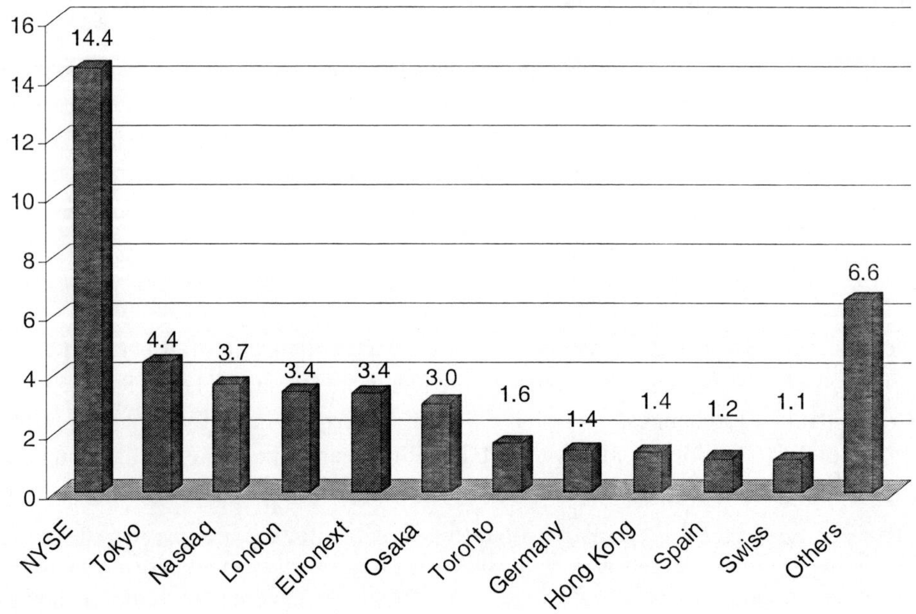

Source: World Federation of Exchanges.

Figure 1. Shares of Global Market Capitalization: September 2006

Trends in EXCHANGE Listings

When a corporation wishes to have its shares traded on an exchange, it applies to be listed. Exchange listing standards are not uniform, but generally include requirements regarding corporate governance practices, financial size or condition, number of shares available for trading, and minimum share price. In addition, listing on an exchange brings a company under the jurisdiction of the national securities regulator.[8] Other things being equal, therefore, an exceptionally onerous regulatory regime ought to discourage growth in the number of listings.

Table 2 presents figures on total exchange listings — both domestic and foreign companies — from the end of 1995 through September 2006, for the largest stock markets. Figure 2 rebases the same data as an index (the number of listings at the end of 1995 is set at 100), and shows the percentage change in the number of listed firms over the period. (Euronext is excluded from the chart, since it was formed by merger in 2000: Hong Kong is substituted.[9])

A glance at Figure 2 suggests that the major U.S. markets have not fared well over the last decade. NYSE listings have barely risen, while Nasdaq listings have fallen sharply. However, factors other than international competition may explain this. The fall in Nasdaq listings reflects the end of the "dot-com" bubble, when thousands of listed firms that had never made money (and that in retrospect probably never should have gone public) collapsed.

In the case of the NYSE, the stability of the listings figure before and after the bust makes it difficult to argue that any single factor, including the response to the Enron scandals, had a major impact. NYSE's listing policy appears to focus on quality rather than quantity — the exchange's annual financial statement for 2005 describes NYSE listing standards as "the most stringent of any securities marketplace in the world," and notes that "[a]ll standards are periodically reviewed to ensure that the NYSE attracts and retains the strongest companies with sustainable business models."[10] In other words, the NYSE may not see growth in the number of listings as a goal to be pursued for its own sake.

Table 2. Number of Companies (Domestic and Foreign) Listed on Seven Major Exchanges: 1995 — September 2006

Market	1995	1996	1997	1998	1999	2000	2001	2002	2003	2004	2005	2006
NYSE	2,242	2,476	2,626	2,670	3,025	2,468	2,400	2,366	2,308	2,293	2,270	2,257
Tokyo	1,791	1,833	1,865	1,890	1,935	2,096	2,141	2,153	2,206	2,306	2,351	2,368
Nasdaq	5,127	5,556	5,487	5,068	4,829	4,734	4,063	3,649	3,294	3,229	3,164	3,130
London	2,502	2,623	2,513	2,423	2,274	2,374	2,332	2,824	2,692	2,837	3,091	3,212
Euronext	NA	NA	NA	NA	NA	1,216	1,195	1,114	1,392	1,333	1,259	1,210
Osaka	1,222	1,256	1,275	1,272	1,281	1,310	1,335	1,312	1,140	1,090	1,064	1,070
Hong Kong	542	583	658	680	708	790	867	978	1,037	1,096	1,135	1,152

Source: World Federation of Exchanges.

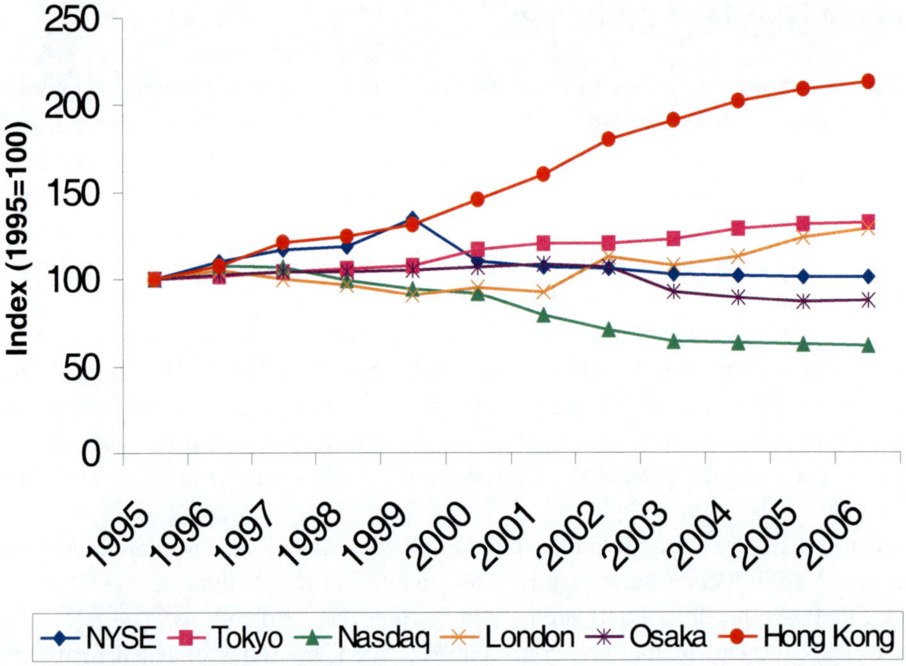

Source: World Federation of Exchanges.

Figure 2. Percentage Change Since 1995 in Listings

What of the markets where listings have increased during the past four years? Has their growth come at the expense of U.S. exchanges, or was it driven by events in those exchanges' home markets? The next set of figures breaks down listings on the leading exchanges into foreign and domestic companies.

Foreign vs. Domestic Listings

International cross listing is a fairly recent phenomenon. Until the late 1980s, only a handful of stocks traded on exchanges in more than one country. In September 2006, by contrast, the tabulation of the World Federation of Exchanges showed that of 40,888 total listings on global exchanges, 2,738 represented foreign companies.[11] Companies seek foreign listings for two reasons: better access to foreign capital markets and to seek a more liquid secondary (or resale) market for their shares, which aids capital formation in their home market.[12] Exchanges seek foreign listings as a source of fee income and for the prestige of being an international financial center.

Competition for foreign listings is intense and cost-driven.[13] How do the NYSE and Nasdaq compare to other major exchanges? Figure 3 shows the percentage of total listings on the major exchanges accounted for by foreign companies, at the end of 1995 (the earliest point in the World Federation of Exchanges data series), at the end of 2002 (shortly after the enactment of Sarbanes-Oxley), and at the end of September 2006.

Several features of Figure 3 are striking. First, international cross-listing is much more common in Europe than elsewhere, as might be expected given the historical economic interdependence of European states, and after more than a decade of economic integration policies.[14] In the Asian markets, on the other hand, nearly all listings are domestic. The trend over time is also interesting: in every market other than the U.S. exchanges, the percentage of foreign listings has fallen since 1995.[15] The decline is most pronounced in the U.K. and German markets, where the percentage of foreign listings was well above U.S. levels in 1995, but is now very similar. On the NYSE and Nasdaq, the percentage of foreign listings climbed between 1995 and 2002, and has since held steady.

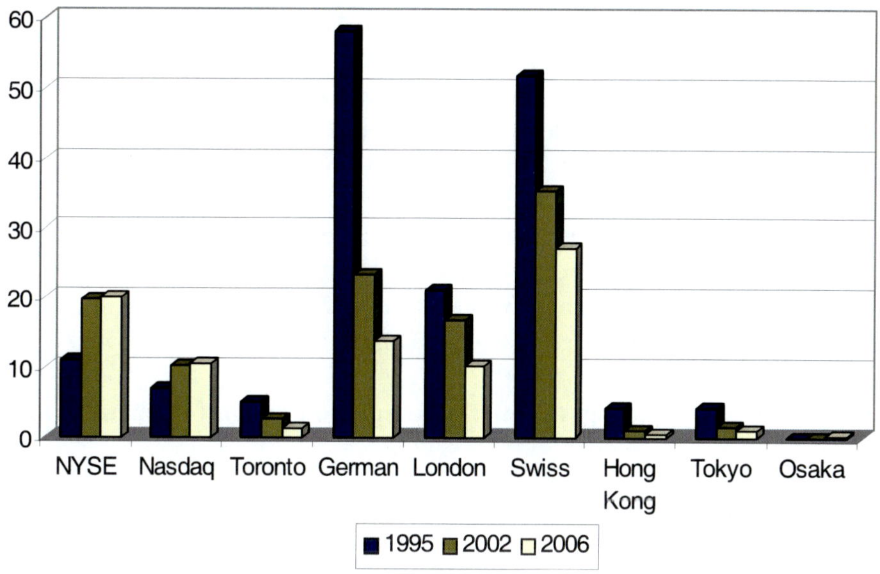

Source: World Federation of Exchanges.

Figure 3. Foreign Listings as a Percentage of Total: 1995, 2002, September 2006

The data in Figure 3 do not provide clear support for a claim that regulatory costs have driven foreign firms away from U.S. stock markets. One might argue that the percentage of foreign listings on Nasdaq and NYSE would have continued their upward trend had U.S. regulation not been tightened in 2002, but is that likely, given that foreign listings appear to be in decline on major markets around the world? A more natural inference from the data would be that Nasdaq and NYSE have remained competitive, since U.S. exchanges have retained foreign listings since 2002, while other markets have been losing them.

With the data in Figure 3 in mind, we might suppose that in the markets (shown in Figure 2) where total listings have risen faster than in the United States — Hong Kong, London, and Tokyo — growth was driven by new listings of domestic companies. In Table 3, which breaks out new foreign and domestic listings on the six largest markets, we can observe this process directly.

New Listings

The data in Table 3 show one common feature: a drop off in new listings after the peak of the bull market of the 1990s. In five of the six markets, there were fewer new listings in 2001 than in 2000. (The exception was the NYSE, where the decline began earlier and 2000 was the trough year.) This is the predictable result of a global bear market — trends and levels of stock prices affect the prices investors are willing to pay for new shares.

The decline in new listings is most dramatic on the Nasdaq and Euronext markets, probably because more highly speculative business ventures were taken public there than elsewhere.[16] There is no consistent pattern among the markets in the recovery from the crash.

Over the 11-year period shown in Table 3, London and Nasdaq are the clear leaders in the number of new listings, and particularly in domestic listings. Since the crash, however, the two markets have fared differently: London recorded record numbers during 2004 and 2005, while Nasdaq remains well below the peak levels of the late 1990s.

Both U.S. markets registered sharp drops in new listings during 2003, the year after Sarbanes-Oxley was enacted, despite the fact that stock prices (as measured by the S&P 500) rose 26% during that year. "Regulatory shock" might explain some of this, or it may be that firms took a wait-and-see attitude as to whether the recovery in stock prices from the trough in October 2002 would last. According to NASDAQ's 2005 Annual Report, "the fluctuation in the number of U.S. IPOs on The Nasdaq Stock Market from 2003 to 2005 was primarily due to market conditions. Over the past few years, competition for new listings has come primarily from the NYSE, although there is also strong international competition."[17] In 2004 and 2005, the number of new listings on both U.S. markets rose above the low figure of 2003.

Table 3. New Exchange Listings (Total, Domestic, and Foreign Companies): 1995-2005

Year	Nasdaq			NYSE			Tokyo			Osaka			Euronext			London		
	Total	Dom.	For.	Total	Dom.	For.	Total	Dom.	For.	Total	Dom.	For.	Total	Dom.	For.	Total	Dom.	For.
1995	476	413	63	173	138	35	32	32	0	27	27	0	28	22	6	330	285	45
1996	655	598	57	278	219	59	61	59	2	38	38	0	74	63	11	397	347	50
1997	648	573	75	273	210	63	51	50	1	27	26	1	121	110	11	254	217	37
1998	487	437	50	205	162	43	57	54	3	13	13	0	287	266	21	202	169	33
1999	614	553	61	151	123	28	75	75	0	24	24	0	119	102	17	187	161	26
2000	605	486	119	122	62	60	206	203	3	61	61	0	108	98	10	399	366	33
2001	144	123	21	144	93	51	93	92	1	55	55	0	49	36	13	245	236	9
2002	121	NA	NA	151	118	33	94	94	0	41	41	0	18	15	3	201	193	8
2003	56	53	3	107	91	16	120	120	0	26	26	0	24	14	10	201	194	7
2004	170	147	23	152	132	20	153	152	1	30	30	0	32	20	12	423	413	10
2005	139	117	22	146	127	19	99	98	1	27	26	1	34	32	2	626	605	21

Note: Euronext figures before 2001 represent the sum of new listings on the Brussels, Amsterdam, and Paris markets.

Source: World Federation of Exchanges.

Comparing Tables 2 and 3 makes clear that the increase in total listings is considerably less than the number of new listings. New listings are offset by delistings, which are set out in Table 4.

Delistings

Table 4 shows no consistent pattern in delisting trends among the six top-tier exchanges between 1995 and 2005. Nasdaq delistings peaked in 1998 and 1999, before the end of the boom; the NYSE peak was a year or two later. Neither market shows an increase in delistings subsequent to 2002.

Table 4. Delistings on Selected Exchanges, 1995-2005

Year	Nasdaq	NYSE	Tokyo	Osaka	Euronext	London
1995	79	136	23	4	63	258
1996	121	98	19	4	97	320
1997	717	171	19	8	94	235
1998	906	194	32	16	88	292
1999	873	254	30	15	100	336
2000	700	286	45	32	124	299
2001	815	215	48	30	140	287
2002	535	145	82	65	99	261
2003	410	111	67	198	82	337
2004	322	107	53	80	67	279
2005	332	135	54	53	65	372

Note: Euronext figures before 2001 represent the sum of delistings on the Brussels, Amsterdam, and Paris markets.

Source: World Federation of Exchanges.

In 2005, 1,011 companies were delisted by the top six exchanges. The exchanges do not publish statistics on the reasons for delisting. Nasdaq and NYSE annual reports provide some information, however. Nasdaq reports that delistings occur for three primary reasons:

- failure to meet listing standards (generally minimum financial criteria);
- mergers and acquisitions, where all of the target company's shares are purchased by another firm (or traded for shares in the merged company); and
- switching to another venue.[18]

Of the 332 firms that ceased listing on Nasdaq during 2005, 85 (25.6%) had failed to comply with minimum share price or other financial criteria, or had failed to file required SEC disclosures on time, which is also grounds for automatic delisting.[19] The NYSE reports a similar percentage: between 2000 and 2005, 27% of all delistings involved failure to maintain the minimum financial criteria required for continued listing.[20]

Of the nearly three-quarters of delistings that happened for reasons other than financial distress, most involved a change of ownership or a change in the form of ownership. This includes several forms of transactions:

- mergers and acquisitions, where two firms become one;
- leveraged buyouts, where a firm's management or outside investors purchase all publicly traded shares in a listed company and take it private; and

- "going dark" transactions, where a company voluntarily delists itself from a major exchange and has its shares traded instead on the over-the-counter, or "pink sheets" market. The firm thus becomes exempt from SEC reporting requirements.

These forms of "voluntary" delistings are where regulatory costs are most likely to be a factor. The next section analyzes trends in mergers and going-private deals and the possible role of Sarbanes-Oxley costs.

Mergers, Leveraged Buyouts, Going Private, Going Dark. In most large corporate mergers, the consolidated firm remains a public company. Thus, regulatory compliance costs are not eliminated, though they may be reduced as a percentage of earnings if two public companies merge into one. Basic data about the corporate merger market, presented in Table 5, do not support an inference that Sarbanes-Oxley costs are a major factor in the volume of deals. The number and reported value of deals increased each year between 2002 and 2005, but remained below the figures for 1998 through 2001, when soaring stock prices encouraged mergers in which target company stockholders received stock in the acquiring firm rather than cash payments for their shares.

Table 5. Completed Mergers and Acquisitions, 1996-2005

Year	Number of Deals	Value ($ in billions)
1996	7,347	563.0
1997	8,479	771.5
1998	10,193	1,373.8
1999	9,173	1,422.9
2000	8,853	1,781.6
2001	6,296	1,155.8
2002	5,497	625.0
2003	5,959	521.5
2004	7,031	857.1
2005	7,298	980.8

Source: Thomson Financial. (Only deals worth more than $10 million are included, and dollar figures include only deals for which price data was made public.)

Table 6. Leveraged Buyouts, 1996-2005

Year	Number of Deals	Value ($ billions)
1996	189	20.1
1997	192	15.4
1998	186	22.3
1999	197	28.7
2000	305	51.2
2001	153	18.9
2002	163	24.8
2003	164	41.4
2004	327	82.0
2005	450	117.4

Source: Thomson Financial. (Only deals worth more than $10 million are included, and dollar figures include only deals for which price data was made public.)

One of the benefits to corporations involved in leveraged buyouts, a subset of corporate mergers in which all public shares are purchased and taken off the market, is the elimination of SEC compliance costs. This market has shown rapid growth since 2001, as shown in Table 6. How much of the rise can be attributed to increased regulatory costs? Several studies have addressed this question by attempting to measure changes in the propensity of U.S. firms to go private before and after Sarbanes-Oxley. Kamar, Karaca-Mandic, and Talley find that small firms were induced to leave the public markets, but that large firms were unaffected.[21] Engel, Hayes, and Wang find a "modest but statistically significant increase in the rate at which firms go private in the post-SOX period," with the effect more pronounced among smaller firms.[22] Other researchers address the difficulty of separating the impact of regulatory costs from other factors:

> Because buyouts occur for many reasons, and SEC disclosures to shareholders in public companies will focus on the value of the consideration to be received compared to current market values, it is difficult to determine what role the costs of compliance with SOX and other securities laws played in these decisions.[23]

An important factor behind the increase in leveraged buyouts is the rise of the private equity market. Private equity investors purchase companies, either private or public, and seek to improve operating results by restructuring or by providing capital. The activity is not new, but is now a more significant factor in the market than ever before. The growth has been driven by institutional investors searching for higher returns. Yields on both debt and equity investment in the public markets have been depressed over the past several years: blue-chip stock indexes remained below 2000 levels until the fall of 2006, while both long- and short-term interest rates have been low by historical standards. At the same time, there has been a "glut" of international capital seeking investment opportunities, making capital abundant at low interest rates.[24] As a result, "alternative" investments have thrived, including private equity funds.

In short, the boom in mergers and private equity has been produced by a combination of economic factors and market conditions. The boom continued in 2006, as a recent Business Week article attests:

> [W]hat's driving this year's merger mania is quite different from what prompted AOL to plop down $182 billion for Time Warner Inc. in 2000. That boom was fueled by inflated stock prices in an overheated equities market that made companies feel like they were playing with funny money. This time the drivers are low interest rates, low valuations, and robust debt markets. One telling difference: 60% of this year's deals have been paid for in cash, vs. 29% in 2000.... The biggest change, though, is the unprecedented heft of private equity firms. Morgan Stanley estimates that buyout shops are now armed with at least $2 trillion in purchasing power, far more than ever before. The number of public-to-private deals in 2006 is set to nearly double the number in 2000, to 205, while their value has soared more than tenfold, says Paul J. Taubman, global head of M&A at Morgan Stanley. Yet there's still plenty of room for the boom to continue. Many companies still look cheap.[25]

Preliminary figures indicate that the value of companies taken private in 2006 reached a record level: $150 billion worldwide, with former NYSE listings representing $38.8 billion; London, $27 billion; and Nasdaq, $11 billion.[26]

Another way a public firm can shed its SEC reporting burden is by "going dark." In this process, firms voluntarily give up their exchange listing and deregister with the SEC.[27] They do not entirely abandon the public markets; their shares continue to trade on the over-the-counter (or "pink sheets") markets. Several studies have linked Sarbanes-Oxley costs to the growing number of going-dark transactions in recent years.[28]

However, firms that go dark are not a representative cross section of listed companies. The studies find that they tend to have serious financial problems (which might have led to an involuntary delisting by the exchange). In addition, Leuz, Triantis, and Wang find evidence that "controlling insiders go dark to protect their private control benefits and decrease outside scrutiny, particularly when corporate governance is weak and outside investors are less protected."[29]

Healthy firms rarely go dark because there is typically a strong negative market reaction. Thus, even if the causal link between rising regulatory costs and going-dark transactions is robust, the competitive position of U.S. markets may not suffer as a result: firms going dark are unlikely to be subject to international competition for listing.

IPOs and Capital Formation

The discussion above has focused on the number of companies listing on U.S. and competing international exchanges, but listing trends are only part of the picture. The basic economic function of a securities market is to intermediate between savers and businesses seeking investment capital. The capacity of an exchange to facilitate capital formation is also an indicator of its competitive position.

One of the most frequent claims regarding the declining competitiveness of U.S. markets is that they now handle a much smaller share of the world's initial public offerings than they once did. Of particular concern is the fact that of the 25 largest IPOs in the world in 2005, only one took place on an American exchange. Have rising regulatory costs driven U.S. firms abroad in search of equity capital, or have foreign firms that might have considered a U.S. offering gone elsewhere?

To begin with the first question, an examination of the 25 largest IPO deals (set out in Table 7) suggests that the answer is no. The only firm on the list domiciled in the United States listed its shares on the NYSE.

Table 7 is dominated by French (five) and Chinese (four) IPOs. Most of these deals, including the China Construction Bank Corporation, the China Shenhua Energy Limited, the Bank of Communications, the China COSCO Holding Company, and France's Electricite de France, Gez de France, Sanef, and Eutelsat, were privatizations of huge state-owned enterprises. It seems unlikely that the French or Chinese governments would look favorably on a foreign listing for these firms.

The table indicates that most of the IPO firms chose to list their shares on domestic exchanges. For example, all the Chinese firms listed on the Hong Kong Stock Exchange and all of the French firms listed on Euronext. The same holds true for the Austrian, Australian, Danish, Dutch, German, and Japanese firms.[30]

It may be noteworthy that the exceptions to this pattern — the two companies from Russia and Kazakhstan — chose to list in London. Regulatory considerations may have been a factor in this choice. Did the NYSE or Nasdaq seek to obtain these listings?[31]

Table 7. The Largest Global IPOs in 2005 (in millions of U.S. $)

Company	Domicile	Industry	Proceeds	Primary Exchange Listing
China Construction Bank Corp.	China	Banks	9,227	Hong Kong
Electricite de France	France	Energy and Power	8,200	Euronext
Gaz de France	France	Energy and Power	4,128	Euronext
China Shenhua Energy Ltd.	China	Mining	3,276	Hong Kong
Bank of Communications	China	Banks	2,165	Hong Kong
Tele Atlas N.V.	Netherlands	High Technology	1,946	Euronext
Partygaming	Gibraltar	Professional Services	1,658	London
Goodman Felder Ltd.	Australia	Consumer Stables	1,599	Australia
AFK Sistema	Russia	High Technology	1,593	London
Huntsman Corp.	U.S.	Materials	1,593	New York
Raiffeisen International Bank	Austria	Financials	1,456	Vienna
Premiere AG	Germany	Media and Entertainment	1,354	Frankfurt
SUMCO Corp.	Japan	High Technology	1,346	Tokyo
China COSCO Holdings	China	Marine Transport	1,227	Hong Kong
Spark Infrastructure Group	Australia	Energy and Power	1,223	Australia
Telenet Holding NV	Belgium	Telecommunications	1,190	Euronext
RHM	UK	Consumer Staples	1,171	London
Kazakhmys	Kazakhstan	Energy and Power	1,166	London
EFG International	Switzerland	Financials	1,097	Swiss Exchange
Sanef	France	Industrials	1,088	Euronext
SP Ausnet	Australia	Energy and Power	1,057	Australia
Eutelsat	France	Telecommunications	1,030	Euronext
EuroCommercial Properties	France	Real Estate	1,026	Euronext
TrygVesta	Denmark	Financials	1,008	Copenhagen

Source: Ernst & Young.

Table 8 presents more comprehensive statistics on the IPO market, showing the value of equity offerings on the six top-tier exchanges and Hong Kong (a second-tier exchange that appears several times in Table 7). Total equity issues include both IPOs and sales of new stock by established public companies.

These figures show considerable year-to-year volatility, reflecting not only the variability of stock prices (which affect the attractiveness of equity sales as a means of raising capital) but also the skewing of single-year data by the presence (or absence) of a few very large transactions. The ratio of IPOs to offerings by established public companies also shows great variation from year to year, probably reflecting the impact of large individual transactions in either category.

Preliminary data suggest that 2006 was a record year for IPOs, with global underwriting exceeding $250 billion.[32] Russian and Chinese firms accounted for just over a quarter of this total. IPO value on Euronext was up 60% (to $24.5 billion) over 2005, and doubled on the Deutsche Börse (to $8.8 billion). IPOs on the NYSE raised a total of $25 billion in proceeds (excluding closed-end mutual funds) in 2006. There were 18 IPOs by non-U.S. companies, raising $6.5 billion.[33] The NYSE continues to be a big fish, but the IPO pond is growing.

The most visible international trend is that all markets show a significant drop in equity underwriting in 2000 or 2001, with the end of the bull market.[34] The performance of the two U.S. exchanges since that time is markedly different: Nasdaq underwritings remain far below the boom levels — 2005 equity issues were less than 10% of the 2000 peak. On the NYSE, by contrast, the 2005 figure was 78% of the 2000 level.

The post-2000 recoveries in equity issuance on the European exchanges have been strong; London experienced only a mild drop-off and reached a record high in 2004, while Euronext in 2005 recorded 75% of its 2000 peak, very similar to the NYSE experience.

What does Table 8 suggest about the competitiveness of U.S. markets? The most striking fact is the dominance of the NYSE as a market for new equity. Its $175 billion in 2005 underwriting was more than double that of the nearest competitor, and in fact accounted for 29.3% of total *global* equity issues. However, the argument is made that the degree of supremacy is diminishing — in 1996, the NYSE accounted for 38.3% of the value of global equity issues.[35]

Table 8. Value of Equity Offerings on Selected Stock Exchanges, 1996-2005 (dollars in billions)

Year	NYSE			Nasdaq			London			Euronext			Tokyo	Osaka			Hong Kong		
	IPO	Other	Total	IPO	Other	Total	IPO	Other	Total	IPO	Other	Total	Total	IPO	Other	Total	IPO	Other	Total
1996	50.0	111.0	161.0	24.1	27.7	51.8	16.7	14.0	30.7	NA	NA	NA	19.0	NA	NA	NA	4.0	8.9	12.9
1997	43.9	133.7	177.6	11.0	25.2	36.2	11.6	10.7	22.3	NA	NA	NA	9.5	NA	NA	NA	10.5	21.1	31.6
1998	43.7	112.7	156.4	13.8	19.7	33.5	6.6	10.8	17.4	NA	NA	NA	11.8	NA	NA	NA	0.8	4.2	5.0
1999	71.4	129.5	200.9	50.4	53.5	103.9	7.4	16.0	23.4	NA	NA	NA	89.2	NA	NA	NA	2.2	17.0	19.2
2000	73.3	149.7	223.0	52.6	80.8	133.4	14.8	21.3	36.1	49.4	38.0	87.4	16.7	NA	NA	NA	17.0	60.0	77.0
2001	28.5	49.3	77.8	7.8	24.0	31.8	7.8	21.0	28.8	32.1	45.3	77.4	16.9	NA	NA	NA	3.3	8.0	11.3
2002	27.2	60.2	87.4	NA	NA	4.5	8.1	26.3	34.4	3.5	32.5	36.0	15.7	0.1	2.2	2.3	6.7	7.5	14.2
2003	27.4	54.2	81.6	NA	NA	6.4	7.8	22.6	30.4	0.7	50.5	51.2	29.0	0.1	4.9	5.0	7.6	19.9	27.5
2004	54.5	93.4	147.9	NA	NA	15.0	13.8	18.6	32.4	11.7	33.2	44.9	25.9	0.3	5.2	5.5	12.5	23.7	36.2
2005	44.1	130.9	175.0	NA	NA	12.2	31.2	20.7	51.9	21.2	44.7	65.9	24.6	0.3	6.2	6.5	21.3	17.0	38.3

Source: World Federation of Exchanges. (Tokyo figures are not broken down into IPOs and follow-on offerings.)

Several factors underlie the growing share of equity issuance going to foreign markets. Many countries in the world did not have well-developed equity markets until recently; these include not only China and Eastern Europe, but also France, Germany, and other continental European states where corporate finance was historically dominated by universal banks. Economic liberalization has provided an impetus for the development of equity financing, and computer technology has made it possible to replicate the sophisticated trading mechanisms of the New York and London exchanges at relatively low cost.[36] Markets have also expanded rapidly in the high-growth emerging economies of Asia and Latin America.

In short, the fact that U.S. stock exchanges are losing market share in global equity trading may reflect positive developments elsewhere, rather than impediments imposed here by regulatory and other burdens. NYSE and Nasdaq have certainly not been complacent in the face of rising competition. On the contrary, they have taken steps like the following:

- pursued mergers with major foreign exchanges (NYSE with Euronext, Nasdaq with London);[37]
- invested heavily in new trading technology to compete with alternative trading systems (cheap, computerized transaction facilities); and
- restructured themselves as for-profit, shareholder-owned corporations, in part to prevent entrenched exchange constituencies (such as the NYSE specialists) with a financial stake in the status quo from blocking innovations needed to remain competitive.

Finally, while equity markets have been an important locus for capital formation for U.S. businesses, they are only part of the larger securities market. Corporations seeking investment funds have many options, and in recent years of low interest rates they have turned increasingly to the bond markets. Figure 4 shows annual dollar figures for U.S. corporate underwriting between 1996 and November of 2006. Total underwriting, which measures funds going directly to firms issuing securities, has shown a fairly steady rise throughout the period, suggesting that costs related to the Sarbanes-Oxley Act's tightening of securities regulation have not materially harmed U.S. businesses' ability to raise funds in securities markets.

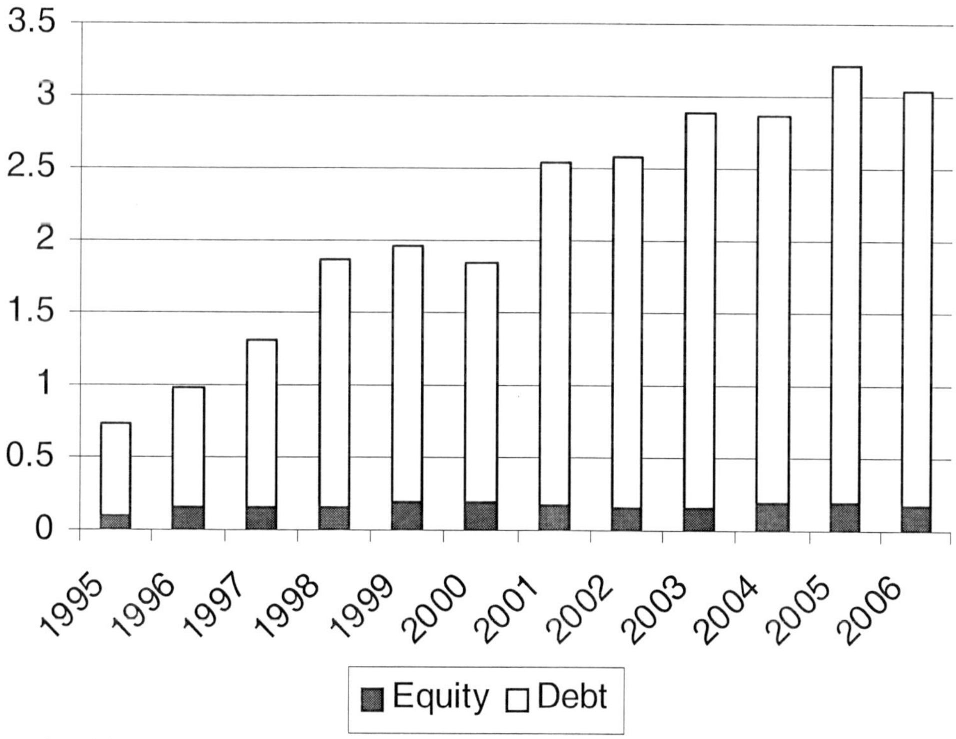

Source: Securities Industry Association.

Figure 4. U.S. Corporate Underwriting, 1995-October 2006

Conclusion

This article has not attempted to make a direct measurement of the impact of Sarbanes-Oxley compliance costs on firm behavior in the equity markets. Instead, the data presented above seek to provide a context for evaluating claims that such costs have put U.S. stock markets at a competitive disadvantage. There have been three developments in recent years that might plausibly be attributed (at least in part) to rising regulatory costs:

- over the past decade, the total number of listed companies on U.S. exchanges has fallen (in the case of Nasdaq) or failed to grow (in the case of the NYSE), while several foreign exchanges (notably Hong Kong, Tokyo, and London) have experienced significant growth in listings;
- there has been a boom in the number and size of going-private transactions, which result in firms being taken off the public markets and outside the SEC's regulatory jurisdiction; and
- the share of global IPO volume handled by U.S. markets has fallen, especially among the very largest deals.

However, there are alternative explanations for each of these phenomena, based on market conditions and global economic trends:

- The drop in Nasdaq listings must be viewed in the context of the aftermath of the 1990s bubble, when thousands of technology firms were taken public even though they had no real prospects of ever turning a profit. The NYSE's stable listings figure, on the other hand, may be due to a policy of maintaining stringent listing standards that exclude all but the largest and most financially sound corporations.
- The private equity boom has been driven by market forces including the availability of relatively abundant and inexpensive debt financing, the pressure on pension fund managers and other institutional investors to seek returns higher than those offered since 2000 by traditional investment classes, and the high compensation levels earned by private equity managers.[38] Research has indicated that rising regulatory costs have a discernible impact on going-private decisions primarily among small firms, particularly those with financial or governance problems.
- Growth in foreign equity underwriting appears to reflect growth in foreign economies (such as China's) and/or the development of equity markets in countries that historically relied on bank financing (such as Germany). Corporations continue to show a strong preference for listing on their domestic market, or the closest major financial center. The data do not suggest that many U.S. firms are choosing to list on foreign exchanges, or that foreign firms have abandoned U.S. markets in significant numbers since Sarbanes-Oxley was enacted.

The impact of Sarbanes-Oxley costs is difficult to measure, but quantification of the benefits is even more elusive. It is worth noting, however, that international competition among stock markets has not up to now taken the form of a regulatory "race to the bottom," in which markets attempt to lure companies by offering a more lax regulatory regime than their competitors. There is no equivalent in equity markets to the offshore banking centers and tax havens that thrive in small jurisdictions like the Dutch Antilles, the Isle of Man, or Vanuatu. This fact reflects a market judgment that investor confidence, which is nurtured by the perception that exchanges and regulators devote significant resources to the prevention of fraud, has real economic value. Where stock market growth has been fastest, as in London and Hong Kong, the securities regulators are generally recognized as capable and vigorous.

The outcome of global stock market competition has different implications for different market participants. If U.S. issuers and traders go overseas, to take advantage of lower regulatory or other costs, the U.S. securities industry will suffer a loss of output and jobs. That industry is concentrated heavily in the greater New York area and, to a lesser extent, Chicago. The cost to the U.S. economy of such a shift, however, would be partially offset by lower trading and underwriting costs, which would mean higher returns for public investors and more efficient business investment spending. To the investors and businesses who use the market, the ranking of the U.S. securities industry in the world market is of secondary importance. If U.S. markets remain competitive, both the industry and its customers can continue to thrive. The United States has been (and continues to be) the world leader in the adoption of new, cost-saving technology and in the elimination of anti-competitive market structures and practices. International market trends over the past several years do not provide strong evidence that a serious loss of competitiveness has occurred, or that such a loss is inevitable unless regulatory costs are reduced

Endnotes

1 For an overview of criticisms, see Henry N. Butler and Larry E. Ribstein, "The Sarbanes-Oxley Debacle: How to Fix It and What We've Learned," Mar. 13, 2006, available at [http://www.aei.org/events/filter.all,eventID.1273/summary.asp].

2 Throughout this report, "public" is used to describe companies that sell their securities to the general public (and thereby come under SEC regulation) and the markets where those securities are traded. "Private" (or "privately held"), on the other hand, refers to corporations that do not report to the SEC because their stock is not available for sale to small investors.

3 See, e.g., Committee on Capital Markets Regulation, *Interim Report*, Nov. 30, 2006, at [http://www.capmktsreg.org/research.html], which argues that "the growth of U.S. regulatory and compliance costs compared to other developed and respected market centers" is "certainly one important factor" in the loss of U.S. competitiveness, (p. x.)

4 Remarks by Treasury Secretary Henry M. Paulson on the Competitiveness of U.S. Capital Markets to the Economic Club of New York, Nov. 20, 2006, available online at [http://www.ustreas.gov/press/releases/hp174.htm].

5 Charles E. Schumer and Michael R. Bloomberg, "To Save New York, Learn From London," *Wall Street Journal*, Nov 1, 2006, p. A18.

6 The market capitalization figures cover domestic companies only, because inclusion of foreign listings would cause double counting.

7 Euronext was formed in 2000 by a merger of the Paris, Brussels, and Amsterdam markets, and absorbed the Lisbon stock exchange in 2002.

[8] For foreign firms, the full range of regulation does not necessarily apply: foreign companies listing on U.S. exchanges, for example, are subject to more stringent reporting requirements when they are raising capital in U.S. markets (i.e., selling new securities to U.S. investors) than if they are simply seeking a venue for secondary trading of shares issued elsewhere.

[9] For other second tier exchanges, consistent data is also a problem: the Canadian, Spanish, and German markets all underwent mergers since 1995.

[10] NYSE Group, Inc., *2005 10-K Report*, p. 8.

[11] See the monthly statistics archive at [http://www.world-exchanges.org]. Note that because a single company may be listed on multiple exchanges, the 2,738 listings represent a smaller number of cross listing firms.

[12] Other things equal, investors will pay a premium for securities that can be resold quickly and inexpensively.

[13] For example, the NYSE has proposed to eliminate listing fees for companies transferring from other markets. See NYSE Group, Inc., "NYSE to Eliminate Listing Fee Applicable to Issuers Transferring from Other Markets," Press Release, Nov. 29, 2006.

[14] Euronext and the BME Spanish exchanges are excluded because consistent and comparable data are not available over the period. The September 2006 percentage of foreign listings on Euronext is 21.2%, but the meaning of "domestic" is not plain where several national exchanges have consolidated.

[15] Actually, the percentage of foreign listings in Osaka rose, but only from zero to 0.1%.

[16] This assumes that the bulge in Euronext listings between 1997 and 2000 is the result of IPO activity, rather than acquisition of new listings through merger with other exchanges. The WFE data do not make this distinction.

[17] Nasdaq, *2005 Annual Report*, p. 9.

[18] Nasdaq describes the third reason as occurring "to a lesser extent." Ibid., p. 10.

[19] Ibid., p. 24.

[20] NYSE Group, Inc., *2005 10-K Report*, p. 8.

[21] Ehud Kamar, Pinar Karaca-Mandic, and Eric L. Talley, "Going-Private Decisions and the Sarbanes-Oxley Act of 2002: A Cross-Country Analysis," USC CLEO Research Paper No. C06-5, August 2006, 60 p.

[22] Ellen Engel, Rachel M. Hayes, and Xue Wang, "The Sarbanes-Oxley Act and Firms' Going-Private Decisions," May 6, 2004, p. 3. Available at SSRN: [http://ssrn.com/abstract=546626]

[23] William J. Carney, "The Costs of Being Public After Sarbanes-Oxley: The Irony of 'Going Private,'" Emory Law and Economics Research Paper No. 05-4, February 2005, p. 13.

[24] See CRS Report RL33140, *Is the U.S. Trade Deficit Caused by a Global Saving Glut?* by Marc Labonte.

[25] Emily Thornton, "What's Behind the Buyout Binge: Merger Monday," *Business Week*, Dec. 4, 2006, p. 38. See also the Committee on Capital Market Regulation's *Interim Report* for discussion of the growing liquidity in the private equity market, with the development of secondary trading of limited partnership interests (pp. 34-38).

[26] Peter Smith and Norma Cohen, "Record $150bn of Delistings," *Financial Times*, Jan. 2, 2007, p. 1.

[27] In order to deregister, firms must have had fewer than 300 shareholders of record (or fewer than 500 shareholders *and* less than $10 million in assets) for the preceding three years. When deregistration is complete, the firm ceases filing financial statements with the SEC.

[28] Christian Leuz, Alexander J. Triantis, and Tracy Yue Wang, "Why do Firms go Dark? Causes and Economic Consequences of Voluntary SEC Deregistrations," Robert H. Smith School Research Paper No. RHS 06-045, March 2006, 58 p. and: Engel, Hayes, and Wang, "The Sarbanes-Oxley Act and Firms' Going-Private Decisions."

[29] "Why do Firms Go Dark? Causes and Economic Consequences of Voluntary SEC Deregistrations," p. 3.

[30] Ernst & Young, which compiled the list, states that the Chinese Government played a role in encouraging firms to list on the Hong Kong Stock Exchange, in order to bolster the firms' good governance credentials. See Ernst & Young, "Accelerating Growth," *Global IPO Trends 2006*, February 2006, p. 15.

[31] A search of periodical databases yields no hint that they did. (Kazakhmys stock trades in the United States on the over-the-counter "pink sheets" market, suggesting that it might not meet Nasdaq listing standards.) On the other hand, the London Stock Exchange appears to have pursued listings from ex-Soviet countries energetically: "More than 40 Russian companies attended a London Stock Exchange 'roadshow' last year. Several are tipped to seek listings in the coming months, including Open Investments, owned by Vladimir Potanin, the Norilsk Nickel billionaire." See Conal Walsh, "Russia's 'Google' aims for London share listing," *The Observer* (London), Jun. 12, 2005, p. 2.

[32] Norma Cohen and Peter Smith, "Upsurge in IPOs and Private Deals," *Financial Times*, Jan. 2, 2007, p. 15. In the authors' view, U.S. regulation does not account for the "relative decline in popularity of U.S. exchanges." Rather, they argue, "companies domiciled outside the U.S. increasingly look to their maturing home markets, or to the largest capital market closest to them, as a listing venue of choice."

[33] NYSE Group, Inc., "2006 Highlights," Press Release, Dec. 29, 2006.

[34] In securities markets, underwriting refers to the process by which companies raise capital by selling (also called issuing) stocks or bonds to investors. This is also known as the primary market, as distinguished from the secondary (or resale) market, where investors trade securities among themselves and the company that originally issued the securities does not share in the proceeds.

[35] Global totals from World Federation of Exchanges, annual statistics archive.

[36] Cheap computer technology has inspired many predictions of the imminent demise of the NYSE over the past decade or so.

[37] In fact, the mergers are driven in large part by the European markets' need to cut their trading costs to U.S. levels, rather than U.S. markets' fear of competition. See "Finance and Economics: A War on Two Fronts; Stock Exchanges," *Economist*, vol. 381, Nov. 18, 2006, p. 92.

[38] Andrew Ross Sorkin and Eric Dash, "Private Firms Lure CEOs with Top Pay," *New York Times*, Jan. 8, 2007, p. A1.

In: Global Stock Exchanges: Stability, Interrelationships... ISBN: 978-60692-184-5
Editor: Paolo B. Cassedes

Chapter 7

ESTIMATION OF VALUE AT RISK FOR HETEROSCEDASTIC AND HEAVY-TAILED ASSET TIME SERIES: EVIDENCE FROM EMERGING ASIAN STOCK MARKETS*

Tzu-Chuan Kao[1] and Chu-Hsiung Lin[2]
[1]Department of Finance and Banking, Kun Shan University, Taiwan
[2]Department of Risk Management and Insurance, National Kaohsiung First University of Science and Technology, Taiwan

Abstract

We propose a two-stage approach for estimating Value-at-Risk (VaR) that can simultaneously reflect two stylized facts displayed by most asset return series: volatility clustering and the heavy-tailedness of conditional return distributions over short horizons. The proposed method combines the bias-corrected exponentially weighted moving average (EWMA) model for estimating the conditional volatility and the extreme value theory (EVT) for estimating the tail of the innovation distribution. In particular, for minimizing bias in the estimation procedure, the proposed method makes minimal assumptions about the underlying innovation distribution and concentrates on modeling its tail using the non-parametric Hill estimator and uses the moment-ratio Hill estimator for the shape parameter of the extreme value distribution. To validate the model, we conducted an empirical investigation on the daily stock market returns of eight emerging Asian markets: China, India, Indonesia, Malaysia, Philippines, South Korea, Taiwan, and Thailand. In addition, the proposed method was compared with J.P. Morgan's RiskMetrics approach. The empirical results show that the proposed method provides a more accurate forecast of VaR for lower probabilities of VaR violation from 0.1% to 1%. Furthermore, we demonstrate that applying the Hill estimator to estimate the tail of the innovation distribution can better capture additional downside risk faced during times of greater fluctuation than the second-order moment-ratio Hill estimator.

---

* A version of this chapter was also published in *Progress in Nonlinear Analysis Research,* edited by Erik T. Hoffmann published by Nova Science Publishers, Inc. It was submitted for appropriate modifications in an effort to encourage wider dissemination of research.

Keywords: Value-at-Risk, bias-corrected EWMA estimator, Extreme value theory, Hill estimator, Moment-ratio Hill estimator

1. Introduction

To ensure a stable financial system, it is important to identify and measure market risk accurately, and to control it. According to the Capital Adequacy Directive produced by the Bank of International Settlement in Basle (Basle Committee, 1996), the risk capital of a bank must be sufficient to cover losses on the bank's trading portfolio over a 10-day holding period on 99% of occasions. The value of risk capital is referred to as Value at Risk (VaR). From a statistical standpoint, VaR is defined as the possible maximum loss over a given holding period with a fixed confidence level. Hence, the VaR at the $100(1-\alpha)$ percent confidence level is the lower 100α percentile of the return distribution. Thus, the VaR is estimated on the basis of the distribution of the expected returns. This entails that one needs to make assumptions concerning the form of the expected return distribution. However, ad-hoc assumptions about the form of return distribution will generate a biased estimate of the VaR. To provide the investment community and risk managers with a more accurate VaR model, this study provides a two-stage approach for reducing the estimation bias that may result from a misspecified model and applies it to the stock market returns of eight emerging Asian markets.

In the literature, we find three approaches to estimating the return distribution (McNeil and Frey, 2000). First, there is the *non-parametric historical simulation method*, in which the actual empirical distribution is considered using observations of past returns as a basis. The method is easy to implement and avoids misspecifications of the form of the return distribution. However, when using it, it is difficult to estimate the extreme VaR quantiles (Beder, 1995; Pritisker, 1997; Danielsson and de Vries, 1997). Second, there are *fully parametric methods* that are based on an econometric model of time varying volatility and that assume conditional normality for the returns. Examples of these methods are J.P. Morgan's RiskMetrics[1], and GARCH-type models. GARCH-type models capture the effects of volatility clustering in the returns, but have the weakness that the assumption of conditional normality does not seem to hold for actual return distributions (Baillie and DeGennaro, 1990; Poon and Taylor, 1992; Danielsson and de Vries, 1997). Third, there are *methods based on extreme value theory* (EVT). EVT-based models model the tails of the return distribution directly and thus have the potential to yield better estimates and forecasts of extreme VaR. However, given the conditional heteroscedasticity of asset return data, EVT-based models cannot reflect the conditional volatility (McNeil and Frey, 2000; Cotter, 2001). A number of authors have attempted to alleviate the weaknesses of each of the above approaches. Barone-Adesi et al. (1998) combine the GARCH model with an historical simulation method to estimate the VaR. They fit a GARCH model to a return series and then apply an historical simulation to infer the distribution of the innovations. McNeil and Frey (2000) estimate the VaR by filtering return series with a GARCH model and then apply

[1] The RiskMetrics approach uses a EWMA model to forecast conditional volatility. Notice that the EWMA model can be viewed as a special case of the simple GARCH model. See the JP Morgan Bank RiskMetrics Technical (1996).

threshold methods from EVT to fit the innovations distribution. McNeil and Frey's (2000) study indicates that the method proposed by Barone-Adesi et al. (1998) may work well for large data sets, but for smaller data sets, threshold methods from EVT can give better estimates of the tails of the residuals. Recently, Gencay et al. (2003), Byström (2004), and Kuester et al. (2006) have demonstrated that McNeil and Frey's (2000) method can yield accurate estimates of the VaR.

In practice, the most widely used approach estimating the VaR is J.P. Morgan's RiskMetrics (Deloitte Touche Tohmatsu, 2002). The RiskMetrics approach to calculating the VaR assumes that returns are conditional normal and uses an exponentially weighted moving average (EWMA) model to forecast conditional volatility. The main advantage of the EWMA model is the simplicity of the estimation procedure with a small number of available observations. However, Harris and Shen (2004) indicate that the EWMA model implicitly assumes that the conditional distribution of real returns is normal, if as is suggested by empirical evidence, the conditional distribution is heavy-tailed, the EWMA estimator will be inefficient.

Taking into account the foregoing, the study presented herein extends the work of McNeil and Frey (2000) and proposes a two-stage approach for estimating the VaR. The proposed method combines the bias-corrected EWMA model proposed by Harris and Shen (2004) for estimating the conditional volatility and EVT for estimating the tail of the innovation distribution. Unlike the methods of J.P. Morgan's RiskMetrics and McNeil and Frey (2000), the two-stage approach presented here possesses two advantages: (a) it can simultaneously reflect two stylized facts that are displayed by most asset return series, namely, volatility clustering and the heavy-tailedness of conditional return distributions over short horizons; and (b) it can minimize the bias in the estimation procedure. These advantages are gained because the proposed method makes minimal assumptions about the underlying innovation distribution and concentrates on modeling its tail using a non-parametric Hill estimator (Hill, 1975) and uses a moment-ratio Hill estimator (Danielsson et al., 1996) for the shape parameter of the extreme value distribution.

In an empirical investigation, the proposed two stage approach was used to measure the downside risk for daily stock market returns of eight emerging Asian markets: China, India, Indonesia, Malaysia, Philippines, South Korea, Taiwan, and Thailand. In addition, the proposed method was compared with the RiskMetrics approach from J.P. Morgan. To assess the predictive performance of the different methods, the study employed a backtesting procedure, which included the test of predictive versus theoretical violation probability, Kupiec's (1995) unconditional coverage testing, and Christofferson's (1998) conditional coverage testing.

The remainder of this paper is organized as follows. Section 2 presents the theoretical foundations used to estimate the downside risk. Section 3 describes the stylized fact of the empirical data. Section 4 presents the empirical results. Section 5 concludes.

2. Methodology

The following subsections (i) describe the bias-corrected EWMA model proposed by Harris and Shen (2004), which was used to measure the conditional volatility; (ii) describe the non-parametric Hill estimator (Hill, 1975) and moment-ratio Hill estimator (Danielsson et al.,

1996) based on EVT for estimating the tail index of the innovations distribution; and (iii) present the backtesting procedure.

2.1. An Alternative VaR Model

Let ($X_t, t \in Z$) be a stationary time series that presents daily observations of the log return on a financial asset price. This study assumes that the dynamics of X are given by:

$$X_t = \mu_t + \sigma_t Z_t \tag{1}$$

where the innovations Z_t are a white noise process with zero mean and unit variance and are independent and identical according to a distribution function $F_Z(z)$ (i.e. iid). This study assumes that the conditional mean μ_t and the conditional standard deviation σ_t are measurable with respect to I_{t-1}, where I_{t-1} is the set of all information through time *t-1*. From Equation (1), the time *t* quantile, x_q^t, can be derived for a given probability level *q*. Therefore, x_q^t is defined such that $q = P(X_t \le x_q | I_{t-1}) = F_{X_t|I_{t-1}}(x_q)$, where $F_X(x)$ denotes the cumulative probability distribution of X_t. Using Equation (1) the probability level *q* can be rewritten as

$$\begin{aligned} q &= P\{\mu_t + \sigma_t Z_t \le x_q | I_{t-1}\} \\ &= P\{Z_t \le (x_q - \mu_t)/\sigma_t | I_{t-1}\} \\ &= F_Z\{(x_q - \mu_t)/\sigma_t\} \ (2) \end{aligned} \tag{2}$$

If the quantile associated with the distribution $F_Z(z)$ is denoted as z_q, namely $z_q = (x_q - \mu_t)/\sigma_t$, the time *t* quantile (or the time *t* VaR at the $100(1-q)$ % confidence level), x_q^t, can be calculated as

$$x_q^t = \mu_t + \sigma_t z_q \tag{3}$$

Via Equation (3), x_q^t is obtained and must estimate μ_t, σ_t, and z_q. To measure x_q^t this study proposes a two-stage approach. The first stage uses the equal-weight moving-average approach to estimate μ_t and applies the bias-corrected EWMA estimator to estimate σ_t. The second stage uses the Hill estimator (Hill, 1975) and moment-ratio Hill estimator based on EVT to estimate z_q. The following subsections detail the proposed two-stage approach.

2.1.1. First Stage: Estimating μ_t and σ_t

For predictive purposes, a rolling window of 500 observations was used to dynamically estimate conditional mean μ_t and conditional standard deviation σ_t. First, this study considers using the equal-weight moving-average approach to estimate the conditional mean μ_t.

$$\mu_t = \sum_{n=1}^{500} x_{t-n} \Big/ 500 \tag{4}$$

Sequentially, this study considers that the conditional variance σ_t^2 follows the bias-corrected EWMA model proposed by Harris and Shen (2004). The EWMA model, known as an integrated GARCH or IGARCH model, is used to estimate the conditional variance σ_t^2 because it relies on one parameter only and thus facilitates estimation. The EWMA estimator is given by:

$$\sigma_t^2 = \lambda\sigma_{t-1}^2 + (1-\lambda)X_{t-1}^2 \tag{5}$$

where the parameter λ is called the decay factor and must be less than unity. The empirical study set $\lambda = 0.94$, which is the value used by RiskMetrics to estimate daily volatility. The EWMA estimator is based on the maximum likelihood estimator of the variance of the normal distribution; hence, if the EWMA model is misspecified, it will generate biased conditional variance forecasts. To generate bias-corrected conditional variance forecasts, Harris and Shen (2004) first estimate the conditional bias in the EWMA model using a realized volatility regression with squared returns, and then apply the estimated regression parameters to obtain new bias-corrected conditional variance forecasts. The theoretical framework for the estimation is detailed in Theil (1966), Mincer and Zarnovitz (1969), and Harris and Shen (2004). The estimation process is summarized as follows:

Step 1: Use Equation (5) to obtain the forecasts of conditional variance $\hat{\sigma}_t^2$.

Step 2: Use the realized volatility measured by the squared returns (X_t^2) and the conditional variance forecasts ($\hat{\sigma}_t^2$) to construct a regression model, as follows:

$$X_t^2 = a + b\hat{\sigma}_t^2 + v_t \tag{6}$$

where v_t denotes the error term. Equation (6) is widely used in the literature on volatility modeling to evaluate the explanatory power of a particular conditional variance model and to correct conditional variance forecasts (Theil, 1966; Mincer and Zarnovitz, 1969). In order to correct the bias of conditional variance forecasts that are generated by the EWMA model, we need to estimate the parameters a and b.

Step 3: Once we have estimated parameter $\hat{a}$ and $\hat{b}$, we can define a new bias-corrected conditional variance forecasts, $\hat{\hat{\sigma}}_t^2$ given by

$$\hat{\hat{\sigma}}_t^2 = \hat{a} + \hat{b}\hat{\sigma}_t^2 \quad (7)$$

2.1.2. Second Stage: Estimating z_q

Following McNeil and Frey (2000), this study assumes that the residuals distribution is not normal and that perhaps it has heavy tails or is leptokurtic. Therefore this study used EVT to model the tail of the residuals distribution and applied this EVT model to estimate z_q. EVT investigates the distribution of tail observations in large samples. In the limit, the shape of the tail follows a Pareto law for a general class of heavy-tailed distributions. The tail fatness of the distribution is characterized by the tail index. As indicated by Dewachter and Gielens (1999) and Cotter (2001), for minimizing model risk, the Hill non-parametric method for estimating the tail index is superior to parametric procedures that require assumptions about the exact distribution type of extreme values. Consequently, this study applies a non-parametric Hill estimator (Hill, 1975) and moment-ratio Hill estimator (Danielsson et al., 1996) to estimate the tail index of residuals distribution and z_q. The process used to estimate z_q is presented below.

This study assumes that the standardized residuals series $(z_{t-n}, z_{t-n+1}, \ldots, z_{t-1}) = \left(\frac{x_{t-n} - \hat{\mu}_{t-n}}{\hat{\sigma}_{t-n}}, \ldots, \frac{x_{t-1} - \hat{\mu}_{t-1}}{\hat{\sigma}_{t-1}}\right)$ follow an extreme value distribution with a tail-index parameter γ and applies the Hill estimator to estimate γ, the desired quantile z_q can be estimated by:

$$\hat{z}_q = z_{(m+1)}\left(\frac{1-q}{m/n}\right)^{-\gamma}. \quad (8)$$

Let $z_{(i)}$ denote the ith decreasing order statistic of the absolute standardized residuals such that $z_{(i)} \geq z_{(i+1)}$ for $i = 2,\ldots,n$. Specifying m as the number of tail observations, the tail estimator γ proposed by Hill (1975) is obtained as follows:

$$\gamma = \frac{1}{m}\sum_{i=1}^{m} \ln z_{(i)} - \ln z_{(m)} \quad (9)$$

For simplicity, we follow Quintos et al. (2001) and set the threshold m to be 10% of the sample size.

In addition, Danielsson et al. (1996) propose a generalization of the Hill estimator, the so-called *k*-order moment-ratio Hill estimator, to estimate the tail index of the distribution. They point out that the moment-ratio Hill estimator has a lower asymptotic bias than the Hill estimator. Moreover, Wagner and Marsh (2004) demonstrate that a second-order moment-ratio Hill estimator performs better. Therefore this study also uses a second-order moment-ratio Hill estimator, ω_2, to estimate the tail-index parameter γ.The *k*-order moment-ratio Hill estimator is given by

$$\omega_k(z_{(m)}) = \frac{\phi_k(z_{(m)})}{k\phi_{k-1}(z_{(m)})} \qquad k = 1,2,... \tag{10}$$

where $\phi_0(z_{(m)}) = 1$ □ $\phi_k(z_{(m)}) = \frac{1}{m}\sum_{i=1}^{k}(\ln z_{(i)} - \ln z_{(m)})^k$. When k=1, the first-order moment-ratio Hill estimator ω_1 is equal to the Hill estimator (Hill, 1975).

Finally, we substitute $\hat{\mu}_t$, $\hat{\sigma}_t$ and $\hat{z}_q$ into Equation (3). Then, the forecasted time t VaR at $100(1-q)\%$ condition level, $\hat{x}_q^t$, is given by

$$\hat{x}_q^t = \hat{\mu}_t + \hat{\hat{\sigma}}_t \hat{z}_q \tag{11}$$

2.2. Backtesting VaRs

To assess the predictive performance of the different risk models and obtain a robust evaluation result, this study employed three backtesting methods, as follows:

First, this study used the test of predictive versus theoretical probability that a VaR violation will occur that is recommended by the Basle Committee of Banking Supervision. Using each of risk models for estimating VaR, given different probabilities that a VaR violation[2] q^* will occur, this study forecasts the daily VaR. These forecasts of the VaR are then compared with the actual returns on the days in question and the number of days on which the actual returns exceed the forecasted VaR is counted. The number of such days, *N*, is called the number of exceedences. The predictive probability that a VaR violation will occur can then be obtained using the number of exceedences divided by the total number of observed returns, *T*. If the predictive probability that a VaR violation will occur that is estimated by a particular risk model is close to the theoretical probability, the risk model in question may be said to perform well for estimating VaRs.

Second, this study used the unconditional coverage test developed by Kupiec (1995). The unconditional coverage hypothesis states that the probability that a VaR violation will occur that is obtained for a particular risk model, call it q, is significantly different from the given

[2] A VaR violation occurs when the actual returns exceed the forecasted VaR.

probability that a VaR violation q^* will occur. Namely, $H_0 : q = q^*$. The likelihood ratio (LR) statistic is

$$LR_{uc} = -2\ln\left[(1-q^*)^{T-N}(q^*)^N\right] + 2\ln\left\{[1-(N/T)]^{T-N}(N/T)^N\right\} \sim \chi^2(1) \quad (12)$$

The LR_{uc} test statistic has a chi-squared distribution with one degree of freedom.

Third, this study used the conditional coverage test developed by Christofferson (1998). The conditional coverage hypothesis is to simultaneously test whether the VaR violations are independent and the average number of violations is correct. Namely, $H_0 : \pi_{01} = \pi_{11} = q^*$. The LR statistic is

$$LR_{cc} = -2\ln(L_A - L_I) \sim \chi^2(2) \quad (13)$$

$$L_A = (1-q^*)^{T-N}(q^*)^N$$

$$L_I = (1-\pi_{01})^{T_{00}}(\pi_{01})^{T_{01}}(1-\pi_{11})^{T_{10}}(\pi_{11})^{T_{11}}$$

$$\pi_{ij} = T_{ij}/(T_{i0} + T_{i1})$$

where T_{ij}, i, j = 0, 1 is the number of times state j follows state i, state 0 denotes an actual return less than the forecasted VaR, and state 1 denotes an actual return that exceeds the forecasted VaR. The LR_{cc} test statistic has a chi-squared distribution with two degrees of freedom.

3. Data Description

To verify the performance of the proposed approach, we conducted an empirical investigation that examined the daily stock market indices of eight emerging Asian markets (China, India, Indonesia, Malaysia, Philippines, South Korea, Taiwan, and Thailand[3]) for the period August 23, 1991 to August 23, 2007. The daily returns were measured by the first difference of the natural logarithm of the stock market index. The dataset was downloaded from Datastream.

Table 1 lists the preliminary statistics of the returns for the eight stock markets. The mean returns for the entire period are almost zero. According to the standard deviation for the returns,

[3] The names of the eight emerging Asian stock market indices are as follows: (1) China: Shanghai SE Composite Price Index (2) India: India BSE National Price Index (3) Indonesia: Jakarta SE Composite Price Index (4) Malaysia: KLCI Composite Price Index (5) Philippines: Philippine SE Price Index (6) South Korea: Korea SE Composite Price Index (7) Taiwan: TSEC Weighted Index (8) Thailand: Bangkok S.E.T. Price Index.

Table 1. Summary statistics of the daily returns for eight emerging Asian stock markets

Statistics	China	India	Indonesia	Malaysia	Philippines	South Korea	Taiwan	Thailand
Mean	0.0004	0.0005	0.0005	0.0002	0.0003	0.0002	0.0002	0.0000
Maximum	0.1522	0.1664	0.1313	0.1492	0.1618	0.0898	0.0617	0.1135
Minimum	-0.1401	-0.1194	-0.1273	-0.1424	-0.0974	-0.1280	-0.0698	-0.1606
Std. Dev.	0.0221	0.0162	0.0152	0.0138	0.0147	0.0182	0.0151	0.0167
Skewness	0.0378	0.0473	0.0114	0.3799	0.5894	-0.1578	-0.1017	0.1949
Kurtosis	10.5611	10.7223	12.5916	19.1659	13.2976	6.5508	5.0820	9.8330
Jarque-Bera [a]	9550.72*	10375.36*	15494.22*	44317.97*	18267.50*	2230.79*	778.79*	7918.29*
ADF [b]	-34.14	-58.43	-53.14	-53.75	-53.87	-60.68	-62.06	-57.45
Ljung-Box Q(6) [c]	43.94*	62.73*	131.59*	66.96*	120.76*	131.59*	30.02*	52.42*
Ljung-Box $Q^2(6)$ [d]	1078*	497.24*	630.63*	1913.80*	2044.6*	871.09*	558.60*	592.84*
Observations	4009	4175	4042	4061	4081	4213	4271	4057

Note: * significant at 1% level

[a] Jarque-Bera is a test statistic for testing whether the series is normally distributed.

[b] ADF indicates augmented Dickey and Fuller (1979,1981) unit root tests for whether the series is stationary.

[c] Ljung-Box $Q(6)$ indicates the Ljung-Box Q-statistics at lag 6 by log return series, it is a test statistic for the null hypothesis that there is no autocorrelation up to order 6.

[d] Ljung-Box $Q^2(6)$ indicates the Ljung-Box Q-statistic at lag 6 by squared log return series, it is a test statistic for the null hypothesis that there is no autocorrelation up to order 6.

investing in firms that are listed on the Chinese stock market carries with it a higher risk than for the stock markets of other countries. The returns distributions are heavy-tailed or leptokurtic, as demonstrated by high kurtosis and highly significant Jargue-Bera statistics. The returns distributions for the South Korean and Taiwanese stock markets display a negative skewness, and for the stock markets of other countries they display a positive skewness. This implies that negative extreme returns are more likely to occur than the normal distribution forecasts in the stock markets of South Korea and Taiwan, while in other countries positive extreme returns are more likely to occur than the normal distribution forecasts. These findings indicate that the returns distributions for the eight emerging Asian stock markets can be characterized by fat-tailed distributions and that the left (or negative) and right (or positive) tails should be treated, respectively[4]. In addition, this investigation also reports the ADF statistics, which indicate that the eight emerging Asian stock market return series are stationary. Ljung-Box statistics for the returns themselves and for the squared returns are also presented. These statistics confirm that the empirical return series contains autocorrelation and volatility clustering, which suggests that the conditional modeling of short run returns is beneficial.

4. Empirical Results

To implement Equation (11), we used a moving window of 500 observations to measure dynamically the forecasts of the VaR given different probabilities of VaR violation, which range from 0.1% to 5%. The proposed two-stage approaches, the B-EWMA-Hill method and B-EWMA-moment-Hill method, were compared with RiskMetrics approach (named EWMA). The B-EWMA-Hill method combines the bias-corrected EWMA model with the Hill estimator, while the B-EWMA-moment-Hill method combines the bias-corrected EWMA model with the second-order moment-ratio Hill estimator. To assess the predictive performance of different VaR models, we used a backtesting procedure that included the test of predictive versus theoretical violation probability, Kupiec's (1995) unconditional coverage test and Christofferson's (1998) conditional coverage test.

Table 2 lists the empirical results for predictive versus theoretical probability that a VaR violation will occur. For all the emerging Asian stock markets, the B-EWMA-Hill method outperformed the other methods when the violation probabilities were below 1%. Furthermore, for violation probabilities of from 0.1% to 1%, the predictive probabilities that a VaR violation will occur that computed by RiskMetrics and the B-EWMA-moment-Hill method exceeded the theoretical probabilities and the predictive probabilities that a VaR violation will occur that were calculated using the B-EWMA-Hill method conditional were equal to or slight higher than the theoretical probabilities. As a result, the forecasts of VaR estimated by RiskMetrics and B-EWMA-moment-Hill methods have an underestimation bias and those estimated by the B-EWMA-Hill method have a slight underestimation bias. Consequently, using the B-EWMA-Hill method to measure VaR can capture the additional downside risk that is faced during times of greater fluctuation.

---

4 Although both the left and right tails of the return distributions are interesting from the perspective of risk management, we chose to focus solely on estimating the left tails of the return distributions to measure the downside risk for the eight emerging Asian stock markets

Table 2. Backtesting results: predictive vs. theoretical VaR violation probability

Country	Method	Theoretical VaR violation probability							
		0.05	0.025	0.01	0.005	0.004	0.003	0.002	0.001
China	EWMA	0.0568#	0.0369#	0.0202#	0.0127	0.0099	0.0091	0.0075	0.0067
	B-EWMA-Hill	0.0742	0.0472	0.0218	0.0115#	0.0075#	0.0060#	0.0044#	0.0024#
	B-EWMA-moment-Hill	0.0798	0.0580	0.0306	0.0187	0.0171	0.0147	0.0099	0.0060
India	EWMA	0.0557#	0.0347#	0.0232	0.0183	0.0157	0.0146	0.0101	0.0090
	B-EWMA-Hill	0.0706	0.0388	0.0198#	0.0086#	0.0078#	0.0064#	0.0045#	0.0026#
	B-EWMA-moment-Hill	0.0740	0.0489	0.0258	0.0157	0.0127	0.0112	0.0075	0.0034
Indonesia	EWMA	0.0535#	0.0366#	0.0228	0.0185	0.0161	0.0149	0.0138	0.0106
	B-EWMA-Hill	0.0704	0.0444	0.0200#	0.0106#	0.0079#	0.0059#	0.0031#	0.0016#
	B-EWMA-moment-Hill	0.0755	0.0507	0.0283	0.0145	0.0122	0.0102	0.0079	0.0028
Malaysia	EWMA	0.0503#	0.0355	0.0226	0.0191	0.0179	0.0152	0.0117	0.0097
	B-EWMA-Hill	0.0659	0.0339#	0.0160#	0.0074#	0.0051#	0.0039#	0.0023#	0.0012#
	B-EWMA-moment-Hill	0.0748	0.0452	0.0269	0.0144	0.0117	0.0105	0.0066	0.0035
Philippines	EWMA	0.0538#	0.0348#	0.0232	0.0151	0.0139	0.0124	0.0108	0.0085
	B-EWMA-Hill	0.0712	0.0418	0.0186#	0.0077#	0.0062#	0.0039#	0.0027#	0.0008#
	B-EWMA-moment-Hill	0.0763	0.0534	0.0294	0.0186	0.0143	0.0108	0.0077	0.0035
South Korea	EWMA	0.0622#	0.0350#	0.0206#	0.0125#	0.0099#	0.0092	0.0070	0.0044
	B-EWMA-Hill	0.0685	0.0468	0.0265	0.0133	0.0099#	0.0081#	0.0055#	0.0022#
	B-EWMA-moment-Hill	0.0700	0.0534	0.0343	0.0210	0.0177	0.0147	0.0118	0.0070
Taiwan	EWMA	0.0552#	0.0386#	0.0216	0.0155	0.0148	0.0133	0.0105	0.0076
	B-EWMA-Hill	0.0700	0.0433	0.0180#	0.0087#	0.0065#	0.0032#	0.0022#	0.0007#
	B-EWMA-moment-Hill	0.0765	0.0523	0.0296	0.0180	0.0141	0.0115	0.0069	0.0040
Thailand	EWMA	0.0449#	0.0297#	0.0156#	0.0106	0.0086	0.0078	0.0066	0.0051
	B-EWMA-Hill	0.0598	0.0344	0.0164	0.0074#	0.0047#	0.0039#	0.0031#	0.0012#
	B-EWMA-moment-Hill	0.0641	0.0426	0.0215	0.0117	0.0109	0.0078	0.0051	0.0035

Note: " # " indicates the predictive VaR violation probability is close to theoretical VaR violation probability.

Table 3. Backtesting results: unconditional coverage test statistics (LR_{uc})

Country	Method	Theoretical VaR violation probability							
		0.05	0.025	0.01	0.005	0.004	0.003	0.002	0.001
China	EWMA	2.3322#	12.8328	20.5967	21.0165	15.6769	20.4081	22.5960	36.0394
	B-EWMA-Hill	27.2845	40.6976	26.6352	15.6694	6.2865#	5.7034#	5.2696#	3.4576#
	B-EWMA-moment-Hill	40.1815	82.3225	69.5371	55.4481	59.3757	59.0054	40.3283	28.6257
India	EWMA	1.7439#	9.3104	34.1521	56.4215	52.5857	61.6824	44.2555	62.8056
	B-EWMA-Hill	21.3250	18.0694	20.1995	5.7073*	7.7441	7.5889	6.0941#	4.8180#
	B-EWMA-moment-Hill	28.3847	49.4017	46.8783	39.1355	32.1852	35.3166	23.5040	9.1945
Indonesia	EWMA	0.6273#	12.2273	30.9007	54.7617	52.9988	61.6270	75.5222	78.8775
	B-EWMA-Hill	19.8201	32.0895	20.0816	12.1644	7.4181	5.5564#	1.4202#	0.7093#
	B-EWMA-moment-Hill	30.2593	53.3971	57.5555	30.6866	27.5888	27.1362	25.0177	5.2662*
Malaysia	EWMA	0.0040#	10.2228	30.3326	59.4982	67.0299	64.3435	56.4484	69.1553
	B-EWMA-Hill	12.4116	7.5244	7.8412	2.5957#	0.6749#	0.6306#	0.1395#	0.0697#
	B-EWMA-moment-Hill	29.0789	34.8110	50.5695	30.2653	25.0341	29.3053	17.0415	9.7359
Philippines	EWMA	0.7724#	9.1644	33.2556	34.2991	38.7966	42.4901	49.1808	99.7529
	B-EWMA-Hill	21.7930	24.9928	15.3405	3.3433#	2.6715#	0.6004#	0.5867#	4.1445#
	B-EWMA-moment-Hill	32.5519	64.9135	64.6887	56.3411	41.3411	31.5975	24.5629	27.6823
South Korea	EWMA	7.9808	9.9086	23.6959	21.7377	16.9971	22.4688	20.5231	17.1286
	B-EWMA-Hill	17.6400	42.2164	51.4942	25.5575	16.9971	16.0811	11.3772	2.9496#
	B-EWMA-moment-Hill	20.4086	68.1483	98.9340	77.4215	68.8995	63.9844	60.6444	41.4626
Taiwan	EWMA	1.5148#	18.0584	28.4604	39.3763	47.7116	53.3724	49.2360	48.6991
	B-EWMA-Hill	20.8025	31.2905	14.5920	6.1042#	3.6306#	0.0545#	0.0363#	0.2391#
	B-EWMA-moment-Hill	35.4062	64.7873	70.3495	56.4709	42.5393	39.0618	19.9493	13.8857
Thailand	EWMA	1.4262#	2.1887	6.9963	11.9956	10.1922	13.7138	17.1067	21.4194
	B-EWMA-Hill	4.8713	8.2987	8.9058	2.6297#	0.2891#	0.6432#	1.3861#	0.0721#
	B-EWMA-moment-Hill	9.8557	26.9299	25.6872	16.8351	20.9485	13.7138	8.4972	9.7712

Note: The critical value of the LR_{uc} statistics at 1% significant level is 6.6349. "#" indicates test results not reject null hypothesis at 1% significant level.

Table 4. Backtesting results: conditional coverage test statistics (LR_{cc})

Country	Method	Theoretical VaR violation probability							
		0.05	**0.025**	**0.01**	**0.005**	**0.004**	**0.003**	**0.002**	**0.001**
China	EWMA	10.9224	22.0800	21.3435	21.6519	17.0067	22.0044	24.8468	38.6934
	B-EWMA-Hill	42.5895	42.6171	26.6726	16.3452	6.5754#	5.8831#	5.3662#	3.4862#
	B-EWMA-moment-Hill	52.0718	88.4909	69.7111	55.4652	59.4654	59.3231	41.6580	28.8054
India	EWMA	30.5209	25.0596	42.8937	62.5868	57.2685	67.1173	53.7739	73.7257
	B-EWMA-Hill	51.2713	38.0375	36.2947	23.5123	27.1014	22.8058	17.3364	4.8547#
	B-EWMA-moment-Hill	55.7928	73.6935	67.0903	51.6681	43.6462	48.7470	36.6623	14.4683
Indonesia	EWMA	20.8270	15.4334	37.3363	61.1549	61.2960	67.0755	81.8390	79.9883
	B-EWMA-Hill	47.9754	38.0748	22.7437	13.2753	7.7352#	5.7344#	1.4707#	0.7219#
	B-EWMA-moment-Hill	58.3914	66.8305	65.6353	36.4131	31.1858	28.3601	25.3347	5.3049*
Malaysia	EWMA	26.9185	39.8781	51.8354	77.1518	86.4028	82.9127	75.2672	85.2367
	B-EWMA-Hill	36.5472	28.5272	25.2184	4.8787#	4.3849#	5.3897#	7.0446#	0.0767#
	B-EWMA-moment-Hill	60.0595	51.1958	74.0748	40.1318	28.8857	33.9049	19.7286	14.9271
Philippines	EWMA	28.1307	28.7716	45.7548	43.4304	49.1232	54.6324	58.0770	101.5379
	B-EWMA-Hill	45.6153	51.5482	16.4065	10.2407	5.5964#	0.6782#	0.6247#	4.1476#
	B-EWMA-moment-Hill	58.7291	89.9826	77.5188	59.5942	41.6828	32.6242	26.6757	27.7453
South Korea	EWMA	7.9808#	9.9086	23.6959	21.7377	16.9971	22.4688	20.5231	17.1286
	B-EWMA-Hill	19.1412	46.0865	57.5430	31.9085	26.5940	22.4210	20.7926	2.9762#
	B-EWMA-moment-Hill	21.5149	72.8063	106.7779	84.6469	75.4326	73.0936	73.1556	48.9540
Taiwan	EWMA	19.2337	26.8263	30.1819	39.5255	47.9325	53.7853	49.8492	49.0197
	B-EWMA-Hill	36.7875	50.5594	15.6314	6.5234#	3.8659#	0.1131#	0.0623#	0.2420#
	B-EWMA-moment-Hill	50.0684	83.5100	76.5823	57.5103	42.8478	39.8093	20.2115	13.9733
Thailand	EWMA	5.4015#	4.8638#	11.9489	21.2636	21.9125	26.6115	25.2672	25.1242
	B-EWMA-Hill	12.6733	12.4725	13.3721	9.8975	4.3096#	5.3971#	7.0615#	0.0791#
	B-EWMA-moment-Hill	15.0062	33.9947	30.1047	24.8886	29.7933	26.6115	12.2021	14.9570

Note: The critical value of the LR_{cc} statistics at 1% significant level is 9.2103. "#" indicates test results not reject null hypothesis at 1% significance level.

To demonstrate that the proposed two-stage approach is reasonably accurate for estimating VaR, we also checked its validity systematically by backtesting, according to the procedures proposed by Kupiec (1995) and Christoffersen (1998). Kupiec's (1995) methodology is an unconditional coverage testing and Christoffersen's (1998) methodology is a conditional coverage testing. Their null hypothesis is that the risk model is correct. Thus, if the test statistics reject the null hypothesis, the proposed risk model is not adequate. The empirical results are presented in Tables 3 and 4. For all emerging Asian stock markets (the Indian and South Korean stock markets excepted), the B-EWMA-Hill method exhibit excellent results given probabilities of VaR violation from 0.1% to 1% because the unconditional and conditional coverage test statistics (i.e. LR_{uc} and LR_{cc}) fail to reject the null hypothesis in almost all cases. However, for the Indian and South Korean stock markets, the use of RiskMetrics, the B-EWMA-Hill method and the B-EWMA-moment-Hill method could not provide more accurate VaR forecasts. Given that the problem of estimating VaR is still related to the estimation of conditional volatility, the results suggest that the decay factor λ in the EWMA and bias-corrected EWMA models may vary across returns series and that the choice of decay factor may lead to variations in performance[5].

Summarizing the above findings, given lower probabilities of VaR violation, the B-EWMA-Hill method for measuring VaR is more accurate than the RiskMetrics and B-EWMA-moment-Hill methods. Furthermore, the results show that using the Hill estimator to estimate the tail of the innovation distribution can better capture the nature of downside risk than can the second-order moment-ratio Hill estimator.

5. Conclusions

Previous empirical research has found that combining the GARCH model and EVT to determine VaR can fully protect against default that results from volatility clustering and extreme price movements. The main contribution of the study reported herein is to provide a two-stage approach that incorporates the non-parametric Hill estimator and the moment-ratio Hill estimator based on EVT into a bias-corrected EWMA model for estimating VaR. This approach is especially appealing because it makes minimal assumptions about the underlying innovation distribution and concentrates on modeling its tail using the non-parametric Hill estimator and use the moment-ratio Hill estimator for the shape parameter of the extreme value distribution. Moreover, rather than using the RiskMetrics approach developed by J.P. Morgan, applying the bias-corrected EWMA model to estimate conditional volatility, as we have done, can reduce the misspecified model risk. The empirical study that involved the eight emerging Asian stock markets demonstrated the accuracy of the proposed approach.

For lower probabilities of VaR violation from 0.1% to 1%, the backtesting showed that the proposed B-EWMA-Hill method produces more accurate forecasts of VaR than the RiskMetrics and B-EWMA-moment-Hill methods. Thus, the proposed B-EWMA-Hill method can ensure adequate prudence for the setting of risk capital. Furthermore, we demonstrate that using the Hill estimator to estimate the tail of the innovation distribution can better capture the additional downside risk faced during times of greater fluctuation than the second-order moment-ratio Hill estimator.

---

[5] We set $\lambda = 0.94$.

References

Baillie, R. & DeGennaro, R. (1990). Stock Returns and Volatility. *Journal of financial and Quantitative Analysis*, **25**, 203-214.

Barone-Adesi, G., Boutgoin, F., & Giannopoulos, K. (1998). Don't Look Back. *Risk*, 11(8).

Base Committee on Banking Supervision (1996). Ammendment to the Capital Accord to Incorporate Market Risks. *Basle Report* **(24),** BIS.

Beder, T, S. (1995). Seductive but Dangerous. *Financial Analysis Journal*, September-October, 12-24.

Byström, H.N.E. (2004). Managing Extreme Risks in Tranquil and Volatile Markets Using Conditional Extreme Value Theory. *International Review of Financial Analysis*, **13**, 133-152.

Christoffersen, P. (1998). Evaluating Interval Forecasts. *International Economic Review*, **39**, 841-862.

Cotter, J. (2001). Margin Exceedences for European Stock Index Futures Using Extreme Value Theory. *Journal of Banking & Finance*, **25**, 1475-1502.

Danielsson, J., Jansen, D.W., & de Vries, C.G. (1996). The Method of Moments Ratio Estimator for the Tail Shape Parameter. *Communication in Statistics Theory and Methods*, **25**(4), 711-720.

Danielsson, J. & De Vires, C. G. (1997). Tail Index and Quantile Estimation with Very High Frequency Data. *Journal of Empirical Finance*, **4**, 241-257.

Dewachter , H. & Gielens, G. (1999). Setting Futures Margins: the Extremes Approach. *Applied Financial Economics*, **9**, 173-181.

Deloitte Touche Tohmatsu. (2002). *Global Risk Management Survey.*

Gencay, R., Selcuk, F., & Ulugülyağci, A. (2003). High Volatility, Thick Tails and Extreme Value Theory in Value-at-Risk Estimation. *Insurance: Mathematics and Economics*, **33**, 337-356.

Harris, R.D.F. & Shen, J. (2004). Estimation of VaR with Bias-Corrected Forecasts of Conditional Volatility. *Journal of Derivatives*, **11**(4), 10-20.

Hill, B.M. (1975). A Simple Approach to Inference About The Tail of A Distribution. *The Annals of Mathematical Statistics*, **3**, 1163-1174.

JP Morgan. (1996). Riskmetrics *TM* Technical Document. (4th ed), New York.

Kuester, K., Mittnik, S., & Paolella, M. S. (2006). Value-at Risk Prediction: A Comparison of Alternative Strategies. *Journal of Financial Econometrics*, **4**, 53-89.

Kupiec, P. (1995). Technique for Verifying the Accuracy of Risk Management Models. *Journal of Derivative*, 3, 73-84.

McNeil, A. & Frey, R. (2000). Estimation of Tail-Related Risk Measure for Heteroscedastic Financial Time Series: An Extreme Value Approach. *Journal of Empirical finance*, **7**, 271-300.

Mincer, J., & Zarnovitz, V. (1969). The Valuation of Economic Forecasts. In J. Mincer, ed., Economic Forecasts and Expectations. Cambridge: National Bureau of Economic Research.

Poon, S. H. & Taylor, S. J. (1992). Stock Returns and Volatility: An Empirical study of the UK Stock Market. *Journal of Banking and Finance*, **16**, 37-59.

Pritsker, M. (1997). Evaluating Value at Risk Methodologies: Accury versus Computational Time. *Journal of Financial Services Research*, **12**(3), 201-243.

Theil, H. (1966). Applied Economic Forecasting. Amsterdam: North Holland.

Quintos, C., Fan, Z., & Phillips, P. C. B. (2001). Structural Change Tests in Tail Behavior and the Asian Crisis. *Review of Economic Studies*, **68**, 633-663.

Wanger, N., & Marsh, T. A. (2004). Tail Index Estimation in Small Samples Simulation Results for Independent and ARCH-type Financial Return Models. *Statistical Paper*, **45**, 545-562.

In: Global Stock Exchanges: Stability, Interrelationships... ISBN: 978-60692-184-5
Editor: Paolo B. Cassedes

Chapter 8

CAPITAL ACCUMULATION IN LESS DEVELOPED COUNTRIES: DOES STOCK MARKET MATTER?*†

***Prabirjit Sarkar*‡**
Jadavpur University, Kolkata, India

Abstract

Our panel data analysis (1988-2002) of a sample of 31 less developed countries shows that the stock market capitalization as a percentage of GDP- an important indicator of stock market development- has no relationship with the growth rates of gross fixed capital formation. Our time series analysis (1976-2005) of 15 countries shows that in at least 10 cases we observe no positive long-run relationship between the stock market turnover ratio and the growth of capital accumulation. Interestingly the countries experiencing the developmental function of stock market are by and large civil law origin countries with alleged poor shareholder protection.

I. Introduction

In the present era of financial liberalisation under the aegis of the three pillars of the Bretton Woods system (IMF, World Bank and WTO) stock market development has been an important part of both internal and external financial liberalisation in the less development countries (LDCs). There is now a call for better corporate governance in order to protect the interests of the shareholders leading to stock market developments and capital accumulation. In a well-known paper La Porta *et al* (1998) – nicknamed LLSV - observed that countries with a 'common law origin' (such as UK) have a higher level of shareholder protection than countries with a civil law origin (such as France) and accordingly, the former group of

---

* A version of this chapter was also published in *Economics of Developing Countries,* edited by Tiago N. Calerira published by Nova Science Publishers, Inc. It was submitted for appropriate modifications in an effort to encourage wider dissemination of research.
† This is a revised version of the paper prepared with the help of CAS project fund (Economics Department, Jadavpur University).
‡ E-mail address: prabirjitsarkar@gmail.com

countries has a lower concentration of stock ownership. In a subsequent paper (Djankov *et al* 2005), the similar line of reasoning is used to explain a positive correlation between the level of shareholder protection and stock market developments. The question is: is there any link between stock market development and economic growth through capital accumulation?

There are many studies supporting the positive link between stock market development and growth. One important study was undertaken by Levine and Zervos (1998). Their cross-country study found that the development of banks and stock markets has a positive effect on growth. In another study Levine (2003) argued that although theory provides an ambiguous relationship between stock market liquidity and economic growth, the cross-country data for 49 countries over the period 1976-93 suggest a strong and positive relationship (see also Levine, 2001). Henry (2000) studied a sample of 11 LDCs and observed that stock market liberalisations lead to private investment boom. Recently, Bekaert *et al* (2005) analysed data of a large number of countries and observed that the stock market liberalisation 'leads to an approximate 1 % increase in annual real per capita GDP growth'. Arestis *et al* (2001) analysed time series data for 5 developed countries and found a favourable role of stock market along with bank in economic growth; but they observed that the favourable role of stock market is exaggerated in different cross-country studies.

There are some economists who are sceptical. Long time back Keynes (1936) compared the stock market with casino and commented: 'when the capital development of a country becomes the by-product of the activities of a casino, the job is likely to be ill-done'.

Referring to the study of World Bank (1993) Singh (1997) pointed out that stock markets have played little role in the post-war industrialisation of Japan, Korea and Taiwan. He argued that the recent move towards stock market liberalisation is 'unlikely to help in achieving quicker industrialisation and faster long-term economic growth' in most of the LDCs.

In this perspective we shall examine the relationship between stock market development and capital accumulation in the LDCs (Section II). We first undertake a panel data analysis of the experience of the LDCs. It will be followed by the time series study of individual country cases. Section III concludes.

II. Relationship between Stock Market Developments and Capital Accumulation

A. Panel Data Analysis

From World Bank (World Development Indicators, various issues – hereafter called WDI) source we obtained a series on stock market capitalization of listed companies (the aggregate market value of stocks of all the companies listed in the domestic stock market) as percentage of GDP (SMC) for 31 LDCs (the full list of countries is in the Appendix) covering 1988-2002 (for some countries we get data for shorter periods). In our study these SMC data are used to indicate the development of stock market in these countries. Since the channel through which stock market development is expected to influence growth is capital accumulation, we would like to examine the relationship between the two. From the above-mentioned source we collected data for the growth of gross domestic fixed capital formation (GKFG).

We have considered three alternative models between the growth of gross domestic fixed capital formation (GKFG) and stock market capitalization of listed companies as percentage of GDP (SMC): between-effects model (BE), the country-fixed effect model (FE) and the random-effect model (RE). The BE model is equivalent to taking the average (mean) of each variable for each case across time and running a regression on the data set of averages. As this averaging procedure results in loss of information, it is not used much in the current literature. Nevertheless we have estimated this BE model and did not observe any significant relationship between the two (details are skipped).

Table 1. Stock Market Development and Capital Accumulation in the Less Developed Countries, 1988-2002[1, 2]

Intercept	SMC	LPCY91	EDUSE	TRD-GDP	FDI-GDP	DCP-GDP	D	SD	R^2	LM Stat[3]
(a)	(b)	(c)	(d)	(e)	(f)	(g)	(h)	(i)		
5.02**	0.01								0.002	3.03
-4.03	0.003		0.18*	0.06	0.47	-0.16*			0.04	1.66
2.24	0.009	0.34							0.002	3.04
-0.68	0.02		0.15*		0.58	-0.11*			0.03	3.02
6.37**	0.02			0.02	0.43	-0.11*			0.02	5.15
4.64**	-0.01			-0.003	0.49				0.007	3.91
							(Dx)	(SDx)		
-2.42	-0.11		0.16*	0.05	0.53	-0.16*	1.58	0.11	0.05	0.57
							(Dy)	(SDy)		
-3.74	-0.01		0.18*	0.06	0.5	-0.16*	1.14	0.01	0.04	1.65
							(Dz)	(SDz)		
-4.53	0.02		0.22*	0.05	0.5	-0.17*	-4.02	-0.01	0.05	0.82
-0.87	-0.03		0.08	0.01	0.6				0.02	1.53

[1] The following equation is fitted:

Growth of Gross Domestic Capital Formation (GGKF)

= a + b. SMC + c. log (PCY91) + d.SE + e. TRDGDP + f.FDIGDP + g.DCPGDP + h.D + i.SD

where D is intercept dummy and SD is the slope dummy = D.SMC. We have used different alternative intercept dummies, Dx, Dy and Dz and SD (SDx, SDy and SDz varies accordingly: Dx = 0 for 15 LO-SMC LDCs with 1992-99 average SMC < 25 per cent and Dx = 1 for other 16 HI-SMC LDCs; Dy = 0 for 24 LDCs with SMC < 50 per cent and Dy = 1 for the seven VHI-SMC LDCs; Dz = 0 for 18 LDCs with 1991 per capita GDP < $ 5000 and = 1 for 13 other rich LDCs.

Setting one or more parameters (b to i) equal to zero, we have fitted alternative regression equations. Details of some of the regression equations are skipped, as the basic conclusion remains unchanged.

[2] Due to the non-availability of data on FDIGDP, DCPGDP and EDUSE, some of the years are deleted for some of the countries.

[3] The Breusch-Pagan Lagrange Multiplier (LM) test statistic is reported in this column.

* Significant at 5 per cent level.

**Significant at 1 per cent level.

The FE is designed to control for omitted variables that differ across countries but are constant over time. This is equivalent to generating dummy variables for each country-cases and including them in a standard linear regression to control for these fixed country-effects. The RE is used if there is a reason to believe that some omitted variables may be constant over time but vary between cases, and others may be fixed between cases but vary over time. The Breusch-Pagan Lagrange multiplier (LM) test has been conducted to choose the appropriate model. It supports the RE model in some cases and the FE model in some other cases. The Hausmann test gives different results not always tallying with the outcome of the LM test. Our conclusion, however, does not change irrespective of whether we choose an RE model or an FE model. We have reported the estimates of the RE model in all the cases (Table 1).

Our estimates show that the growth of capital accumulation has no significant (positive or negative) relationship with stock market capitalisation. The result does not change if we include the log values of 1991 GDP per capita (purchasing power parity constant 2000 international $), LPCY91 (obtained from the WDI source) in the regression to control for the influence of initial condition in the tradition of 'Barro regression' of convergence/catching up debate literature.

We have also considered other factors such as openness index (share of trade – export plus imports – in GDP, TRDGDP), the importance of foreign direct investment in GDP (FDIGDP) and the indicator of banking sector development as measured by the ratio of domestic credit provided to the private sector to GDP (DCPGDP), which may be expected to influence growth and capital formation (1992-99 averages of all these data are presented in the Appendix). Furthermore to accommodate the state of human capital development we have included educational factor – secondary school enrolment ratio (SE) in 2000 or 2001 (available from the same WDI source for 27 countries of our sample). Only this factor has been found to have a positive relationship with the growth of capital accumulation in many alternative models (fitted by changing the set of independent variables considered here). Surprisingly we got significant negative relationship between domestic credit (DCPGDP) and the growth of capital accumulation. But the basic conclusion of no relationship between stock market developments and capital accumulation remains.

This finding is important in view of the fact that the independent variables (expected to have positive relationships with capital accumulation) considered here have high positive correlations among themselves favouring the case for a positive relationship between GGKF and SMC. As we observed a negative relationship between DCPGDP and GGKF, we have dropped it from the set of independent variables and re-estimated the regression. Similarly many other alternative regressions are fitted (including or excluding a number of independent variables). Our basic conclusion remains (details are skipped).

In the next stage we have divided the sample into two groups – 'developed' and 'less developed' stock market - on the basis of the 1992-99 average values of SMC - 16 'HI-SMC' (SMC > 25 per cent) countries and 15 'LO-SMC' (others) countries. Within the HI-SMC group, we have made a further division – seven countries (Chile, Hong Kong, Jordan, Malaysia, Singapore, Philippines and Thailand) belong to the category of 'very highly developed stock market' ('VHI-SMC') with 1992-99 average SMC greater than 50 per cent. Remaining nine countries belong to the HI-SMC category (with SMC greater than 25 per cent and less than or equal to 50 per cent): Brazil, India, Indonesia, Jamaica, Korea, Mexico, Mauritius, Trinidad & Tobago and Zimbabwe.

We have used a binary variable intercept dummy (for example, intercept dummy = 1 for 'HI-SMC' and = 0 for 'LO-SMC') and/or slope dummy (intercept dummy multiplied by SMC) and observed that none of the dummies are significant. Similar is the outcome if we use dummies for the VHI-SMC group.

Furthermore our conclusion does not change if we use dummies for 13 rich countries (as indicated by higher than $5000 per capita GDP in 1991 – the countries belonging to this category are underlined in the Appendix). We have considered all the dummies or a sub-set of dummies with or without other independent variables (such as DCPGDP and/or FDIGDP etc). In no case do we find a significant relationship between GGKF and SMC.

B. Time Series Analysis

With this over-all picture of panel data analysis we set ourselves to examine individual country experiences. It is, however, very difficult to get a long time series data for different indicators of stock market development. From the Financial Structure Dataset of World Bank (available on-line) we have been able to collect annual data on the most important indicator of stock market development for 15 countries (out of 31 countries covered in our panel data study) since the mid-1970s (for some countries since the early 1980s). It is the turnover ratio (TURN) defined as the ratio of the value of total shares traded in a country's stock market to average real market capitalization.[1] We have collected the WDI data for the growth of gross capital formation (GKFG) for all these countries.[2] Our objective is to examine whether there is any meaningful long-run relationship between this indicator of stock market development (TURN) and the growth of capital accumulation (GGKF) for all these 15 LDCs over the period since the mid-1970s or early 1980s till 2005 for which we have the relevant data.

We shall use Autoregressive Distributive Lag (ARDL) approach to cointegration developed by Pesaran and Shin (1999) to test for the existence of a long run relationship between two variables irrespective of whether they are stationary or stochastic. This approach does not require any pre-testing of the variables to determine the order of their integration (how many times the data are to be differenced to achieve the stationary property of the data). This approach is especially useful here as the standard tests of stationarity have very low power for a small sample.

First, we shall include no other variables that are expected to influence capital accumulation. The following ARDL (p, q) model is fitted:

$$G_t = a + b.t + \sum_{i=1}^{p} b_i G_{t-i} + \sum_{j=0}^{q} c_j S_{t-j} \qquad (1)$$

where G is the growth rate of gross capital formation (GKFG), S is the stock market turnover ratio (TURN), t is the time trend which captures the effect of other explanatory variables (it is omitted from the ARDL equation when its coefficient is found to be insignificant), the

[1] Turnover Ratio (TURN) is the ratio of the value of total shares traded to average real market capitalization. It is calculated using the following method: $T_t/P\_a_t/\{(0.5)*[Mt/P\_e_t + M_{t-1}/P\_e_{t-1}]$ where T is total value of stock trading, M is stock market capitalization, P_e is the end-of period CPI, P_a is average annual CPI.

[2] For Korea we have calculated GKFG from the data on gross capital formation available in International Financial Statistics published by IMF.

subscripts t, t-i, t-j, indicate different time periods and p and q are unknown lags to be determined by Schwarz Bayesian criterion (SBC) as suggested by Pesaran and Shin (1999).

Table 2. Capital Accumulation and Stock Market Development: Estimates of Long-term Relationships through ARDL Method[1], 1976-2005

Country/Period (Model)	TURN	DCBGDP	FDIGDP	a	t
I. *HI-SMC Group*					
BRAZIL					
1977-2005 (0,0)	20.34			-8.42	
1977-2005 (0,0,0,0)	19.59	0.001	-0.48	-7.29	
CHILE					
1978-2005 (0,0)	64.95			4.77	
1978-2005 (4,3,4,3)	329.05**	0.3	-3.87**	-4.21	
INDIA					
1976-2005 (2,0)	0.58			-3.2	0.22*
1976-2005 (3,4,2,3)	-4.16*	0.41**	26.21**	14.48*	-0.75**
1976-2005 (2,1)[2]	-5.36			22.07**	
1976-2002 (4,3,4,1)[2]	-5.08	-1.24	10.43	10.43	
INDONESIA					
1977-2005 (0,0)	0.06			4.69	
1977-2005 (3,4,4,4)	-4149.5	110.05	-2488.2	-340.42	
JORDAN					
1977-2005 (1,0)	91.29**			-13.17**	
1977-2005 (1,0,0,0)	92.99**	-0.01	-0.22	-12.35	
KOREA					
1976-2005 (3,4)	-6.32*			15.31**	
1976-2005 (2,4)[3]	-1.23			11.49**	
1976-2005 (3,4,4,4)[4]	-12.79**	-0.04	25.25**	20.19**	
MALAYSIA					
1976-2005 (0,0)	16.17			1.99	
1976-2005 (0,0,0,0)	21.27	-0.24	1.21	26.31	
MEXICO					
1977-2005 (0,0)	3.38			0.93	
1977-2005 (0,0,1,0)	19.79*	-1.86**	-5.63	83.74	
PHILIPPINES					
1976-2005 (0,0)	29.77			-4.27	
1976-2005 (5,5,5,5)	203.92	0.79	-10.42	-70.15	
THAILAND					
1976-2005 (0,1)	28.74*			37.14	-1.15*
1976-2005 (0,1,0,0)	21.76*	-0.21	-2.71	18.23	
ZIMBABWE					
1980-2005 (2,0)	-116.58**			10.35**	
1980-2005 (4,2,3,4)	-58.7	-0.72	4.35	37.41	

Table 2. Continued

Country/Period (Model)	TURN	DCBGDP	FDIGDP	a	t
II. *LO-SMC Group*					
ARGENTINA					
1977-2005 (0,0)	24.37			-3.49	
1977-2005 (1,0,2,4)	24.41	-0.63	2.61	18.45	
PAKISTAN					
1984-2005 (1,0)	-1.22**			4.12**	
1984-2005 (1,1,2,3)	0.43	0.39	-3.61	-13.76	
PERU					
1981-2005 (3,0)	38.31*			-2.46	
1981-2005 (4,4,4,4)	-119.96	-4.36	-10.01	134.28	
VENEZUELA					
1977-2005 (2,0)	69.08*			-5.81	
1977-2005 (3,1,0,0)	71.04**	1.12*	2.19	-134.53*	1.99

[1] The following ARDL (p, q, r, s) model has been fitted:

$$G_t = a + b.t + \sum_{i=1}^{p} b_i G_{t-i} + \sum_{j=0}^{q} c_j S_{t-j} + \sum_{k=0}^{r} d_k F_{t-k} + \sum_{l=0}^{s} e_l B_{t-l}$$

where G = GKFG, S =TURN, F = FDIGDP and B = DCBGDP; the subscripts t, t-i, t-j, t-k, t-l, indicate different time periods and p, q, r and s are unknown lags to be determined by the SBC.

Setting the coefficients such as b, d_k and e_l (for all k, l) we have fitted alternative ARDL equations such as ARDL (p, q), ARDL (p, q, r, s) with or without time trend.

[2] Instead of GGKF data we used data on growth of private fixed capital formation, GPGKF.

[3] Intercept dummy, D97 is added to the ARDL equation; it is 0 for 1976-96 and =1 for 1997-05. Its estimate is -8.95 significant at 10 per cent level.

[4] We have used intercept dummy (D97) and/or slope dummy (SD97=D97*t) and observed that the basic conclusion holds.

** Significant at 1 per cent level (based on asymptotic standard errors).

* Significant at 5 per cent level (based on asymptotic standard errors).

The estimates of the long-term coefficients are reported in Table 2. Estimates show that for 4 countries (2 from HI-SMC group: Jordon and Thailand and 2 from LO-SMC group: Peru and Venezuela) a positive long-run relationship exists between stock market development (indicated by turnover ratio, TURN) and capital accumulation (GGKF).

For three countries, Korea, Zimbabwe and Pakistan we find negative relationships! For all others there is no significant relationship.

Next we have extended the ARDL analysis to accommodate other factors that are often expected to influence the growth of capital accumulation such as domestic credit provided by the banking sector (relative to GDP), DCBGDP and foreign direct investment (relative to GDP), FDIGDP. We have not considered trade openness (TRDGDP) as we find very strong positive relationships between FDIGDP and TRDGDP in most of the cases: a higher openness attracts more FDI and vice versa.

The following ARDL (p, q, r, s) model has been fitted:

$$G_t = a + b.t + \sum_{i=1}^{p} b_i G_{t-i} + \sum_{j=0}^{q} c_j S_{t-j} + \sum_{k=0}^{r} d_k F_{t-k} + \sum_{l=0}^{s} e_l B_{t-l} \qquad (2)$$

where G = GKFG, S = TURN, F = FDIGDP and B = DCBGDP; the subscripts t, t-i, t-j, t-k, t-l, indicate different time periods and p, q, r and t are unknown lags to be determined by the SBC.

The estimates of the long-term coefficients show that our observation of positive relationship based on our earlier analysis can be maintained for Jordon, Thailand and Venezuela. Two more countries join the list: Chile and Mexico. India, however, joins with Korea to exhibit a negative relationship (Zimbabwe and Pakistan now exhibit no relationship).

For Korea the negative relationship vanishes through the re-estimate of the ARDL (p, q) equation by incorporating intercept dummy for the 1997 crisis. But the negative relationship remains for the ARDL (p, q, r, s) equation in spite of using intercept and/or slope dummies for the 1997 crisis. This requires further investigation beyond the scope of the present paper.

For India we observe that during our period of analysis (since the mid-1980s) the importance of public capital formation started declining (our GGKF data covers both private and public capital formation). We have looked into the Indian data on the growth of private fixed capital formation (calculated from the relevant data available from Government of India, Economic Survey). Fitting both ARDL equations to these data we observed neither negative nor positive relationship between private fixed capital formation and stock market turnover ratio. In our earlier study on Indian experience (Sarkar, 2007a) we have used many other indicators of stock market development and found no relationship between stock market behaviour and private capital accumulation.

To sum up our time series analysis, only for four to five out of 15 countries we have observed a positive link between growth of capital accumulation and stock market developments (as indicated by the turnover ratio). All these countries (excepting Venezuela) belong to the HI-SMC group. Among these countries, Chile, Jordan and Thailand belong to VHI-SMC group.

Another interesting feature is that all these countries (excepting Thailand) are so-called ‘civil-law’ countries with relatively ‘poor’ protection of shareholders compared to ‘English-origin common law’ countries *a la* the controversial theory of LLSV (La Porta *et al*, 1998). There are some leximetric studies, which question this LLSV proposition (see Fagernas-Sarkar-Singh, 2007, Sarkar, 2007a). It is beyond the scope of the present paper to go into the details. But we have done some casual empiricism on the basis of some available leximetric data on shareholder protection for seven countries out of these 15 countries.

Available data (presented in Table 3) show that India and Malaysia belonging to ‘English’ heritage had high levels of shareholder protection while Pakistan with the same heritage had a very low level of shareholder protection. None of them experienced a positive link between stock market development and capital formation. Chile, Mexico, Brazil and Argentina had the other heritage and had a much lower level of shareholder protection. For Chile and Mexico we observed a positive long run relationship between capital formation and stock market development while for Argentina and Brazil we get no relationship between stock market development and capital accumulation. All these provide some evidence against the LLSV-Djankov (et al., 2005) type generalisation (see also Sarkar, 2007b).

Table 3. Shareholder Protection index, 1995-2005: Selected Countries

Countries	Average Shareholder Protection Index[1]
I. 'Common law' origin countries	
Malaysia	6.05
India	5.35
Pakistan	2.23
II. 'Civil Law' origin countries	
Brazil	4.89
Argentina	3.91
Chile	3.25
Mexico	2.67

[1] Legal scholars of Centre for Business Research (CBR), University of Cambridge have compiled a large time-series dataset on shareholder protection as a part of the project on Law, Finance and Development. For details of the construction of these leximetric data see Lele and Siems (2007). In these CBR data, originally 60 indicators of shareholder protection were considered and finally these were reduced to 10 important variables. We have added the 10 variables to get the aggregate index. Then it is averaged over the period for which the data are available. For maximum protection the index would assume the value 10 (as 1 is the maximum value for each of the 10 indicators). So the lower the value the lower is the level of protection

III. Conclusion

The stock market has become an integral part of a mature capitalist society. It is expected to provide a market mechanism for financing a new venture, which is profitable on the basis of private cost calculations. As a part of the development strategy many less developed countries try to promote the growth of stock market, often under the advice of the proponents of the Washington Consensus. However a lot of speculative activities and movements of speculative capital take place in the stock market particularly for stock trading. Accordingly stock prices move up and down and in many cases it has no connection with real economic activities. That's why Keynes compared this with casino and long-term investment decision taken on the basis of this gambling is harmful for the economy. Stock market booms and slumps do not guide long-term investment decisions. The source of long-term real growth does not lie in the activities of the stock market.

Our panel data study finds no positive link between the indicator of stock market development (SMC) and growth of fixed capital formation (GGKF) even after controlling for the level of per capita GDP, trade openness, FDI and banking sector development.

In our time series study of individual country cases of LDC group, based on the ARDL method, we observe that in the majority of cases there is no positive relationship between the growth of capital formation and stock market turnover ratio- an important indicator of stock market development incorporating both market capitalisation and the value of stock trade. Given this lack of relationship between stock market development and capital accumulation, there is a limited usefulness of the policy of promoting stock market for achieving the developmental goals of the LDCs.

Appendix

Per Capita GDP, Capital Accumulation and the Ratios of Stock Market Capitalisation, Trade, Foreign Direct Investment and Bank Credit to GDP, 1992-1999: Selected Less Developed Countries

Country[1]\Series*	DCP-GDP	FDI-GDP	PCY-91	TRD-GDP	GGKF	SMC	SE
I.HI-SMC Group (1992-99 SMC > 25 %)							
BRAZIL	49.56	1.92	6425	18.54	2.39	26.62	69
CHILE	56.75	5.81	6167	57.86	9.14	96.79	75
HONG KONG[2]	153.7	12.12	20872	268.8	4.35	252.9	71
INDIA	24.28	0.48	1687	22.16	7.87	33.47	--
INDONESIA	48.76	1.06	2675	59.57	-1.41	26.45	54
JAMAICA[3]	26.38	3.47	3897	102.2	29	36.55	74
JORDAN	71.96	1.43	3639	121.8	5.38	72.47	81
KOREA[3]	68.69	0.69	9985	62.16	8.67	38.65	91
MALAYSIA	132.0	5.61	5937	184.4	4.34	215.5	69
MEXICO	27.14	2.48	7662	51.98	6.56	34.45	58
MAURITIUS	49.91	0.7	6759	125.9	5.04	34.95	70
PHILIPPINES	44.44	2.03	3734	87.57	4.17	65.5	52
SINGAPORE	108.8	11.46	15285	275	7.59	165.7	--
THAILAND	134.8	2.61	4791	89.55	-2.54	60.22	87
TRINIDAD & TOBAGO	44.69	9.08	7100	91.66	8.8	32.74	72
ZIMBABWE	32.22	1.77	2795	77.24	-1.88	27.6	37
II.LO-SMC Group (1992-99 SMC < 25 %)							
ARGENTINA	20.64	2.91	9766	19.78	8.42	17.14	79
BANGLADESH	19.77	0.16	1190	27.17	9.51	3.51	43
BOTSWANA	12.62	0.09	5704	92.18	4.88	10.58	55
COLOMBIA	34.44	2.38	5889	35.47	3.34	15.94	56
COTE D'IVOIRE	20.19	1.61	1733	69.3	9.24	8.23	21
ECUADOR	24.62	2.88	3527	54.01	-1.64	7.7	48
EGYPT	40.62	1.27	2842	49.25	7.16	19.06	78
GHANA	7.03	2.03	1678	67.8	1.37	16.45	30
KENYA	32.84	0.22	1128	65.85	3.18	20.16	23
PAKISTAN	27.31	0.95	1630	36.2	1.66	16.53	--
PANAMA	74.78	6.05	4940	175.1	26.76	16.59	61
PERU	19.51	3.82	4026	30.52	7.61	20.04	66
SRI LANKA	22.28	1.38	2445	78.41	6.97	15.87	--
TUNISIA	66.12	2.43	4653	89.14	4.53	13.57	70
VENEZUELA	15.51	2.8	6150	49.81	4.5	10.45	58

[1] Relatively Rich (with PCY91 > $5000) countries are underlined.

[2] FDIGDP data for 1998-99.

[3] GGKF data are calculated from the data available in International Financial Statistics (IMF).

Source: Calculated from World Development Indicators (World Bank).

References

Arestis, Philip, Panicos O. Demetriades and Kul B. Luintel (2001). 'Financial Development and Economic Growth: The Role of Stock Markets,' *Journal of Money, Credit and Banking*, 33(1): 16-41.

Bekaert, Geert and Christian Lundblad (2005). 'Does financial liberalization spur growth,' *Journal of Financial Economics*, 77(1): 3-55.

Djankov, S., La Porta, R., Lopez de Silanes, F., Shleifer, A. (2005). The Law and Economics of Self-Dealing. *NBER Working Paper* No. W11883.

Fagernas, Sonja, Prabirjit Sarkar and Ajit Singh (2007). 'Legal Origin, Shareholder Protection and the Stock Market: New Challenges from Time Series Analysis', *Working Paper*, CBR, Cambridge (available online at *http://ssrn.com/abstract=987850*).

Henry, Peter Blair (2000). 'Do stock market liberalizations cause investment booms?,' *Journal of Financial Economics,* 58, (1–2 ,October): 301–34.

Keynes, J.M. (1936). *The General Theory of Employment, Interest and Money*, Harcourt Brace, New York.

La Porta, R., F.Lopez-de-Silanes, A. Shleifer and R.W. Vishny (1998).'Law and Finance', *Journal of Political Economy*, 106 (6): 1113-1155.

Levine, Ross (2003). 'Stock markets liquidity and economic growth: theory and evidence,' in Luigi Paganetto and Edmond S. Phelps (eds), *Finance, Research, Education and Growth*, Palgrave Macmillan, New York.

__________, (2001). 'International financial liberalisation and economic growth,' *Review of International Economics*, 9 (4): 688-702.

Levine, Ross and Sara Zervos (1998). 'Stock markets, banks, and economic growth,' *American Economic Review,* 88 (3): 537-558.

Pesaran, M.H. and Y. Shin (1999). 'An autoregressive distributed lag-modeling approach to co integration analysis.' In: Strom, S. (Ed.), *Econometrics and Economic Theory in the 20th Century*: The Ragnar Frisch Centennial Symposium. Cambridge University Press, Cambridge.

Sarkar, Prabirjit (2007a). 'Corporate Governance, Stock Market Development and Private Capital Accumulation: A Case Study of India', paper presented at the conference: "Corporate Accountability, Limited Liability and the Future of Globalisation' at The Centre for International Studies and Diplomacy (CISD), SOAS, London (20-21 July, 2007), vvailable online at *http://www.cisd.soas.ac.uk/Editor/assets/prabirjitsarkar.pdf*

Sarkar, Prabirjit (2007b). 'Trend of Legal Globalisation and Stock Market Development', paper presented at the Second Annual International Conference on "Globalization and Its Discontents," at the State University of New York College at Cortland (June 8-9, 2007), forthcoming in the conference volume.

Singh, Ajit (1997). 'Financial Liberalisation, Stock Markets and Economic Development,' *The Economic Journal* 107(May): 771-782.

World Bank (1993). *The East Asian Miracle*, Oxford University Press, New York.

In: Global Stock Exchanges: Stability, Interrelationships... ISBN: 978-60692-184-5
Editor: Paolo B. Cassedes

Chapter 9

DO INTERNATIONAL STOCK PRICES REFLECT INTERNATIONAL BUSINESS CYCLES?*

Shigeyuki Hamori
Faculty of Economics, Kobe University, Rokkodai, Nada-Ku, Kobe, Japan

Abstract

This paper empirically analyzes the relationship between international stock prices and international business cycles, specifically focusing on the number of cointegration vectors of each variable. The empirical data were taken from statistics on Germany, Japan, the UK, and the USA tabulated from January 1980 to May 2001. No cointegrating vectors were identified in indices of international stock prices, whereas several were identified in indices of international industrial production. These empirical results suggest that international stock prices do not necessarily reflect international business cycles.

Introduction

Many studies have sought to identify and enumerate the common trends, or what are known as cointegrating relations, in international stock markets. Prominent examples include the studies by Kasa (1992), Corhay, Rad and Urbain (1993), Engsted and Lud (1997), and Ahlgren and Antell (2002).

Kasa (1992) identified a number of common stochastic trends among the equity markets of Canada, Germany, Japan, the UK, and the USA using monthly and quarterly data covering the period from January 1974 through August 1990. Cointegration tests to analyze the long-run co-movements in these five stock markets identified a single stochastic trend common to all of the markets, and estimates based on loading factors suggested that this trend was most important in the Japanese market and least important in the Canadian market.

---

* A version of this chapter was also published in *Business Fluctuations and Cycles,* edited by T. Nagakawa published by Nova Science Publishers, Inc. It was submitted for appropriate modifications in an effort to encourage wider dissemination of research.

Corhay, Rad and Urbain (1993) used bi-weekly data from France, Germany, Italy, the Netherlands, and the UK collected between March 1, 1975 and September 30, 1991 to investigate whether European stock markets displayed a common long-run trend in behavior. In their cointegration test for empirical analysis, they identified several common stochastic trends among the five countries.

By showing cointegration in stock prices, these two earlier studies (Kasa, 1992; Corhay, Rad and Ubain, 1993) proved that world stock markets were at least partially driven by one or more common stochastic trends. The presence of a common trend can be interpreted as a natural consequence of well-functioning, well-integrated capital markets freely accessible to both domestic and foreign investors.

Several years later, Engsted and Lud (1997) performed a similar study using annual data from 1950 to 1988 from Denmark, Germany, Sweden, and the UK. According to empirical results derived from a vector error correction model (VECM), several common trends could be found in the dividends in these four countries.

In a more recent study, however, Ahlgren and Antell (2002) reexamined earlier findings using small sample corrections and found no evidence of cointegration among international stock prices. They applied the cointegration test to monthly and quarterly stock price data from Finland, France, Germany, Sweden, the UK, and the USA collected from January 1980 to February 1997. According to their findings, the cointegration test was sensitive to the lag length specification in the VAR model, and the previous empirical results such as those of Kasa (1992) and Corhay, Rad and Urbain (1993) could be explained by the small-sample bias and size-distortion of the cointegration test.

This paper takes a different tack in analyzing the issue of common trends in international stock markets by focusing on whether the number of common trends in international stock markets is equal to the number of common trends in international industrial production. If the international stock market is an integrated capital market freely accessible to both domestic and foreign investors, then the market should accurately reflect actual business cycles, i.e., investment, consumption, and other economic activities. If international stock prices contain abundant noise or bubbles, on the other hand, then the market would not reflect the actual economic activities. As the number of common trends in international stock markets can only equal the number of common trends in international industrial production if the former case holds true, we can rule out such an equivalence. This paper analyzes the problem for four major industrial countries, i.e., Germany, Japan, the UK, and the USA. This approach is an alternative to the usual method of empirically testing the efficiency of international stock markets.

Data

The data consist of monthly observations of the aggregate stock price index and industrial production index for Germany, Japan, the UK, and the USA from January 1980 to May 2001, taken from the International Financial Statistics of the International Monetary Fund. Based on Fama (1990) and Schwert (1990), industrial production is used to both measure real economic activity and define the business cycle of each country. Real stock prices are obtained by dividing the nominal stock price index by the consumer price index during the study period.

Table 1 summarizes the statistics on the real growth of stock prices and industrial production. The real growth of each variable is calculated as: $\{\ln(y_t) - \ln(y_{t-1})\} \times 100$, where y_t is the real stock price index or the industrial production index.

Table 1. Summary Statistics

	Real Stock Price Index			
	Germany	**Japan**	**UK**	**USA**
Mean	0.564	0.300	0.527	0.642
Std. Dev.	5.335	4.363	3.894	3.605
Skewness	-0.858	-0.235	-1.278	-0.702
Kurtosis	5.822	3.727	9.713	5.778
Jarque-Bera	116.383	7.998	550.339	103.351
P-value	0.000	0.018	0.000	0.000
	Industrial Production Index			
	Germany	**Japan**	**UK**	**USA**
Mean	0.094	0.133	0.091	0.221
Std. Dev.	1.770	1.670	1.033	0.676
Skewness	0.246	-0.034	-0.382	-0.365
Kurtosis	11.723	3.269	3.965	4.203
Jarque-Bera	814.128	0.821	16.161	21.108
P-value	0.000	0.663	0.000	0.000

P-value is the probability value of Jarque-Bera test.

The average growth rates for stock prices are 0.564 for Germany, 0.300 for Japan, 0.527 for the UK, and 0.642 for the USA. The standard deviations are 5.335 for Germany, 4.363 for Japan, 3.894 for the UK, and 3.605 for the USA. The skewnesses are -0.858 for Germany, -0.235 for Japan, -1.278 for the UK, and -0.702 for the USA. The kurtoses are 5.822 for Germany, 3.727 for Japan, 9.713 for the UK, and 5.778 for the USA. The Jarque-Bera statistics (its associated *P*-value) are 116.383 (0.000) for Germany, 7.998 (0.018) for Japan, 550.339 (0.000) for the UK, and 103.351 (0.000) for the USA. Thus, the null hypothesis of normal distribution is rejected for every country at the 5 percent significance level.

The average growth rates of industrial production are 0.094 for Germany, 0.133 for Japan, 0.091 for the UK, and 0.221 for the USA. The standard deviations are 1.770 for Germany, 1.670 for Japan, 1.033 for the UK, and 0.676 for the USA. The skewnesses are 0.246 for Germany, -0.034 for Japan, -0.382 for the UK, and -0.365 for the USA. The kurtoses are 11.723 for Germany, 3.269 for Japan, 3.965 for the UK, and 4.203 for the USA. The Jarque-Bera statistics (its associated *P*-value) are 814.128 (0.000) for Germany, 0.821 (0.663) for Japan, 16.161 (0.000) for the UK, and 21.108 (0.000) for the USA. Thus, the null hypothesis of normal distribution is rejected for every country except Japan at the 5 percent significance level.

Empirical Results

The unit root test developed by Phillips and Perron (1988) is used to test whether each variable has a unit root. The unit root test statistic is the t-value of γ obtained from the following regressions:

$$\Delta y_t = \mu + \delta t + \gamma y_{t-1} + u_t, \quad \text{(CT)}$$

$$\Delta y_t = \mu + \gamma y_{t-1} + u_t, \quad \text{(C)}$$

$$\Delta y_t = \gamma y_{t-1} + u_t, \quad \text{(None)}$$

where Δ is a difference operator, i.e., $\Delta y_t = y_t - y_{t-1}$, t is the time trend, and u_t is a disturbance term. The first equation (CT) includes a constant term and a time trend, the second equation (C) includes a constant term, and the third equation (None) includes no deterministic term. The null hypothesis (H_0) and the alternative hypothesis (H_A) are shown as follows:

$$H_0 : \gamma = 0,$$

$$H_A : \gamma < 0.$$

Thus, the null hypothesis shows that a unit root is included and the alternative hypothesis shows that a unit root is not included. Each equation is applied to both the level and the first difference of the log of the real stock price index and the log of the industrial production index. The empirical results are shown in Table 2. Taking Japan as an example, we find that the test statistics for the level and first difference of the real stock price index are -1.336 and -11.237 for CT, -1.843. and -11.232 for C, and -1.887 and -11.222 for None, respectively, while the test statistics for the level and first difference of the industrial production index are -1.027 and -22.971 for CT, -1.814 and -22.692 for C, and 1.568 and -22.441 for None. Thus, the null hypothesis of a unit root is not rejected for any of the specifications on the levels of the real stock price index and industrial production index, whereas it is rejected for all specifications on the first difference of the real stock price index and the industrial production index. As these results are robust to all countries, the real stock price index and industrial production are found to be a I(1) process for all countries.

The theory of non-stationary time series was developed soon after researchers discovered that multiple macro time series may obtain a unit root. Engle and Granger (1987) pointed out that a linear combination of non-stationary series may be stationary. When such a stationary linear combination exists, the non-stationary variables are said to be cointegrated. The stationary linear combination is called the cointegrating equation and is interpreted as a long-run equilibrium relationship among the variables. Given that the variables in an equilibrium relationship cannot move independently of each other, any equilibrium relationship among a set of non-stationary variables implies that the stochastic trends of the variables must be linked. This linkage among the stochastic trends necessitates that the variables be cointegrated. Since the trends of cointegrated variables are linked, the dynamic paths of such variables must bear some relation to the current deviation from the equilibrium relationship.

Table 2. Unit Root Test

Variable	Country	Test Statistics		
		CT	C	None
Real Stock Price Index		**Level**		
	Germany	-2.301	-1.011	-1.173
	Japan	-1.336	-1.843	-1.887
	UK	-2.299	-1.510	-2.247
	USA	-2.520	-0.009	-1.091
		First Difference		
	Germany	-14.782†	-14.810†	-14.708†
	Japan	-11.237†	-11.232†	-11.222†
	UK	-12.682†	-12.691†	-12.597†
	USA	-11.530†	-11.539†	-11.398†
Industrial Production Index		**Level**		
	Germany	-3.183	-0.391	1.331
	Japan	-1.027	-1.814	1.568
	UK	-3.253	-0.341	1.582
	USA	-2.557	0.799	3.467
		First Difference		
	Germany	-24.997†	-25.364†	-25.916†
	Japan	-22.971†	-22.692†	-22.441†
	UK	-19.526†	-19.562†	-19.288†
	USA	-12.526†	-12.417†	-12.068†

* shows that the null hypothesis of a unit root is rejected at the 5 percent significance level.

† shows that the null hypothesis of a unit root is rejected at the 1 percent significance level.

CT corresponds to the following regression: $\Delta y_t = \mu + \delta t + \gamma y_{t-1} + u_t$.

C corresponds to the following regression: $\Delta y_t = \mu + \gamma y_{t-1} + u_t$.

None corresponds to the following regression: $\Delta y_t = \gamma y_{t-1} + u_t$.

The cointegration test is applied to determine whether a group of non-stationary series are cointegrated or not. The presence of a cointegrating relation forms the basis of the vector error correction (VEC) specification. Consider a VAR of order p

$$y_t = A_1 y_{t-1} + \cdots A_p y_{t-p} + Bx_t + u_t$$

where y_t is a k-vector of non-stationary I(1) variables, x_t is a vector of deterministic variables, and u_t is a vector of innovations. We can rewrite this VAR as

$$\Delta y_t = \Pi y_{t-1} + \sum_{i=1}^{p-1} \Gamma_i \Delta y_{t-i} + Bx_t + u_t$$

where

$$\Pi = \sum_{i=1}^{p} A_i - I,\ \Gamma_i = -\sum_{j=i+1}^{p} A_j .$$

Granger's representation theorem asserts that if the coefficient matrix Π has reduced rank $r < k$, we come up with $k \times r$ matrices α and β, each with rank r such that $\Pi = \alpha\beta'$ and $\beta' y_t$ is I(0). r is the number of cointegrating relations, and each column of β is the cointegrating vector. Johansen's method is used to estimate the Π matrix from an unrestricted VAR and to test whether we can reject the restrictions implied by the reduced rank of Π (Johansen, 1988, and Johansen and Juselius, 1990).

Johansen (1988) considers the following five cases for the deterministic trend:[1]

(case 1)	$\Pi y_{t-1} + Bx_t = \alpha\beta' y_{t-1}$
(case 2)	$\Pi y_{t-1} + Bx_t = \alpha(\beta' y_{t-1} + \rho_0)$
(case 3)	$\Pi y_{t-1} + Bx_t = \alpha(\beta' y_{t-1} + \rho_0) + \alpha \perp \gamma_0$
(case 4)	$\Pi y_{t-1} + Bx_t = \alpha(\beta' y_{t-1} + \rho_0 + \rho_1 t) + \alpha \perp \gamma_0$
(case 5)	$\Pi y_{t-1} + Bx_t = \alpha(\beta' y_{t-1} + \rho_0 + \rho_1 t) + \alpha \perp (\gamma_0 + \gamma_1 t)$

where the term associated with $\alpha \perp$ is the deterministic term outside the cointegrating relations.[2] In case 1, the level data y_t have no deterministic trends and the cointegrating equations have no intercepts. In case 2, the level data y_t have no deterministic trends and the cointegrating equations have intercepts. In case 3, the level data y_t have linear trends but the cointegrating equations have only intercepts. In case 4, both the level data y_t and cointegrating equations have linear trends. In case 5, the level data y_t have quadratic trends and the cointegrating equations have linear trends.

Thus, the cointegration test developed by Johansen (1988) and Johansen and Juselius (1990) is applied to two data sets, i.e., a log of the stock price indices and a log of the industrial price indices of the four countries. This necessitates estimations of four-variable VAR models for the stock price and industrial production indices. Care must be taken in selecting the model, as the test results can be sensitive to the lag length of VAR. The common procedure is to estimate a VAR using the undifferenced data and then to select the lag length using the Akaike information criterion (AIC), a criterion often used to select the appropriate

---

[1] See EViews 4 User's Guide.

[2] When a deterministic term appears both inside and outside the cointegrating relation, the decomposition is not uniquely identified. Johansen (1995) identifies the part that belongs inside the error correction term by orthogonally projecting the exogenous terms onto the α space so that $\alpha \perp$ is the null space of α such that $\alpha' \alpha \perp = 0$

model. As clearly shown in Table 3, a lag length (p) of two is selected for the stock price indices and a lag length of three is selected for the industrial production indices.

Table 3. AIC

Number of Lag	Real Stock Price Index	Industrial Production Index
1	-14.816	-24.202
2	-14.920*	-24.571
3	-14.852	-24.576*
4	-14.718	-24.561
5	-14.619	-24.480
6	-14.492	-24.389

* shows the smallest value of AIC.

Table 4 shows the results of the cointegration test for the aggregate index of real stock prices in the four countries. Two test statistics are reported, i.e., the trace test statistic and the maximum eigenvalue test statistic. The critical values for these tests were tabulated by Osterwald-Lenum (1992). The specification (Case 5) is used for empirical analysis. For the null hypothesis of no cointegration, the test statistics are 43.635 for the trace test and 24.450 for the maximum eigenvalue test. As both these values fall below the corresponding 5 percent critical value (54.64 for the trace test and 30.33 for the maximum eigenvalue test), the null hypothesis of no cointegration is statistically accepted at the 5 percent significance level.

Table 4a. Trace Test for Cointegration: Real Stock Price Index

Hypothesized No. of CE(s)	Eigenvalue	Trace Statistic	5 Percent Critical Value	1 Percent Critical Value
None	0.091	43.635	54.64	61.24
At most 1	0.040	19.185	34.55	40.49
At most 2	0.022	8.739	18.17	23.46
At most 3	0.012	3.048	3.74	6.40

*(†) shows the rejection of the null hypothesis at the 5%(1%) level.

Table 4b. Maximum Eigenvalue Test for Cointegration: Real Stock Price Index

Hypothesized No. of CE(s)	Eigenvalue	Trace Statistic	5 Percent Critical Value	1 Percent Critical Value
None	0.091	24.450	30.33	35.68
At most 1	0.040	10.446	23.78	28.83
At most 2	0.022	5.691	16.87	21.47
At most 3	0.012	3.048	3.74	6.40

*(†) shows the rejection of the null hypothesis at the 5%(1%) level.

Table 5 shows the results of the cointegration test for the aggregate index of industrial production in the four countries. For the null hypothesis of no cointegration, the test statistics are 80.300 for the trace test and 41.242 for the maximum eigenvalue test. As both these values are larger than the corresponding 5 percent critical value (54.64 for the trace test and 30.33 for the maximum eigenvalue test), the null hypothesis of no cointegration is statistically rejected at the 5 percent significance level. For the null hypothesis of at most one cointegration relation, the test statistics are 39.058 for the trace test and 25.355 for the maximum eigenvalue test. As both values are larger than the corresponding 5 percent critical value (34.55 for the trace test and 23.78 for the maximum eigenvalue test), the null hypothesis of at most one cointegration relation is statistically rejected at the 5 percent significance level. For the null hypothesis of at most two cointegration relations, the test statistics are 13.703 for the trace test and 13.312 for the maximum eigenvalue test. As both values are smaller than the corresponding 5 percent critical value (18.17 for the trace test and 16.87 for the maximum eigenvalue test), the null hypothesis of at most two cointegration relations is statistically accepted at the 5 percent significance level.

Table 5a. Trace Test for Cointegration: Industrial Production Index

Hypothesized No. of CE(s)	Eigenvalue	Trace Statistic	5 Percent Critical Value	1 Percent Critical Value
None †	0.150	80.300	54.64	61.24
At most 1 *	0.095	39.058	34.55	40.49
At most 2	0.051	13.703	18.17	23.46
At most 3	0.002	0.391	3.74	6.40

*(†) shows the rejection of the null hypothesis at the 5%(1%) level.

Table 5b. Maximum Eigenvalue Test for Cointegration: Industrial Production Index

Hypothesized No. of CE(s)	Eigenvalue	Trace Statistic	5 Percent Critical Value	1 Percent Critical Value
None †	0.150	41.242	30.33	35.68
At most 1 *	0.095	25.355	23.78	28.83
At most 2	0.051	13.312	16.87	21.47
At most 3	0.002	0.391	3.74	6.40

*(†) shows the rejection of the null hypothesis at the 5%(1%) level.

According to these results, the number of cointegration relations is zero for the stock price index and two for the industrial production index. Thus, the number of common trends for the real stock price index is not equal to the number of common trends for the industrial production index.

Given that the results of the cointegration test depend on the model specification, this paper carries out the cointegration test for various specification to check the robustness of the empirical results. Table 6 and Table 7 show the number of cointegrations for five types of specification. As the table clearly illustrates, the number of cointegrating relations is zero in every case for stock prices, versus one or two in most cases for industrial production. These values are not equal in most cases, hence the number of common trends for the real stock price index does not equal the number of common trends for the industrial production index.

Table 6. Selected (5% level) Number of Cointegrating Relations by Model: Real Stock Price Index

	(Case 1)	(Case 2)	(Case 3)	(Case 4)	(Case 5)
Trace	0	0	0	0	0
Max-Eig	0	0	0	0	0

Trace is the trace test.
Max-Eig is the maximum eigenvalue test.

Table 7. Selected (5% level) Number of Cointegrating Relations by Model: Industrial Production Index

	(Case 1)	(Case 2)	(Case 3)	(Case 4)	(Case 5)
Trace	1	1	1	2	2
Max-Eig	1	1	0	1	2

Trace is the trace test.
Max-Eig is the maximum eigenvalue test.

Some Concluding Remarks

This paper empirically analyzes the relationship between international stock prices and international industrial production, specifically focusing on the number of cointegration vectors of each variable. The empirical data were taken from statistics on Germany, Japan, the UK, and the USA covering the period from January 1980 to May 2001.

The indices of international industrial production were found to have several cointegrating vectors, whereas the international stock price indices had none. If international stock prices contain abundant noise or bubbles, the market will not reflect actual economic activities; hence the number of common trends in international stock markets cannot be equal to the number of common trends in international industrial production. These empirical results suggest that international stock prices do not necessarily reflect international business cycles.

References

Ahlgren, N. and Antell, J., (2002), Testing for cointegration between international stock prices, *Applied Financial Economics,* Vol. 12, pp. 851-861.

Corhay, A., Rad, A. T., and Urbain, J. P., (1993), Common stochastic trends in European stock markets, *Economics Letters*, Vol. 42, pp. 385-390.

Engle, R. F. and Granger, C. W. J., (1987), Cointegration and error correction: representation, estimation and testing, *Econometrica*, Vo. 55, pp. 251-276.

Engsted, T. and Lund, J., (1997), Common stochastic trends in international stock prices and dividends: an example of testing overidentifying restrictions on multiple cointegration vectors, *Applied Financial Economics*, Vol. 7, pp. 659-665.

Fama, E. F., (1990), Stock returns, expected returns, and real activity, *Journal of Finance*, Vol. 45, pp. 1089-1108.

Johansen, S., (1988), Statistical analysis of cointegration vectors, *Journal of Economic Dynamics and Control,* Vol. 12, pp. 231-254.

Johansen, S., (1995), *Likelihood-based Inference in Cointegrated Vector Autoregressive Models,* Oxford University Press, Oxford.

Johansen, S. and Juselius, K., (1990), Maximum likelihood estimation and inference on cointegration with application to the demand for money, *Oxford Bulletin of Economic and Statistics*, Vol. 52, pp. 169-209.

Kasa, K., (1992), Common stochastic trends in international stock markets, *Journal of Monetary Economics,* Vol. 29, pp. 95-124.

Osterwald-Lenum M., (1992), A note with quantiles of the asymptotic distribution of the maximum likelihood cointegration rank test statistics, *Oxford Bulletin of Economic and Statistics*, Vol. 54, pp. 461-472.

Phillips, P. C. B. and Perron, P., (1988), Testing for a unit root in time series regression, *Biometrika*, Vol. 75, pp. 335-346.

Quantitative Micro Software, (2000), *EViews 4 User's Guide.*

Schwert, G. W., (1990), Stock returns and real activity: a century of evidence, *Journal of Finance,* Vol. 45, pp. 1237-1257.

INDEX

C

D

G

H

I

R

T

U

V

W

Y

Z